PROBLEMS IN THE PHILOSOPHY OF RELIGION:
CRITICAL STUDIES OF THE WORK OF JOHN HICK

Problems in the Philosophy of Religion

Critical Studies of the Work of
John Hick

Edited by

Harold Hewitt, Jr.

St. Martin's Press   New York

© The Claremont Graduate School 1991

First published in the United States of America in 1991

Printed in Hong Kong

ISBN 0–312–06137–4

Library of Congress Cataloging-in-Publication Data
Problems in the philosophy of religion: critical studies of the work
   of John Hick / edited by Harold Hewitt, Jr.
      p.   cm.
      Includes index.
      ISBN 0–312–06137–4
      1. Hick, John—Contributions in philosophy of religion.
   2. Religion—philosophy—History—20th century.   I. Hewitt, Harold,
   1955–
   BL51.P735   1991
   200'.1—dc20   90–26889
                                                              CIP

Contents

Contents

Preface

For two days, 7 and 8 April 1989, religious scholars from around the world gathered on the campus of Claremont McKenna College. This gathering has become something of an annual event since, in the spring of 1979, John Hick accepted his appointment as Danforth Professor of the Philosophy of Religion at The Claremont Graduate School. Under Hick's direction, the annual "Philosophy of Religion Conference" addresses a wide range of topics related to the philosophy of religion. Several of the conference proceedings have found their way into publication.

But in this particular year there was to be a difference. The topic was John Hick's own work, following a suggestion from his academic colleagues in Claremont that it would be fitting to celebrate the achievements of a long and distinguished career, most recently recognized in the publication of Hick's 1986 Gifford Lectures under the title *An Interpretation of Religion: Human Responses to the Transcendent*. His colleagues thought it best to honour Hick not with a *Festschrift* (one is, incidentally, already in progress), but with the type of intellectual exchange by means of which Hick has invigorated those around him: the respectful but candid critique, replete with direct responses from the person whose ideas and works are being criticized.

This collection of essays follows generally the pattern of the conference. During the conference, a paper analysing Hick's ideas was presented. It was followed by the reading of a prepared critical response. Then all conference participants, including John Hick, were invited to raise questions and offer insights. Finally, Hick was provided the opportunity to bring the discussion to a close by offering his final reply to the session. Similarly, each chapter presented here begins with a paper, is followed by a "Critical Response", and concludes with Hick's "Reply". I think the reader will be especially interested in Hick's "Reply" to each of the papers; each one is characteristically pointed and clear. This format will, I hope, not only prove useful to the reader, but also prove faithful to the spirited exchanges which characterized the conference.

The only exception to this format occurs in the case of Gerard Loughlin's paper. Loughlin, alas, could not attend the conference, and consequently there is no "Critical Response" to his essay.

The papers in this collection address a wide variety of topics. Some of them renew discussion of familiar themes and criticisms. For example, there is Gerard Loughlin's critique of Hick's writings about the Incarnation; or William Rowe's excellent presentation of Hick on the problem of evil; or Frank Dilley's and Dan Stiver's discussions of the replica theory and life after death.

However, most of the papers address *An Interpretation of Religion*. Gavin D'Costa argues that Hick's position in the work is ultimately self-contradictory. Chester Gillis provides a survey of what he regards as the new insights, possible shortcomings, and lasting contributions of the work. Robert Mesle argues that Hick's claim to have considered all intellectual and social movements appropriate to the task he defines for himself is insupportable in the case of humanism. June O'Connor echoes this concern in the case of feminist theology. Paul Badham analyses the work from a philosophical perspective. Finally, this book closes with two delightful narratives. The first, by Julius Lipner, challenges Hick's assertion that one cannot ascribe personal or non-personal attributes to the Real *an sich*. The second, by Joseph Prabhu, offers an alternative theology to that of Lipner and that of Hick.

My review of the contents of this book is intentionally brief. The essays are lucid and can be appreciated by all interested readers, from scholars in related fields to students of religious studies to "laypersons" whose interest, perhaps, has been aroused by reading *An Interpretation of Religion*.

I wish to acknowledge the contributions of Steven T. Davis, who served as Chair and organizer of the conference. The conference would not have been possible without the continuing support of The Claremont Graduate School, Claremont McKenna College, and Pomona College's Department of Religion. Ellen Sun was especially helpful with conference logistics. The editorial staff of Macmillan Press have exhibited grace, patience and professionalism. Special thanks go to Sophie Lillington of Macmillan and to Graham Eyre, whose careful review of the text was most helpful. Linda Carlson-Hewitt ably helped with the page proofs. And, last but not least, I would like to thank each of the contributors for placing their trust in me and forgoing the customary privileges of the author in order to produce this volume in a relatively timely manner. I also bear responsibility for any errors in the text.

Finally, this work is dedicated, appropriately I believe, by means of its title. Although this sentiment has been expressed in several of the individual essays, on behalf of all contributors, I wish to express gratitude once more to John Hick for providing us all with years of challenging thoughts, carefully expressed in his many published works. If this volume succeeds in furthering the discussion which John started, it will prove to be the fitting tribute that his colleagues intended.

Claremont, California HAROLD HEWITT, JR
4 March 1990

Note on References

The notes to the papers and critical responses collected in this book have been placed at the end of the contributions to which they relate and include all relevant source references. The notes to each contribution are self-contained (with, for each work cited, full publication details on first citation), except that references to the more frequently cited publications of John Hick generally consist of title (or short title) and location (page, chapter, etc.) only. To this is added, where necessary, an indication of the edition cited. The works in question are as follows:

Death and Eternal Life (London: Collins; New York: Harper and Row, 1976; reissued London: Macmillan, 1985).

Evil and the God of Love (London: Macmillan, 1966).

Evil and the God of Love, 2nd edn (London: Macmillan; New York: Harper and Row, 1978).

Faith and Knowledge, 2nd edn (London: Macmillan; Ithaca, NY: Cornell University Press, 1966).

Faith and Knowledge, 2nd edn, Fount pbk (London: Collins, 1974).

God and the Universe of Faiths (London: Macmillan; New York: St Martin's Press, 1973).

God and the Universe of Faiths, Fount pbk (London: Collins, 1977).

God Has Many Names (London: Macmillan, 1980; Philadelphia: Westminster Press, 1982).

Interpretation of Religion: abbreviated title for *An Interpretation of Religion: Human Responses to the Transcendent* (London: Macmillan; New Haven, Conn.: Yale University Press, 1989).

Philosophy of Religion (Englewood Cliffs, NJ: Prentice-Hall, 1963).

Philosophy of Religion, 2nd edn (Englewood Cliffs, NJ: Prentice-Hall, 1973).

Philosophy of Religion, 3rd edn (Englewood Cliffs, NJ: Prentice-Hall, 1983).

Philosophy of Religion, 4th edn (Englewood Cliffs, NJ: Prentice-Hall, 1989).

Problems of Religious Pluralism (London: Macmillan; New York: St Martin's Press, 1985).

The Second Christianity (London: SCM, 1983).

Notes on the Contributors

Paul Badham studied theology at the universities of Oxford, Cambridge, and Birmingham, in the latter two cases as a student of John Hick. He spent five years as an Anglican clergyman in the diocese of Birmingham, and since 1973 has been teaching at St David's University College, Lampeter, in the University of Wales, where he is a Reader in Theology and Religious Studies and Chairman of Religion and Ethics. He has published widely on ideas about death and immortality, and is the editor of *A John Hick Reader* and of *Religion, State and Society in Modern Britain*.

L. Stafford Betty is Professor of Religious Studies at California State University, Bakersfield. Born a Roman Catholic, presently worshipping as an Episcopalian, he is in fact an ecumenical theist very much in the mould of John Hick and is almost as comfortable worshipping in a Hindu temple as a Christian church. He has published a book, *Vadiraga's Refutation of Sankara's Non-Dualism*, and numerous articles on Asian philosophy, philosophy of religion, and parapsychology. He has also published three fictional works on religious themes.

Stephen T. Davis is Professor of Philosophy and Religion at Claremont McKenna College and an ordained United Presbyterian minister. He is the author of five books and many scholarly articles. His books are *The Debate about the Bible: Inerrancy versus Infallibility; Faith, Skepticism and Evidence: An Essay in Religious Epistemology; Encountering Evil: Live Options in Theodicy; Logic and the Nature of God;* and *Encountering Jesus: A Debate in Christology.* He is also associate editor of the *International Journal for Philosophy of Religion* and *TSF Bulletin*.

Gavin D'Costa is an Indian Roman Catholic theologian who gained his doctorate from the University of Cambridge and now lectures in Religious Studies at the West London Institute of Higher Education. He is secretary to the British Council of Churches Committee for Relations with People of Other Faiths (Theological Issues Consultative Group) and a member of the

Roman Catholic Committee for Other Faiths (England and Wales). His published works include *Theology and Religious Pluralism* and *John Hick's Theology of Religions.* He has also edited a book in response to John Hick and Paul Knitter (eds), *The Myth of Christian Uniqueness,* for Orbis: *Christian Uniqueness Reconsidered: The Myth of a Pluralistic Theology of Religions.*

Frank B. Dilley is Professor and Chairperson, Department of Philosophy, University of Delaware. He is the author of *Metaphysics and Religious Language* and various articles on the proofs for God's existence, the free will/theodicy problem and philosophical parapsychology. His earlier article "Resurrection and the 'Replica Objection' " (*Religious Studies,* 1983), is closely related to his contribution here.

Carl W. Ernst received his Ph.D. in Comparative Religion and Islamic Studies from Harvard University, and has specialized in the study of classical Sufism and Indo-Muslim history and culture. His writings include *Words of Ecstasy in Sufism* and *Sufism and History at Khuldabad.* He is Associate Professor of Religion at Pomona College, Claremont, California.

Chester Gillis holds a Ph.D. from the University of Chicago Divinity School. He has taught at Drew University Graduate and Theological Schools and is currently Assistant Professor of Theology at Georgetown University in Washington, DC. He is the author of a number of articles and *A Question of Final Belief: John Hick's Pluralistic Theory of Salvation.*

Harold Hewitt, Jr, is completing his doctorate in the Philosophy of Religion at the Claremont Graduate School and is Vice President for Business and Finance at Whittier College, Whittier, California. His dissertation addresses the philosophical foundation of John Hick's global theology.

John Hick is Danforth Professor of the Philosophy of Religion, and Director of the Blaisdell Programs in World Religions and Cultures, at the Claremont Graduate School, California. He is the author of numerous books and articles on theology and the philosophy of religion.

James Kellenberger is Professor of Philosophy at California State University, Northridge. He is the author of *Religious Discovery;*

Faith and Knowledge; The Cognitivity of Religion: Three Perspectives; and *God-Relationships with and without God*. He has published articles in *Religious Studies, Philosophy, Faith and Philosophy* and other journals.

Julius Lipner lectures in the comparative study of religion, with special interests in the Buddhist, Hindu and Christian traditions, in the Faculty of Divinity, University of Cambridge. He is the author of *The Face of Truth: A Study of Meaning and Metaphysics in the Vedāntic Theology of Rāmānuja*, co-author of *Hindu Ethics: Purity, Abortion and Euthanasia*, and editor of *A Net Cast Wide: Investigations into Indian Thought in Memory of David Friedman*.

Gerard Loughlin is a Lecturer in Religious Studies at the University of Newcastle upon Tyne, where he teaches Christian theology and philosophy of religion. He was a student at both the University of Wales and the University of Cambridge, where he undertook his doctoral research on the theology and philosophy of John Hick. He has published in a number of leading journals, including *Theology, Modern Theology, Religious Studies* and *New Blackfriars*.

C. Robert Mesle is a "process" naturalist with deep appreciation for the value and power of religious traditions. His articles relating to John Hick have appeared in the *Journal of Religion*, the *International Journal for Philosophy of Religion* and *The Christian Century*. Macmillan will soon be publishing his book on John Hick, *Does God Hide from Us?* Mesle is currently Associate Professor of Philosophy and Religion at Graceland College.

June O'Connor is Associate Professor and Chair of the Program in Religious Studies at the University of California, Riverside. Her publications include *The Quest for Political and Spiritual Liberation: A Study in the Thought of Sri Aurobindo Ghose* and articles on theology and ethics in the *Journal of Religious Ethics, Religious Studies Review, Union Seminary Quarterly Review, Women's Studies: An Interdisciplinary Journal*, and other journals.

Joseph Prabhu studied economics and politics at Delhi University, and philosophy and theology at the universities of Heidelberg, Munich and Cambridge. His doctoral dissertation at Boston University was on Hegel's philosophy of Christianity. He is the author of *The Dark Side of Modernity: Hegel's Political Theology and the Non-European World*, editor of *The Cross-Cultural Understanding* *of Raimundo Panikkar,* and co-editor with P. Bilimoria of *Indian Ethics* (all forthcoming).

William Rowe is Professor and Head of the Department of Philosophy at Purdue University. He has taught at the University of Illinois and held visiting appointments at Wayne State University and the University of Michigan. His publications include *Religious Symbols and God, The Cosmological Argument, Philosophy of Religion,* and numerous articles. He has held a Guggenheim Fellowship, been a fellow at the National Humanities Center, and is a past president of the Central Division of the American Philosophical Association.

Dan R. Stiver received his doctorate from Southern Baptist Theological Seminary, Louisville, Kentucky, and now teaches Christian Philosophy there. He has conducted research at Regent's Park College, Oxford University, at the University of Chicago Divinity School, and in the Philosophy Department of the University of Notre Dame. His special interests are phenomenological hermeneutics, the philosophy of religious language, and the problem of evil.

Linda Zagzebski received her doctorate from the University of California at Los Angeles, and is Associate Professor of Philosophy at Loyola Marymount University in Los Angeles. Her publications include *The Dilemma of Freedom and Foreknowledge,* as well as articles on metaphysics and philosophy of religion. She has directed three conferences of the Society of Christian Philosophers and has served on the executive committees of the Society of Christian Philosophers and the Philosophy of Religion Society. She is on the editorial board of *Faith and Philosophy.*

Part I
On *An Interpretation of Religion*

1

John Hick and Religious Pluralism: Yet Another Revolution

GAVIN D'COSTA

INTRODUCTION

John Hick's *An Interpretation of Religion* (based on the Gifford Lectures of 1986–7) offers us his latest and most systematic reflections on religious pluralism. Hick has been a major contributor to the debate on religious pluralism since the 1970s and his position has evolved gradually, although since the 1970s he has always championed a "pluralist" approach as opposed to an "exclusivist" or "inclusivist" one.[1] These terms are inadequate, but help in mapping out fundamental issues. The basic orientation of the pluralist is to affirm the great religious traditions as valid and different paths to salvation. Exclusivists, by contrast, believe that only one religion or revelation is true and that the others are false, while Christian inclusivists allow for salvation within other religions but relate this salvific grace to the Christ event in a representative or causative fashion.

In this essay, I do not want to conduct an archaeological excavation of Hick's work, but shall rather concentrate on the most recent developments of his Copernican revolution, first proposed in *God and the Universe of Faiths* (1973) and culminating in his *An Interpretation of Religion*. However, archaeology does help in understanding the present – and to that extent some reference to Hick's previous positions will be inevitable. After setting out his current position, I shall then outline some problems with his pluralism that still force me to be an inclusivist. These criticisms are intended as a respectful dialogue between scholars concerned with the same perplexing problem: what is and should be

Christianity's attitude to the other great world religions? This is an immensely practical and urgent question in our multi-faith world.

HICK'S COPERNICAN REVOLUTION AND CONSEQUENT KANTIAN REVOLUTION

In 1973, using an astronomical analogy, Hick suggested a Copernican revolution in the Christian theology of religions whereby Christians should "shift from the dogma that Christianity is at the centre to the realization that it is *God* who is at the centre, and that all religions . . . including our own, serve and revolve around him".[2] The earlier Ptolemaic "dogmas" placed the Church and Christ as the source and centre of salvation. According to Hick, these dogmas became increasingly implausible in the light of the truth and holiness evident in other religions, and the Christian belief in a God who loves all people and therefore would not deny them the means to salvation. Hence the Copernican revolution marked a shift from *ecclesio*centrism and *Christo*centrism to one of *theo*centrism – analogous to the monumental paradigm shift in astronomy precipitated by Copernicus. Hick argued that this paradigmatic shift would facilitate a new understanding of religions whereby claims to superiority and exclusivity would dissolve, as would mission. A new era of inter-religious ecumenism would dawn, similar to that experienced within the Christian churches.

In the 1980s, Hick developed this theory, culminating in *An Interpretation of Religion* and in what I shall argue is yet another revolution.[3] I shall call this a "Kantian revolution", in that Kant focused on human subjectivity as opposed to the pre-Kantian traditions of attention to the object of reflection. Analogously, God is removed from the centre of the universe of faiths and is replaced by human transformation. Furthermore, a Kantian-type epistemology lies at the heart of Hick's new strategy. Hence it is inappropriate to characterize this development as an "epicycle" of the Copernican revolution when such a radical paradigm shift is involved.

Hick introduced a Kantian-type distinction between the "*noumenal* world, which exists independently, and outside man's perception of it, and the *phenomenal* world, which is that world as it appears to our human consciousness" (emphasis added).[4] The

"Real" occupies the centre of the universe of faiths and is analogous to the *noumenal* realm. The varying *phenomenal* responses within the different religious traditions, both theistic and nontheistic, are to be viewed as authentic but different responses to this noumenal Real.

This Kantian revolution developed in response to two types of criticisms aimed at the Copernican revolution. It circumvented the charge that it was a covert Christian God inhabiting the centre of the universe of faiths and thereby excluding non-theistic religions. It also allowed Hick to distinguish his position from that of the Hindu Advaita Vedanta view, which holds that God is ultimately "non-personal . . . and that the worship of personal gods belongs to a lower and preliminary stage of religious life which is eventually to be left behind".[5] His new position attempts to transcend both these views. Hence the "Real is *equally authentically thought* and *experienced* as *personal* and *non-personal*" (emphasis added).[6] Furthermore, the Real is expressed through various concretizations. In theistic traditions the Real is manifested in various "personae", such as Yahweh, Krishna, Siva, Allah and the Father of Jesus Christ. In non-theistic religions the divine "impersonae" are experienced as Brahman, *nirvāṇa, śūnyatā*, the *dharma*, and so on.[7]

Within this philosophical framework, Hick argues that the great world religions

are fundamentally alike in exhibiting a soteriological structure. That is to say, they are all concerned with salvation/liberation/enlightenment/fulfilment. . . . Along each path the great transition is from the sin and error of self-enclosed existence to the liberation and bliss of Reality-centredness.[8]

In effect, this common soteriological structure can be typified as exhibiting a turning from "self-centredness to Reality-centredness".[9] Over the years Hick has therefore moved from *Christocentrism* to *theocentrism* to a *Realocentrism*.

CRITICAL EXPOSITION

In what follows I wish to explore a single question: does Hick's new post-Copernican pluralism perpetuate a vague form of agnosticism? I shall suggest that it does for a number of reasons: first, because of his increased attention to human transformation at the cost of attention to the Reality which transforms it; secondly, because of his Kantian epistemology; and thirdly, because it is precisely through a covert agnosticism that he has attempted to transcend criticisms of covert theism and his fear of importing a covert non-theism. This latter option is unlikely to be acceptable to either theists or non-theists. Furthermore, Hick's position undermines *his own* defence of the cognitive status of religious language, as well as imposing a solution contrary to the intentions of most religious people in using such language.[10]

Hick is led into agnosticism when he presses the distinction between the Real *in itself* and the various phenomenal manifestations of it perceived by humankind. Hick writes, "It follows from this distinction between the Real as it is in itself and as it is thought and experienced through our religious concepts that we cannot apply to the Real *an sich* the characteristics encountered in its *personae* and *impersonae*."[11] As noted above, this strategy is undertaken for a number of reasons. Hence, for Hick, one cannot argue that ultimately *either* the theistic *or* the non-theistic traditions have more appropriate images (personae/impersonae) of the Real. Both are equally appropriate, for the Real cannot be known apart from the various personae and impersonae. What is at stake here is a "religious" rather than a "non-religious" (or naturalistic) view of reality.[12]

Hick's eschatological dilemma

Here we begin to notice the tensions generated in Hick's post-Copernican position between the idea that the Real cannot be known in itself, and his claim that religions make cognitive claims about the Real that are in principle eschatologically verifiable. From the beginning of his career Hick has been a strong defender of the cognitive status of theistic language. Now he has had to enlarge this defence to include non-theistic language, while at the same time denying that theistic and non-theistic claims are claims about Reality! This is exemplified in the early part of *An Interpretation of Religion*, where Hick defends minimalist eschatological scenarios for Christian, Hindu and Buddhist outlooks in the course of defending the cognitive import of religious language.[13] I say "minimalist" as Hick disqualifies "concrete pictures", or specific details of eschatological expectations. He writes, "any acceptable theory of the eschatological verification of theism must make [the] distinction between the basic notion of an 'unlimitedly good end-state in communion with God' and the various concrete pictures of such a state produced by our human traditions".[14] However, even this statement affirming "communion with God" surely implies a theistic *ontology* requiring separate although related persons in communion with a separate although related God, running contrary to non-theistic claims. It is odd that Hick supportively refers to *Death and Eternal Life* in *An Interpretation of Religion*[15] when in the former he frankly acknowledges that even such a minimalist eschatological scenario (which he defends) "implicitly rejects the *advaitist* view that Atman *is* Brahman, the collective self being ultimately identical with God".[16]

This difficulty is only overcome by a sleight of hand. On the one hand Hick defends the cognitive status of religious claims by means of eschatological verification, and on the other he deems these eschatologies "mythological", thereby truncating their cognitive claims about the nature of reality.[17] In thus diverting attention from the religious referent of language, Hick concentrates on all that remains: the transformation that takes place in the person in response to the religious reality. Hence all that Hick can say now is that "the eastern and western paths constitute different forms of self-transcendence in response to the Real" and that they *all* affirm a "limitlessly good fulfilment of the project of human existence".[18] This Kantian revolution has come full circle. The cognitive claims upon which many of the religions are founded are no longer significant; only the apparent effects of these claims on the believer are. Later, even this much will be denied. Religious truth-claims are forced into agnosticism.

Hick and "transcendental agnosticism"

Hick's suggestion that the eschaton may be beyond the anticipations of *any* of our "earthly religious traditions" and possibly "beyond the present range of our imaginations" is in keeping with a tendency towards what I shall call *transcendental agnosticism*.[19] Transcendental agnosticism affirms the *transcendent* divine Reality over against *naturalistic* positions, while refusing to state that the eschaton may eventually be theistic rather than non-theistic, in however minimalist a sense. The transcendental agnostic prefers to remain agnostic on this question – and, by implication, *agnostic* as to the *ultimate nature* of the transcendent Reality.

This transcendental agnosticism is confirmed when Hick finally deals with religious conflicts on at least three different levels.[20] Hick responds similarly to all levels of conflict with three suggestions: (1) "that we should all school ourselves to tolerate and live with such disagreements"; (2) that the other person with his or her differences "might nevertheless be closer to the divine Reality than I"; (3) that such ultimate beliefs are "evidently not essential to our salvation or liberation".[21] This third suggestion implies a transcendental agnosticism concerning the ultimate cognitive value and significance of religious beliefs. Hick thereby seems to suggest that the way of life and effects precipitated by beliefs is minimal. Hick is approving when he notes that "the Buddhists adopt an attitude of agnosticism to the question of a personal creator".[22] He goes on to say, "Indeed it seems to me that the Buddha's doctrine of the undetermined questions, to know the answer to which is not necessary for liberation, is one from which non-Buddhists also could profit."[23] It would appear then that, while on one level a belief in God may be true, on another it is not important for salvation – as ultimate Reality is beyond "human picturing".[24]

This form of transcendental agnosticism has as its counterpart a pragmatic import, in that Hick wishes to focus upon the "transformation of human existence from self-centredness to Reality-centredness" (soteriology) instead of theological and philosophical questions that are, according to him, unnecessary for liberation/ salvation. Realocentrism has as its practical counterpart soterio-centrism.

I wish to pursue two related lines of criticism. First, this transcendental agnosticism at the heart of the new universe of faiths poses major philosophical, theological and epistemological difficulties – many of which run counter to the thrust of Hick's pluralist thesis. Secondly, the shift of attention to the soteriological *process* or *practice* of "self-centredness to Reality-centredness" cannot be intelligibly sustained without attention to the precise nature of the Real which informs and gives such a process meaning. In effect I shall argue that a transcendental agnostic pragmatism is ultimately self-contradictory.

The theoretical aspect of transcendental agnosticism

Let me develop the first criticism regarding the resultant transcendental agnosticism. Hick's sharp distinction between the *noumenal Real* and the *phenomenal images* framed by the human mind within particular cultures reminds me of David Hume's comment on the supposed religious object of mystics. Hume writes of mystical claims that the Reality confronted is ineffable: "Is the name, without any meaning, of such mighty importance? Or how do you MYSTICS who maintain the absolute incomprehensibility of the deity, differ from sceptics or atheists?"[25] It is precisely this "absolute incomprehensibility" regarding the nature of reality that threatens Hick's whole pluralist project by further *mystifying* rather than *illuminating* the nature of the Real through this Kantian development.[26] One may ask with Hume whether such a position as Hick's is any different from atheism or scepticism or, equivalently, a transcendental agnosticism.

This kind of problem is inevitable owing to Hick's adoption of a Kantian framework, for Kant's noumenon, like Hick's Real, encountered the same difficulties. How can Kant, writes Wedberg, "claim to know that there is a correspondence between phenomena and things in themselves, and that the latter act upon consciousness?"[27] Reformulating this question, one may ask how Hick can claim to know that there is a correspondence between the Real and any particular personae or impersonae.

Can Hick defend himself from the type of criticisms levelled by Hume at mystics, and by Wedberg at Kant? Can Hick even justify the supposition that there is a noumenon "behind" the various phenomena – for it has been persuasively argued that the very existence of religious plurality and the "many incompatibilities between the claims made about the nature of the religious ultimate and the way to salvation in the world faiths" leads to a "sceptic's response, which is to deny truth to any of them", which "seems more plausible than granting truth to all".[28] One may therefore ask whether the Real's invulnerability also leads to its redundancy. There are a number of further potential strategies within Hick's writing that can be utilized by him to try to circumvent these difficulties. However, these strategies are potentially problematic – as I shall try to demonstrate.

One way in which Hick could counter the charge of total scepticism or agnosticism would be to point out his firm and constant belief in the cognitive value of religious language. Consequently, he could maintain that the charge of transcendental agnosticism is illegitimate. Hick has always argued that in our present life we cannot show that our beliefs are actually true – inasmuch as they relate to reality as it is. Nevertheless, he has always assumed that "the importance of religious beliefs to the believer lies ultimately in the assumption that they are substantially *true references* to the *nature of reality*" (emphasis added).[29] Hence, on one level it would be incorrect to accuse Hick of scepticism or agnosticism, as it is clear that he accepts that many of the religions do make valid claims about a transcendent reality.

But how does one even justify the possibility that one's religious beliefs may be true in an ambiguous universe? The answer, for Hick, lies in eschatological verification! And I have shown above that Hick is eventually led to undermine the cognitive import of eschatological verification, thereby cutting off the branch on which he is perched. However, Hick may rightly protest that he does allow a minimalist eschatological claim regarding the "limitlessly good fulfilment of the project of human existence".[30]

But, if this is Hick's defence against the charge of scepticism or atheism (or transcendental agnosticism), then it surely concedes too much. First, it is questionable whether the contention that eschatological verification *per se* could be used to counter "a naturalistic interpretation of the universe" is credible or consistent.[31] Such a bare affirmation that the universe is "religious" amounts to nothing if certain predicative descriptions are not applicable to this quality of being "religious". For instance, the naturalist may ask whether this religious reality can be described as "intelligent, personal and loving". If Hick was to reply affirmatively, then certain religious traditions would be excluded by this definition of "religious". Furthermore, if eschatological verification can apparently be used to defend Christian theism against naturalism, it is not clear why eschatological verification is not relevant to defending Christian theism over against, let us say, non-theistic Advaita. Secondly, even the sense of conviction that most religious believers have, that their beliefs are "substantially true references to the nature of reality", is jettisoned in Hick's transcendental agnostic option.[32] Surely this in itself is a major cause for concern, as it contradicts Hick's own principle that the convictions of religious believers should and can be seen as relating to Reality. Ironically, it was this principle which led in part to the formulation of the pluralist position. Hick could be criticized on the same grounds as those on which he criticized Cupitt and Phillips's non-realist understanding of language – as introducing an "unintended elitism".[33] The "unintended elitism" present in Hick's pluralism stems from the fact that, while it allows religious people to make their claims, arguing that this is permissible and the claims basically true, it permits this only within a framework that undermines any ontological affirmation implicit in these claims about the nature of Reality.

The main point I have been driving at is this: either Hick jettisons his professed belief in the cognitive status of religious language and thereby escapes the eschatological dilemma that I have posed; or he maintains that religious language is cognitive, with the result that the eschatological dilemma confounds the Kantian revolution.

The pragmatic counterpart to Hick's theoretical transcendental agnosticism

Having examined the theoretical aspect of this soteriological emphasis I shall now turn to the praxis-based soteriological argument. My criticism here concerns Hick's shift of attention to the *soteriological process* of turning from "self-centredness to Reality-centredness" which is apparently present in the world religions. This emphasis is in line with the Buddhist insight concerning undetermined questions such as the existence of God, "namely that it is not necessary for liberation to know the answer to them".[34] I shall try to state what may be the strongest possible utilization of Hick's soteriological emphasis to overcome my objections to his new revolution. Such a hypothetical defence is based on clues from within Hick's own works.[35] The defence would have three stages. In the first, Hick argues that, despite the many levels of conflicting truth-claims, these differences "are not of great *religious*, i.e. soteriological, importance".[36] The second step would be the confirmation of such an insight from Hick's own experience. His meetings with, among others, "Nyanaponika Mahathera, a Buddhist monk" and "Kushdeva Singh, a Sikh mystic", have impressed upon Hick the priority of the life lived, rather than of the doctrines held – exemplifying the principle, "by their fruits ye shall know them".[37] The third step maintains that the focus must now be on liberation, the practice of self-giving love within the religions.[38] Paul Knitter, holding a similar view, has put it aptly:

> for Christians, that which constitutes the basis and goal for interreligious dialogue . . . is *not* how they [non-Christian religions] are related to the church (invisibly through "baptism of desire"), or how they are related to Christ (anonymously [Rahner] or normatively [Küng]), nor even how they respond to and conceive of God, but rather, to what extent they are promoting *Soteria* (in Christian images, the *basileia*) – to what extent they are engaged in promoting human welfare and bringing about liberation with and for the poor and non-persons.[39]

I believe that Hick would be in agreement with Knitter's statement, although he could not be classified as a liberation theologian, owing to his method. There are a number of problems involved in this soteriological emphasis. Does Hick not render the notion of *soteria* or salvation/liberation hopelessly vague, undialectical and without basis? Hick's emphasis on praxis still begs the question of the *basis* for the *recognition* of what *constitutes* a turning from "self-centredness to Reality-centredness" – which leads back to doctrinal formulations and their validity, and then, finally, back to the eschatological dilemma.

Before developing this criticism, I would grant the following: that ultimately, only *grace* is required for salvation, so that strictly speaking one's "beliefs and mythologies" are ultimately invalid indicators of whether salvation takes place. There is no guarantee that one who holds Christian beliefs is saved by virtue of formally professing such beliefs. Existential appropriation is all-important, as is the priority and freedom of God's grace. On a formal level, the deepest desires and promptings of a person's heart in his or her response to grace freely offered is hermeneutically inaccessible to us, but not to God or the person in question. However, and this is all-important, the argument of this paragraph is based on a set of beliefs about the nature of God's reality, based on the revelation of Jesus; hence my inclusivist position.

My first criticism concerns a tension within Hick's epicycle. On the one hand, he deems that differences in belief are ultimately unimportant for salvation, while, on the other, he uses the notion of a common salvific process to affirm the validity of the different beliefs. (Logically, he cannot have it both ways!) Secondly, Küng's implicit criticism of Knitter's position is applicable to Hick's thesis:

> the Christian community may allow itself to be persuaded to replace an ecclesio-centricism with a Christo-centricism or theo-centricism (which for Christians amount to the same thing!) but they are hardly likely to be persuaded to take up some vague soterio-centricism. Practice should not be made the norm of theory undialectically and social questions be expounded as the basis and centre of the theology of religions.[40]

If praxis, or "Reality-centredness", is made into an undialectical norm-determining theory, then the problematic transcendental agnosticism that I criticized earlier creeps back. We then encounter the problem that the notion of liberation cannot be useful as a basis for pluralism if it remains "vague" and theoretically unfounded.

Hick's view of "Reality-centredness" sometimes seems vague and lacking a clear foundation and justification. He defines "Reality-centredness" as that which "consists in a new and limitlessly better quality of existence" so that,

> if one believes that God is gracious and merciful, one may imitate the divine love and compassion [a Christian response]. If one believes that one is, in one's deepest being, identical with the infinite and eternal Brahman, one will seek to negate the present false ego and its distorting vision in order to attain that which both transcends and underlies it [an Advaitin Hindu response].[41]

And so on. This soteriological communality would lead to liberating "social structures", nobility, justice and beauty.[42]

There are some major difficulties with these formulations. The first conflates value with truth. It, perhaps too easily, identifies a common *phenomenological* or *psychological* process and mistakes it for an *ontological* similarity. It confuses a similar *process* with a common *goal*. It also assumes that there is a neutral position or common bank of acceptable criteria for defining and recognizing salvation which are not ultimately founded and grounded within a specific paradigmatic basis – and therefore are acceptable to all.

Kraemer argues against the pragmatic tradition in which value is equated with truth, because "fictions and even lies have been extraordinarily successful" and also because it is "philosophically superficial to equate the psychic experience of satisfaction with the certainty that [the experience] is therefore true in the deepest sense, or is related to realities which are true".[43] One may apply Kraemer's comments to Hick's soteriocentrism. There is a danger of Hick's assuming that similar forms of *psychological* and *phenomenological* behaviour must participate in and tend towards the *same ontological* reality. Not only is there a confusion of behavioural categories with ontological goals but there is also the assumption of the hermeneutical penetrability of the heart.

However, one cannot minimize the relation of categorical expression with the inner happenings of the heart, or minimize the importance of praxis in the acceptance of grace. The fundamental difficulty with Hick's thesis at this stage is the *basis* for identifying and recognizing the valid activity of God's saving grace operative in the religious traditions of the world. In this respect Knitter is more sensitive to the criteriological difficulties at hand when he acknowledges that

> every theocentric or soteriocentric approach remains, in a sense, inherently Christocentric. . . . But what makes the soteriocentric approach different from Christocentricism or theocentricism is its explicit recognition that before the mystery of *Soteria*, no mediator or symbol system is absolute.[44]

However, Knitter fails to overcome my objections and his own alleged disavowal of absolutes, for one sentence later he writes, "the absolute, that which all else must serve and clarify, is not the church or Christ or even God . . . but rather, the Kingdom and its justice". But from where does Knitter's notion of "the Kingdom and its justice" derive? And from where does Hick's notion of what constitutes "Reality-centredness" derive? If it is not from a secularist "modern liberal moral outlook", as Hick sometimes suggests,[45] what is it that makes the values of "acceptance, compassion, love for all humankind, or even for all life" normative?[46]

In answering these questions and defining more precisely the terms *soteria*, Kingdom, love, and so on, we are inevitably driven back to theory and the particularities of each tradition. Theory, of course, retains a dialogical relation to praxis. If Hick follows the route of transcendental agnosticism he cannot answer this question. If, on the other hand, one discovers that the Buddhist notion of *annata*, the Advaitin notion of *ātman* and the Christian notion of *agape* have different, and possibly conflicting, ontological contexts, then we are forced back to the problems that I have posed earlier – which are inevitably highlighted in the eschatological dilemma. And Hick certainly seems to succumb to the eschatological dilemma when he writes of his "pragmatic" soteriological test of the world's religions, "They accordingly test themselves by their failure in fulfilling this soteriological function. The final verification is thus *eschatological*."[47]

CONCLUSION

My argument in this essay is not meant to deny the possibility and probable reality that saving grace is operative in non-Christian religions. That it is is a perfectly legitimate affirmation within an inclusivist theology of religions, such as I hold and have defended elsewhere.[48] Rather, my arguments are a *theological* critique of Hick's reflections upon this likely reality. Elsewhere I have criticized the early stages in Hick's development to a pluralist position (from Christocentrism to theocentrism).[49] His recent strategy to avoid a theocentric solution is also problematic. His "epicycles" eventually leading to this Kantian revolution introduce what I have called an "eschatological dilemma", leading back to a covert theocentrism or non-theism. Alternatively, he is led into a "transcendental agnosticism": an agnosticism concerning the "divine Reality" coupled with an unfounded pragmatic soteriology.

My arguments are an attempt to suggest that Hick's pluralism does not provide an adequate theological explanation of the presence of God's grace outside Christianity. These arguments are not a warning against mutual co-operation by religions for justice, peace and a loving community. While the Christian may work together with the Buddhist and find himself or herself in deeper agreement about what "justice" or "liberation" constitutes in a particular situation, such an agreement does not mean that the normative and decisive nature of Christ's revelation is thereby called into question. Nor does it mean that such Christological criteria will not be enlarged and enriched through mutual action and reflection, or that the Buddhist's beliefs are false. This latter judgemental aspect of dialogue can only be clarified *in dialogue*. Theologically, however, the Christian must necessarily admit that the grace and truth within Buddhism can only be recognized, acknowledged and embraced as the grace of God – made known definitively, but not exclusively, in Christ. Soteriocentrism or Realocentrism cannot be divorced from theocentrism, which cannot be divorced from Christocentrism or finally from ecclesiocentrism. Such would be my contention. We should be grateful for John Hick's careful consideration of these problems and for the stimulus his ideas present to all those interested in religious pluralism.

NOTES

I am grateful to Dr Gerard Loughlin for his helpful criticisms – and to the Spaldings Trust for financial assistance in writing this essay.

1.   *Problems of Religious Pluralism*, pp. 31–4.
2.   *God and the Universe of Faiths*, p. 131.
3.   Although the following account is construed from various works, the position outlined is that held in *An Interpretation of Religion*.
4.   *God Has Many Names* p. 105.
5.   Ibid., p. 110.
6.   John Hick, "The Theology of Religious Pluralism", *Theology*, 86, no. 713 (1983) 337; *Interpretation of Religion*, chs 14–16.
7.   *Interpretation of Religion*, chs 15, 16.
8.   *The Second Christianity*, pp. 86–7.
9.   *Problems of Religious Pluralism*, p. 95.
10. See *An Interpretation of Religion*, ch. 11, for his understanding of religious language.
11. Ibid., p. 246; and John Hick, "Religious Pluralism and Salvation" and "A Concluding Comment", *Faith and Philosophy*, 5, no. 4 (1988) 452, ("A Concluding Comment").
12. *Interpretation of Religion*, pt 3, esp. chs 11, 13.
13. Ibid., pp. 177–88.
14. Ibid., p. 180.
15. Ibid., p. 361 n. 7.
16. *Death and Eternal Life*, p. 464.

17. *Interpretation of Religion*, p. 353 ff.
18. Ibid., pp. 356, 361.
19. Ibid., p. 361.
20. These levels are matters of history, quasi-historical, and experiential: see ibid., ch. 20.
21. *Problems of Religious Pluralism*, pp. 89–90. See also *An Interpretation of Religion*, pp. 374–6; and Hick, "Religious Pluralism and Salvation" and "A Concluding Comment", *Faith and Philosophy*, 5, no. 4, pp. 365–77, 449–55.
22. *Problems of Religious Pluralism*, p. 93.
23. Ibid. See also *An Interpretation of Religion*, p. 354; "Religious Pluralism and Salvation", *Faith and Philosophy*, 5, no. 4, p. 373.
24. *Problems of Religious Pluralism*, p. 94.
25. David Hume, *Dialogues Concerning Natural Religion* (1779), ed. Norman Kemp Smith (Indianapolis: Bobbs-Merrill, 1947) IV.1.
26. Admittedly, the apophatic tradition within Christianity affirms the incomprehensibility of God, as do Aquinas and other major theologians (as noted by Hick, but in a somewhat one-sided fashion, in *An Interpretation of Religion*, p. 247). However, Aquinas and others equally speak of God's self-disclosure to human beings in revelation; hence the important tradition that the economic Trinity is the immanent Trinity.
27. A. Wedberg, *A History of Philosophy* (Oxford: Oxford University Press, 1982) II, 174.
28. Peter Byrne, "John Hick's Philosophy of Religion", *Scottish Journal of Theology*, 35, no. 4 (1982) 289–301.
29. *Problems of Religious Pluralism*, p. 16; *Interpretation of Religion*, ch. 11.
30. *Interpretation of Religion*, p. 361.
31. *Problems of Religious Pluralism*, p. 125.
32. Ibid., p. 16.
33. *Interpretation of Religion*, p. 207.
34. Ibid., p. 344; and *Problems of Religious Pluralism*, p. 73.
35. These three steps are present in *An Interpretation of Religion*, chs 17–20.
36. *Interpretation of Religion*, pp. 344ff, 375; and "Religious Pluralism and Salvation", *Faith and Philosophy*, 5, no. 4, p. 373.
37. *The Second Christianity*, p. 87; *Interpretation of Religion*, ch. 18.
38. *Interpretation of Religion*, ch. 18.
39. Paul Knitter, "Towards a Liberation Theology of Religions", in John Hick and Paul Knitter (eds), *The Myth of Christian Uniqueness* (London: SCM, 1987).
40. Hans Küng, "Towards an Ecumenical Theology of Religion: Some Theses for Clarification", in Hans Küng and Jürgen Moltmann, *Christianity among World Religions, Concilium* 183 (Edinburgh: T. & T. Clark, 1986) p. 123.
41. *Problems of Religious Pluralism*, p. 70; *Interpretation of Religion*, chs 17–18.
42. *Problems of Religious Pluralism*, p. 79.

43.   H. Kraemer, *Religion and the Christian Faith* (London: Lutterworth, 1956) p. 85. Interestingly, Hick acknowledges that his criterion is "pragmatic" in *Problems of Religious Pluralism*, p. 80, and *Interpretation of Religion*, ch. 18.

44.   Knitter, "Towards a Liberation Theology of Religions", in Hick and Knitter, *The Myth of Christian Uniqueness*, p. 190.

45.   *Problems of Religious Pluralism*, p. 76.

46.   Ibid., p. 81.

47.   Ibid., p. 80.

48.   See Gavin D'Costa, *Theology and Religious Pluralism: The Challenge of Other Religions* (Oxford: Basil Blackwell, 1986); and "Christ, the Trinity and Religious Plurality", in G. D'Costa (ed.), *Christian Uniqueness Reconsidered: The Myth of a Pluralistic Theology of Religions* (New York: Orbis, 1990) ch. 2.

49.   Gavin D'Costa, *John Hick's Theology of Religions: A Critical Evaluation* (New York: University Press of America, 1987) chs 3, 4.

Critical Response

JAMES KELLENBERGER

Gavin D'Costa, as much as John Hick, allows that those in religious traditions other than Christianity may attain salvation. Both D'Costa and Hick oppose exclusivism. However, they do so from different positions, D'Costa from a Christian inclusivist position, Hick from a pluralist position. For D'Costa the possibility of non-Christians finding salvation in non-Christian religions is a matter of the "probable reality" that God's saving grace is at work in those religions.[1] But, he argues, "Hick's pluralism does not provide an adequate theological explanation of the presence of God's grace outside Christianity".[2] D'Costa's paper is in fact a sustained critical examination of Hick's pluralism. He, not without sympathy, argues against Hick's view. Also, along the way, he identifies several significant issues, including one that may be pivotal in the controversy between Hick's pluralism and his own inclusivism.

As D'Costa sees it, Hick's pluralism has evolved since its inception. The Copernican revolution earlier proposed by Hick, which put God or divine Reality at the centre of the universe of faiths, has given way to a "Kantian revolution". This Kantian revolution leads, however, D'Costa argues, to an "eschatological dilemma", which in turn leads to a "transcendental agnosticism", which, finally, requires the rejection of pluralism as it has evolved. Briefly, this is the movement of D'Costa's reasoning. I want to look at that reasoning and raise some questions about it, but also, and more importantly, I want to focus on some issues that D'Costa rightly brings to our attention.

What D'Costa means by a "Kantian revolution" has two main parts. One is that "God is removed from the centre of the universe of faiths and is replaced by human transformation". The second is that a "Kantian-type epistemology" is adopted.[3] This Kantian-type epistemology posits a distinction between the Real as experienced and the Real *an sich*. The Real as experienced is known differently in various religious traditions, as God the Father or Allah or as Brahman or the Tao, in accordance with the concepts that fashion experience in these traditions; the Real *an sich* is not

19

experienced in itself, on Hick's view.[4] This epistemological position, D'Costa argues, leads to an eschatological dilemma: on the
one hand Hick defends the cognitive status of religious language
in theistic and non-theistic traditions, but on the other hand he
denies "that theistic and non-theistic claims are claims about
Reality".[5] It must be admitted that there is a tension between these
two; but does Hick deny that all religious claims are about Reality?
John Hick himself can answer this question definitively. However,
I will venture to say that on one reading his position allows, even
insists, that various religious claims – many of the "metaphysical"
ones – are cognitive claims about Reality. It is in order to
guarantee the cognitive and "factual" status of such claims that
Hick insists upon the possibility of eschatological verification.[6]
What Hick rules out is that we human beings are in a position *now*
to assess the truth of such conflicting truth-claims. D'Costa quotes
Hick as saying in *An Interpretation of Religion*, "It follows from this
distinction between the Real as it is in itself and as it is thought
and experienced through our religious concepts that we cannot
apply to the Real *an sich* the characteristics encountered in its
personae and *impersonae*."[7] However, there is a question about
what this means. Does Hick mean that *we* (before the eschaton)
cannot apply such characteristics to the Real *an sich*, or does he
mean that logically such characteristics are not applicable to the
Real *an sich*? D'Costa understands Hick as saying the second. But,
as I read his entire position, it may well involve the first and not
the second. Hick at one point allows that, though unlikely, it is
logically possible that "some present set of dogmas (Catholic . . .
Mormon . . . Mahayana [etc.]) will turn out to correspond precisely with reality".[8] Of course he said this before *An Interpretation
of Religion*. Are things different now? At bottom I think not,
although now, in *An Interpretation of Religion*, Hick says that
phenomenally experienced attributes of Reality, such as love in
the Christian tradition, if they are authentic phenomenal manifestations of the Real, have their ground or source in the Real.
Either of two models may be employed to think about this, Hick
suggests. Such experienced attributes as love and bliss may be
different "aspects of the Real" or it may be that the love and bliss
of the Real are "super analogues" of the love and bliss we
experience.[9] On his earlier view, then, central metaphysical religious claims are cognitive claims about a correspondence with
"reality"; on his later view they are claims about the Real as the

noumenal ground of the attributes phenomenally experienced. In either case, though, Hick ends up recognizing that central metaphysical religious claims are cognitive claims about the Real. In short, it seems to me that Hick may be able to escape the eschatological dilemma. But perhaps I have failed to appreciate its full force, and I shall leave its further consideration for subsequent discussions. In any case, D'Costa sees this dilemma as leading to what he calls "transcendental agnosticism".

"Transcendental agnosticism", in D'Costa's words, "affirms the *transcendent* divine reality over against *naturalistic* positions, while refusing to state that the eschaton may eventually be theistic rather than non-theistic, in however minimalist a sense."[10] It is true, as D'Costa also observes, that Hick suggests the eschaton may be beyond the anticipations of any religious tradition; and it is true, as D'Costa says, that Hick suggests the eschaton is possibly beyond the present range of our imaginations. But, as I have indicated, Hick has also allowed that it is logically possible that the eschaton may be theistic, even precisely Christian, and as far as I can see he still allows this in the sense that he does not deny the logical possibility that the Real in itself may be the noumenal ground for, precisely, Christianity alone. It is just that Hick does not claim to know now, and that he thinks, moreover, that we cannot now know.[11] Thus, if Hick's position is indicted for transcendental agnosticism, it is only as it relates to human understanding of the Real *an sich* before the eschaton. His view, we may say, has no transcendent problem of transcendental agnosticism.

However, there may be a related problem in the area that D'Costa draws to our attention. He reminds us of Hick's strong support for the cognitive status of religious language.[12] Why is it important to insist upon the cognitivity of religious language? It is because, arguably, religious language must be cognitive for the self-understanding of religious persons. For instance, their own trust in God and their own prayer, as these are understood by traditional Christians, require for their coherence the cognitive beliefs that there is a God and that God receives prayers. Also, of course, the cognitivity of religious language is necessary for that form of religious commitment that expresses itself in such utterances as Job's cry of faith "I know my Redeemer liveth". The question that arises here is this: is religious commitment in such a Job-like expression open to a Christian, or a member of any other particular religion, who subscribes to Hick's philosophy of religious pluralism? It would appear not to be, for as a pluralist the individual believer would not profess to know that his Redeemer liveth or that Christ is Lord or that Allah is God. Perhaps Hick could at this point draw attention to his analysis of faith as interpretation, which also is knowledge, for him.[13] Such knowledge, though, as Hick emphasizes, is "fallible" knowledge. That is, for him, it is knowledge that may be mistaken. So it is that one with such knowledge might enter into dialogue with another who holds conflicting beliefs and consistently believe that the partner in dialogue, in Hick's words, "might . . . be closer to the divine Reality".[14] For the same reason, though, this sense of "knowledge" does not allow for a Job-like expression of commitment. Job, I submit, would fail to express his faith by saying, "I know my Redeemer liveth, although I may be mistaken." Now, to be sure, there are other ways to express religious commitment, even the commitment of faith, such as, "Lord, I believe. Help thou my unbelief." However it remains that there is a tension between Hick's pluralism and the not-unimportant form of religious commitment embodied in Job's utterance. It seems to me that D'Costa's discussion of transcendental agnosticism helps us to identify this tension.

D'Costa more explicitly raises other issues. The most serious issue he raises, it seems to me, has to do with the first part of the Kantian revolution: the new central emphasis on soteriological movement in Hick's pluralism. As Hick sees it, human transformation is taking place in all the main traditions and, as far as can be humanly judged, to about the same extent in all of them.[15] This soteriological movement, then, being found in various traditions, cannot be defined in terms that would limit it to just one religion. It must be given a very broad sense in order to apply as widely as Hick requires. The result, as D'Costa sees it, is that Hick ends up with a vague concept of *soteria*, one that is even "hopelessly vague".[16] The issue that D'Costa raises may be put this way: what are the criteria for, or indications of, human transformation? It does not help, or help enough, to call human transformation "salvation/liberation". Moreover, in order to appreciate the full force of the issue, we should appreciate that, for Hick, human transformation may also be taking place within naturalistic Marxism and humanism.[17] So the notion he needs must be exceptionally broad. In each case of human transformation Hick would say that a movement from "self-centredness to Reality-centredness" is taking place, but, while this helps, it still leaves it fairly vague what will and will not count as an instance of this movement, as D'Costa sees.

Let me elaborate the issue slightly to bring out its importance. Are there religion-neutral criteria for salvation? Or, alternatively, are the particular notions of salvation (or liberation) in the different traditions so different that they cannot be reconciled? Hick accepts the first. His position may even require it. At best the second alternative would be uncomfortable for his pluralism. D'Costa regards the first alternative as mistaken and would not be unhappy with the second alternative since, for him, the ultimate criteria for salvation are Christian. In this way this issue is one that cuts between pluralism and inclusivism. Not that the issue is easy. D'Costa at the end of his paper allows that Christological criteria may be enlarged and enriched through contact with other religions.[18] If a similar point can be made about the criteria for salvation in other traditions, then the indicators of salvation in the various traditions may be in a process of change. If so, a resolution of this issue will, among other things, require assessing the direction of that change.

NOTES

1.   Gavin D'Costa, above, p. 15.
2.   Ibid.
3.   D'Costa, above, p. 4.
4.   Hick, *Problems of Religious Pluralism*, pp. 41–4.
5.   D'Costa, above, p. 6.
6.   *Problems of Religious Pluralism*, p. 95.
7.   D'Costa, above, p. 6.
8.   *Problems of Religious Pluralism*, p. 100.
9.   *Interpretation of Religion*, pp. 246–7.
10.   D'Costa, above, pp. 7–8.
11.   *Interpretation of Religion*, p. 341, n. 8.
12.   D'Costa, above, p. 6.
13.   *Faith and Knowledge*, 2nd edn, ch. 9.
14.   *Problems of Religious Pluralism*, pp. 89–90; as quoted by D'Costa, p. 8.
15.   Ibid., pp. 86–7.
16.   D'Costa, above, p. 12.
17.   *Problems of Religious Pluralism*, p. 44; and *Interpretation of Religion*, p.308.
18.   D'Costa, above, p. 16.

Reply

JOHN HICK

Gavin D'Costa poses, as always, important questions, and James Kellenberger suggests how they can be answered from the standpoint of the *Interpretation of Religion* (IR) hypothesis. My contribution here is to put these answers into a somewhat wider context.

The basic idea of eschatological verification is simply that different conceptions of the nature or structure of the universe, religious and naturalistic, are correlated with different expectations concerning future human experience, and are to this extent open to experiential confirmation or disconfirmation. They involve, in particular, beliefs as to whether there will be any experiences beyond our present life; and, if there are, beliefs about the nature of such experiences. There are thus various stages at which expectations may be wholly or partly confirmed or disconfirmed in the light of experience. If we find, after physical death, that we exist as conscious minds, though without physical bodies, the materialistic conception of the universe will have been falsified. (If, on the other hand, we cease to exist at death we shall not be able to verify that this is so. There is thus at this point an unavoidable asymmetry.)

If there are post-mortem experiences, these could take many possible forms. The eschatological claims made by the different religious traditions are made in terms of their own belief systems, built around the experience of particular divine personae or metaphysical impersonae. They accordingly present distinctively Christian or Muslim or Buddhist (or whatever) expectations. Each of these will – according to the IR hypothesis – prove to be correct in comparison with the naturalistic view that "when you're dead you're dead". But, on the other hand, each of them will almost certainly turn out to be *extremely* inadequate as an account of what actually happens, so that all of these pictures will probably have to undergo considerable amendment, or radical reconstruction, in the light of future post-mortem experience. It is possible, for example, that in an immediately post-mortem phase the different expectations generated by the different traditions will each to some extent be fulfilled in different individuals' mind-dependent

24

bardo worlds; but that beyond this there are other phases whose nature we cannot presently imagine. All that the IR hypothesis affirms, on the basis of the "cosmic optimism" of the great traditions, is that the process moves towards "a limitlessly good fulfilment of the project of human existence".[1] "Good" here means good from our human point of view, bearing in mind, however, that this point of view may itself develop through time in harmony with increasing insight and wisdom – perhaps even finally to the point at which separate ego identity is no longer valued. If we are indeed part of such a cosmic process, this will become increasingly evident as its goal is approached. (If, on the other hand, no such process is occurring, it is less easy to see how this negative fact could be established; again there is an unavoidable asymmetry.)

D'Costa holds that so general a prediction as "a limitlessly good fulfilment of the project of human existence" is "no longer significant".[2] But is not this a considerable overstatement on his part? Consider the various specifically Christian pictures of heaven – such as the picture in Revelation 21, in which we read concerning the heavenly city that "The wall was built of jasper, while the city was pure gold, clear as glass . . . . And the twelve gates were twelve pearls, each of the gates made of a single pearl . . ." (vv. 18, 21). Would D'Costa say that, if all such images are highly inadequate, the not-further-specified Christian expectation of an end-state. expressing the limitless love of God is "no longer significant"? Surely not. Why then should he think that the general expectation of a limitlessly good end-state is no longer significant?

It is of course theoretically possible – as Kellenberger notes – that one of the religious traditions has a literally true belief system (all other belief systems being false in so far as they differ from this); and this includes the possibility that the eschatological beliefs of that tradition are literally true (and all others false in so far as they differ). Indeed, each tradition has generally claimed this for its own beliefs. But there is no way of establishing at present that one of these claims is justified; and the very evident fact that the belief systems are all strongly culturally conditioned prompts the development of a different and more complex hypothesis, such as I have tried to formulate.

D'Costa also makes a "charge of total scepticism or agnosticism".[3] The characterization of the IR hypothesis as "agnostic as to the ultimate nature of the transcendent reality",[4] whilst correct in a sense, is in another sense misleading. It is misleading if it presupposes that the Ultimate must be either personal or impersonal, purposive or non-purposive, good or evil, and so on, and regards the IR hypothesis as professing not to know which. The hypothesis is in fact, however, rather different, namely that the Real in itself is beyond the scope of our human concepts, so that none of these pairs of opposites applies to it. In Buddhist terms it is *śūnya*, empty – that is, empty of all that human thought projects as it seeks to grasp reality. In Western terms, the Ultimate is ineffable, not describable in human terms.

But this does not mean that the concept of the Real is a mere blank. It is the concept of the inexperienceable and indescribable ground of the range of human religious experience in so far as this is more than purely human projection. The Real is that which there must be if this range of experience is not *in toto* delusory. We thus postulate the noumenal Real as our way of affirming that the religious experience of humanity is our response – always historically and culturally conditioned – to a transcendent Reality.

It should perhaps at this point be reiterated, in response to D'Costa, that according to the IR hypothesis religious beliefs can be true or false in two different senses and in two different contexts. They are literally or analogically true or false (analogy being a stretched literality) of the manifestation of the Real which is their intentional object – for example, the Christian Trinity, the Allah of Islam, the Brahman of Hindu thought. And, in so far as they are literally (or analogically) true of a manifestation of the Real, they are mythologically true of the Real in itself. They are "mythologically true" in so far as the dispositional response which they tend to evoke is appropriate to an authentic manifestation of the Real, and so to the Real in itself. For that such a manifestation is authentic means that it is in "soteriological alignment" with the Real. The circular movement here from the postulated noumenal Real to its phenomenal manifestations, to appropriate responses to these, which are also appropriate responses to the Real in itself, is, I suggest, an example of a "benign" as distinguished from a "vicious" circle.

Finally, D'Costa's suggestion that the move from Christocentrism to theocentrism to "Realocentrism" (his word, not mine) is now extended to "soteriocentrism" involves a category mistake on his part. The "centre" of all things is the Real, not human transformation; the salvific transformation is the form taken by our response to that central Reality. The transcendent Reality, and our human responses to it, should not be confused.

NOTES

1. *Interpretation of Religion*, p. 361.
2. Gavin D'Costa, above, p. 7.
3. D'Costa, above, p. 9.
4. D'Costa, above, p. 8.

2

An Interpretation of
An Interpretation of Religion

CHESTER GILLIS

INTRODUCTION

It is a great honour to be chosen to deliver the Gifford Lectures, which are arguably the most prestigious lectureship on religion in the English-speaking world. One immediately thinks of past publications of lectures that have now achieved classic status – William James's *Varieties of Religious Experience* and Reinhold Niebuhr's *Nature and Destiny of Man*, to name just two. These lectures often represent the culmination of a career of scholarship. But many Gifford Lectures are period pieces that are remanded to obscurity and distant memory. Only the test of time will judge the fate of John Hick's 1986–7 Gifford Lectures, titled *An Interpretation of Religion: Human Responses to the Transcendent*. My attempt to interpret, appreciate and criticize them comes at the time of their publication, making me one of the first to offer an assessment of the contribution this work makes to scholarship.

The book presents the conclusions of a lifetime of critical thought, and in general fulfils the expectations raised by such a work. It is carefully crafted, tightly written, coherent, provocative, readable and scholarly. Producing a volume with these characteristics is a rare enough accomplishment among scholars of religion. Hick's style has a clarity one can only admire. His book is one that colleagues in the field will certainly consider a benchmark work. At the same time it is a text that also lends itself to use in the classroom by students in a number of fields of inquiry, notably philosophy, theology, history of religions and comparative studies.

It is a book that has the patina of decades of thought and scholarship. The text itself has been refined by the author through dialogue with his students at Claremont, and his sympathetic and unsympathetic commentators and critics who are fellow scholars. It is a piece to be proud of, a contribution, a culmination, a challenge, an interpretation and a vision. While it is not the conclusion of John Hick's career as a productive scholar, it is the crowning work.

In this paper I shall attempt to substantiate my view that *An Interpretation of Religion* is the most polished version of its author's thinking and constitutes a significant contribution to the scholarly treatment of religion. My appreciation, however, does not preclude criticism of Hick's work. While I intend to indicate what I think are his lasting contributions, I also intend to point to problems and difficulties in his thought process in general and in this work in particular. Also, rather like Hick himself in the book, I shall offer some suggestions for future directions of inquiry.

POSITIVE POINTS

I begin this section with an assessment of the improvements Hick has made in this work as a result primarily of nuancing of his established position on a number of different issues and aspects of his examination of religion. I shall then indicate those ideas that are either genuinely new for Hick or, in the form in which he now presents them, so radically altered as to represent not simply a nuancing of an established position but a quite new position.

Changes of nuance

DEFINITION OF RELIGION

In the introduction of one of his early works, *Philosophy of Religion* (1963), Hick wrote, "There is . . . no universally accepted definition of religion, and quite possibly there never will be."[1] While he held that position with regard to a phenomenological description of religion, for practical purposes he adopted fairly strict criteria for what should be considered a religion in the formal sense. He proposed "a working definition of religion as an understanding of the universe, together with an appropriate way of living within it, which involves reference beyond the natural world to God or gods or to the Absolute or to a transcendent order or process".[2]

This definition included the major traditions (Judaism, Christianity, Islam, Hinduism, Buddhism) but excluded naturalistic systems of belief such as Marxism. His definition of a religion is narrowed further by his insistence on the concept that a genuine encounter with the divine (Real) is limited to one which "has come out of a great revelatory religious experience and has been tested through a long tradition of worship, and has sustained human faith over centuries of time in millions of lives".[3] This restriction eliminated consideration of archaic or primitive religions, and religious movements founded in the modern era. In a more recent work (*Problems of Religious Pluralism*) Hick acknowledges this lacuna with the assurance that he is aware of these other possibilities and consideration of them is "among the many important questions which any complete philosophy of religious pluralism must answer".[4]

In *An Interpretation of Religion* he finally addresses this issue. He does this in four ways: (1) by admitting outright that he has given less attention to primal religion than it deserves;[5] (2) by making it clear that archaic religion is not (necessarily) an inferior form of religion;[6] (3) by recognising the potential soteriological character of minor and new religious movements;[7] (4) and perhaps most importantly, by relying on Wittgenstein's concept of family resemblances to describe religion.[8] By using Wittgenstein's concept he expands his previously rigid criteria for what constitutes religion so that he is able to accommodate religious traditions or expressions that do not speak explicitly of the transcendent (for example, Theravāda Buddhism) or that reject a transcendent or divine reality (for example, Marxism) while having many characteristics in common with explicitly religious traditions.

As the subtitle of the book, "Human Responses to the Transcendent", indicates, Hick still prefers to focus on those religious expressions that acknowledge transcendent reality, and that is his legitimate prerogative. At least in this presentation he does not deny the possibility of legitimacy in the religious world for other expressions that are also comprehensive world views. In relation to his previous work, this acknowledgement represents a significant concession and advance.

NEW SOURCES

For the first time, to my knowledge, Hick takes into account the contributions of some highly regarded scholars whom he has previously ignored. The recognition and appropriation of this material makes a clear difference to his own presentation. It adds depth, complexity and breadth to his work. Although there may well be others who serve as new sources of insight in the research for this book, the two scholars whose significance is most obvious here are Robert Bellah and Mircea Eliade. The influence of Bellah, besides supporting the inclusion of Marxism under the rubric of religion,[9] is most clearly apparent in Hick's description of the pre-axial period. He further nuances his position on the pre-axial and axial period (a designation derived from Karl Jaspers), indicating that pre-axial religion did not completely end with the advent of the axial age and that archaic religion is not to be dismissed as insignificant or inferior. This greater appreciation of archaic religion is, I think, largely owing to the influence of Eliade's writing, which Hick cites extensively in the book. This acknowledgement of a scholar recognized for a long time by others as an authoritative source is a welcome addition to Hick's research. In my more critical comments later I shall mention a few other world-class scholars whose work I think Hick might also have employed to improve his argument.

RESPONSES TO CRITICS

In a number of places, and on a number of issues, Hick uses *An Interpretation of Religion* to answer his critics. Such responses are not a novelty in his work, since Hick has often in the past written to answer specific objections and criticisms. In this work he does not shy away from critics but attempts to respond to some of the most recent criticism of his thought. He does this when and where he believes that the criticism is wrong and should not be heeded, or is right in some respects and requires him to adjust his position, as he has done so adeptly on a number of issues in the book. When he clearly differs with critics he employs argument to make (or maintain) his point. He also chooses central issues to defend. The citation of a few instances should serve to illustrate this character of the work. For instance, his expanded use of Wittgenstein's concept of "seeing-as", interpreted as "experiencing-as", is central to Hick's religious epistemology. If it were to be denied or refuted it would undermine an essential element of Hick's interpretation of religion. In his defence Hick takes the opportunity to rehearse[10] and support his position. In another instance[11] he enlists the support of other recent scholarship to support his position against attacks. In this case it again deals with his epistemology, specifically on the nature of experience. Yet he is careful to distinguish his position from that of others who may appear to agree with him but upon closer examination do not.[12] He also attempts to refute recent positions which contradict his own.[13]

CROSS-DISCIPLINARY APPROACH

The college student who ventures to read *An Interpretation of Religion,* and I hope that there will be many, may be attracted to the work by its lucid style and its comprehensive scope. However, were he or she asked to categorize the work as one of philosophy, theology, philosophy of religion or history of religion, or the author as philosopher, theologian or historian, he or she would probably have a difficult time responding. This is not meant as a criticism of the work as unfocused but as a compliment to its breadth and the author's range of interest and competence. So much of Hick's early work was philosophy of religion or theology considered from the Western Christian perspective exclusively. The second half of his academic career has been increasingly dedicated to theological and philosophical study of traditions other than Christianity. All of this effort bears fruit in this volume. It is a balanced, well-chosen and well-thought-out presentation of religion across a broad spectrum of the religious enterprise. Further, the marshalling of insights from various disciplines (and anthropology could be included with philosophy, theology and history of religions) is masterfully done. It is a feat few contemporary authors have accomplished as well as Hick. It is also precisely because he turned his attention to traditions other than Christianity that this work is so valuable. It is on the cutting edge of contemporary theology. The issues it raises, even if not fully resolved to everyone's satisfaction, are the issues that those thinking theologically within the religions face. It confronts these issues boldly with creative suggestions for resolutions or new directions.

New ideas and radical changes

There are two (at least two, perhaps more) developments in *An Interpretation of Religion* which are simply not in evidence in Hick's previous work. The first is his effort to take seriously the contributions of feminist theology. The second is his attempt to address the issues of cross-cultural ethics. The first is, in my opinion, long overdue. The second is a beginning of an effort that will require much more ink on his part and from other scholars involved with inter-religious dialogue.

ACKNOWLEDGEMENT OF FEMINIST CRITICISM

For most of his career Hick has either employed exclusively male language in his work or at best used non-gender-specific pronouns. In this book a significant new awareness is present in a dynamic way. It is one which I welcome, though I do think its late appearance reflects a serious flaw in his previous scholarship.

For someone who is so sensitive to religious language and theological terminology he has been less than sensitive to the dangers of theologizing as if the world were male. However, he corrects this flaw in the present work in a number of ways. First, he uses the feminine form of the pronoun alongside the male form in a number of places in the text[14] and sometimes even uses it on its own.[15] This is no small advance and certainly will not be overlooked by readers who are wisely aware of feminist views concerning language and its careful use. Secondly, and perhaps more importantly, Hick takes seriously, in a number of places in the text, the issues raised by feminist theologians. This indicates that more conscious use of language is not simply a superficial nod to feminism or an editorial directive. At one point in his discourse he describes feminist theologians as those "who are today contributing major and sometimes startling insights which would be a serious mistake for others to ignore",[16] even though he himself has previously ignored them.

There are two places in the text that I would cite as evidence of this new consciousness and attitude. In his chapter "Soteriology/ Liberation as Human Transformation" he argues that religions encourage a movement away from ego-centredness or a denial of the ego. After articulating and presenting evidence for this point, the author himself raises and responds to the potential objections. The first objection centres around the prominence he gives to mystical tradition in his analysis. This is an objection that may be raised by any number of theologians. But I shall not address it here. The second objection is the feminist criticism of such an understanding of salvation/liberation. The feminists see self-assertion or ego-centredness as a characteristic not of all human beings but of *male* human beings. The female, by contrast, is more likely to lack assertiveness and to deny her own self-fulfilment or ego. Here Hick responds that one must first be a self to be able to respond to religion's call to self-denial. Thus he concludes that, in so far as feminism is attempting to support or restore the often suppressed or underdeveloped ego of women, it is a healthy contribution that must precede religious conversion to ways of salvation as he describes them. He goes far in his praise for feminism when he writes, "This means that the contemporary women's liberation movement, as a part of the larger movement for human liberation, is in the front line of salvific change in our world today."[17]

CROSS-CULTURAL ETHICS

The issue of cross-cultural ethics is something to which the unfolding of a pluralistic soteriology has been leading for quite some time. Hick broadly indicates this concern at the beginning of his book when he writes, "the recognition of the human element in all religion emphasizes the need for rational and *ethical criticism and discrimination*" (emphasis added). But it is, appropriately, at the end of the book that the issue of an ethical criterion is addressed.[18] Here Hick lays out his ethical/soteriological criteria to evaluate his claim that religions promote the transformation of persons from self-centredness to Reality-centredness. This he does under the rubric of two foci: spiritual fruits and moral fruits. In the first of these, the spiritual dimension, holy persons transcend their own egoistic point of view and concentrate instead on the Real (the divine). This generates compassion/love for other persons and for the environment. Thus Hick depicts the call to holiness or saintliness common to all traditions in these terms. However he does not ignore the issues of systemic evil that need also to be overcome. Drawing on the insights of liberation theology (another new development for Hick) he acknowledges the necessity to transform unjust or oppressive social structures as well. Here he talks of "political saints" whose role it is to reform political and social structures. He distinguishes between a pre- and a post-sociological consciousness. The effort or holiness of the saint in the pre-sociological consciousness is conceived in terms of individual charity, while in the post-sociological consciousness it is conceived as an *agape/karuna* that demands justice. Hick argues that both the pre- and post-sociological consciousnesses are attempting to address the central problem of human suffering, from which we seek to be delivered or which we hope to help transform. He posits that "The basic criterion, then, for judging religious phenomena is soteriological."[19] All the religions, in different formulations, subscribe to a golden rule to the effect that you should not do to others what you do not wish done to you.

However I find that this ethical criterion goes only so far. While its general character gives it a wide applicability, it also permits it to be vacuous and unspecified. Hick addresses the issue of possible different intentions of persons who perform the same ethical actions motivated by different beliefs.[20] He contends that different beliefs may lead to similar actions. However, is it not sometimes the case that apparently similar ethical/religious beliefs result in different and even opposite actions? For example, if one takes the idea of "liberation" as a starting-point in seeking to show the solidarity of different religions, one faces the problem that this norm is interpreted in different ways in different traditions. Some would view it as a this-worldly norm meant to affirm the intrinsic value of persons here and now, and would therefore consider it a basic duty of the religious person to strive to alleviate poverty or hunger. Others, with religious beliefs and practices focusing on a world beyond this world, would not recognize such a duty. For example, in the Hindu tradition the distribution of wealth and material goods is often seen as a consequence of previous lives and so not something that religion should question. The Christian tradition, however, stresses the welfare of the poor as a constitutive part of the Christian's obligations. If the formal norm is considered to be "liberation" and under this rubric many and sometimes opposing postures and actions can be assumed or defended, what is the common denominator that makes it possible to speak of it as a norm cutting across different traditions?

Or take the example of "justice": if this is a norm for different religions, then what sort of justice is it? Christian biblical justice that registers disapproval but allows for forgiveness? Strict Qur'ānic justice that calls for amputation of the thief's hand or stoning of the adulterer? Hindu justice that can logically attribute circumstances of poverty or depravity to *karma?* And what about the Buddhist traditions, in which it is difficult to find a concept analogous to the Western conception of justice at all? Do ideas of justice in diverse cultures and religious traditions have a consistent-enough meaning or content for us to be able to recognize in them a norm determining when and where salvation/ liberation is truly occurring?

These are the hard cases. Hick does address them,[21] condemning specific practices particular to each religion that he considers to be evil. Among these are, for example, racism (Christianity), persecution (Islam), and designation of outcasts (Hinduism). He bases his condemnation upon "the common criterion of true *Menschlichkeit,* expressed in agape or karuna".[22] Hick has great, if not exaggerated, confidence in science and "the modern liberal moral outlook" to transform societies and permeate religions. One quality of the modern liberal ethical outlook is the intrinsic equality of persons. This may appear true to a Western Christian living in a democratic state. But does Hinduism, for example, consider individuals intrinsically equal, or does it view the matter in just the opposite terms: that is, that persons are not equal, intellectually, physically, morally or politically. In other words, inequality is the presumption. Or do present-day Iranian Muslims consider the scientific picture of the world accurate, desirable or inviting? I think not.

Hick speaks to these moral differences by concluding that each of the religions has a mixture of good and evil on different issues, and that this mixture is itself variable over time. Therefore no one religion can be judged to be better over all, or more salvific, than another. Each does strive to move persons from self-centredness to Reality-centredness. Each enjoys successes and endures failures in the process.

PROBLEMS AND DEFICIENCIES

Thus far I have indicated differences, subtle or striking, between *An Interpretation of Religion* and Hick's earlier work. In general, the changes registered strengthen and solidify his position as a major voice in contemporary theological conversation. *An Interpretation of Religion* is not without weaknesses, however. In this section I shall indicate what I consider to be its most serious deficiencies.

Some relate to what it continues to claim; some, to what the work lacks; some, to what it concludes and how it reaches those conclusions.

Questionable positions that continue to be held

The book is very carefully written. Hick has painstakingly nuanced his position on a number of significant issues. However, some positions, no matter how nuanced, are not worth upholding and should be abandoned altogether. In a few instances he has tenaciously clung to positions which continue to be problematic, or unnecessary. Hick's continued concern with empiricism, particularly of the logical-positivist variety, seems to me to be a concession to the validity of the whole enterprise of logical positivism. Most scholars have dismissed this long ago as ill-fated and unworthy of further consideration. The criteria of the logical positivists are simply not well founded or acceptable. To continue to try to answer the question of the referent of religion on the grounds established by logical positivism is to concede validity to those grounds. Hick's nuanced version of eschatological verification[23] still constitutes an attempt to respond to this positivist critique.

A second issue, which I have addressed more extensively elsewhere,[24] is Hick's understanding of myth and metaphor. He distinguishes between "literal" and "mythological" truth. Literal truth is a kind of truth-as-correspondence theory. Literal statements conform to empirical fact. What he calls mythological truth is more of a psychological conception, or, as Hick prefers to call it, an existential truth. Statements which evoke what are deemed to be appropriate dispositional attitudes are said to be mythologically true, though not literally true. He further divides myth into two types, expository myths and those which respond to mysteries. Expository myths make a statement that can be expressed in liberal terms but for which the mythical version may be preferred, simply for its creativity. Among a number of examples cited by Hick is the story of the fall of Adam and Eve, which conveys a message about the alienation present in life. Myths which address mysteries respond to questions which do not allow for a literal response. This kind of mythological language is used to talk about the noumenal Real *an sich*. As Hick puts it, "we speak mytholo-

gically about the noumenal Real by speaking literally or analogously about its phenomenological manifestations".[25] Religious
myths, then, orient us properly in relation to the Real. Hick calls
those myths that orient us properly "true religious myths".

The role of myth is further analysed in relation to its use of levels
of religious language. On the narrative level the mythological
references are more concrete (for example, the anthropomorphic
rendering of God the creator in the Hebrew Scriptures, or Allah
giving direction to the Muslims in the Qur'ān). On the abstract
level, in which theological and philosophical discourse serve, the
mythological takes a different form (for example, discussion of the
Trinity in Christian theology or of Brahman in Hinduism), but
does not disappear.

Religious language uses both concrete and abstract forms but is
consistently mythological since it is discourse "about that which
transcends the literal scope of human language".[26] In this understanding of myth in religious language, truth is construed in
terms of (or reduced to) appropriateness or inappropriateness or
the practical disposition it engenders. So myth is not truth-
disclosive or able to make a claim to reality, but is more of a tool
properly to orient the feelings and actions of a religious person.
"True myths", then, evoke proper practical attitudes or dispositions. Mythical language, therefore, is non-cognitive, non-factual
language. It is not to be considered in itself true or false, since it
does not make these types of claims.

However, using different sources (for example, Paul Ricoeur)
one could claim that mythical language can and does disclose
something which can be true or false. Whether or not a disclosure
or claim is determined ultimately to be true or false is a matter that
is to be adjudicated by evidence and argument. But my contention
is that myths do disclose something that is either true or false and
that they are not merely linguistic tools for the proper orientation
of attitudes or dispositions. They are not simply practical, as Hick
insists, but make truth-claims like other forms of language. Myths,
like literal language, also make cognitive claims.

Method

I have just mentioned the issue of the use of sources. My argument
here with Hick is one of method. Before considering the issue of

method and sources I do concede that it is the rightful prerogative of an author to select sources that will inform and support a particular hypothesis, theory or argument. So, indeed, it is Hick's right to marshal ideas and evidence directly or indirectly from the work of predecessors and contemporaries in a number of fields. However, my point is that the selection of specific scholars and sources to inform and corroborate a work is always a process also of elimination. In that selection, however well-informed, one omits other and sometimes competing ideas, theories or arguments. This can be done consciously or unconsciously. Judging from the care and breadth of Hick's scholarship in general, and in *An Interpretation of Religion* in particular, I can only conclude that Hick has made an informed selection of sources. To suggest ignorance of some major commentators would be unfair. So I must presume then that Hick has consciously chosen to omit or ignore the work of a number of prominent thinkers.

No one (certainly not I) expects him to consult or refer to all possible critical sources before attempting to write. Given the current abundance of critical scholarship on religion, this is a near-impossible task. Yet the selection of sources does in fact help to determine the conclusion of a constructive effort. In a book that cites the ideas or texts of scholars from Masao Abe to R.C. Zaehner alphabetically and from Abraham to Bowker chronologically it is risky to say that something has been omitted. However, there are sources that Hick ignores. The tradition of contemporary hermeneutical understanding derived from Gadamer, Ricoeur and Tracy is not considered. Hick seems more interested in responding to issues of empiricism than in investigating a hermeneutics of disclosure such as proposed by these thinkers. Use of these authors' work might have led to a different understanding of religious language and interpretation, as I have indicated.

Another flaw is the reverse side of a strength. Hick's clarity of style, a quality I genuinely admire, sometimes allows for little ambiguity and lacks subtlety. While I would not always and wholly agree with David Tracy's interpretation of the tradition, I do think that his point (in works such as *Plurality and Ambiguity*) that there is much ambiguity in the Christian tradition and consequently great diversity of interpretation is largely correct. This ambiguity in the Christian tradition is not always so clearly acknowledged by Hick. I suspect that there is significant ambiguity in the other major traditions also. Hick's presentation is so crisp and clear-cut that it may mask some ambiguity. For example, are Hinduism or Buddhism as unified in their understanding of the Real as he proposes? Are the traditions not more rife with subtle differences and interpretations then he lets on?

My final criticism concerns a presumption in Hick's work that directs or underlies his project. That presumption is about the nature of the Real. It is obvious that the religions do not agree explicitly in their beliefs about the divine (personal or impersonal, for example). Hick's appropriation of Kant's distinction between noumenon and phenomenon, while it may shed light on the conflicting claims, may not actually resolve the issue. The doctrines of the various religions claim to be descriptions of the nature of the Real. Is it not possible that one of these is correct and therefore disclosive?

Could not the Real disclose itself in a definitive revelation? The suggestion echoes Barth's scandal of particularity. Hick's response to this objection is that a single true revelation is logically possible but unlikely, given the presumption and conditions he describes concerning the Real and revelation. His argument is that the Real would want to be known to and salvific for all and that a single, universal revelation in history is impossible. Yet is it not important for a believer to consider definitive or absolute the revelation known to him or her, in order to be capable of total commitment? This is an issue that will continue to challenge Hick's conception of the Real and revelation.

FUTURE DIRECTIONS OF INQUIRY

In the epilogue of Hick's book he makes some comments about the future direction of the pluralistic hypothesis and theology. He describes what he perceives to be a growing split between those who are moving in the direction of pluralism and those who are increasingly strong in their defence of either the theological *status quo* or a religious fundamentalism. Comparing the situation to the nineteenth-century debates on evolution, Hick concludes that the pluralistic viewpoint will eventually gain wide (though, just like the evolutionary theory, not total) acceptance. The movement towards a global ecumenical viewpoint will mean confrontation and change for each of the religions. It will not, however, in the end mean one world religion. Rather, each religion will view itself as one way or path to salvation/liberation alongside other equally legitimate and effective paths. Hick foresees some difficulty with this transition, because of the tension with people's principal convictions and commitments within each individual tradition. He thinks that the problem will not be theological but on the level of emotion and imagination. I think he is naïve in expecting a relatively easy theological transition and only partially correct about the difficulty of the emotional transition.

The theological transition

In dismissing the theological tension, Hick lists a number of theologians (for example, Küng, Rahner, John Baillie and Maurice Wiles) who have developed Christologies that are not exclusivist, but omits to observe that some of these are not pluralists but inclusivists. Others adopt very controversial positions, often disputed by many respected theologians. I think that the battle for a shift from a Christocentric understanding to a theocentric or soteriocentric understanding will be much like what Thomas Kuhn in *The Structure of Scientific Revolutions* has described as a paradigm shift in science. There is competition with, and therefore resistance from, the established position and established theologians who have a great deal invested in the traditional interpretation. The intellectual dispute is far from resolved. Maybe if a truly new paradigm is about to replace an existing one, it will only happen when the most respected defenders of the *status quo* die out. I do not think that it will be easy or that it is imminent.

Political tension

While I agree with Hick that emotion and imagination present troublesome barriers to the acceptance of a pluralistic vision, I think that they are accompanied by a tension not mentioned by Hick – that is, a political tension. This tension exists among both theologians and members of the community of faith. Theologians, faithful persons and churches have a great deal invested and at stake in the discussion of the truth-claims of their religion. This is most often supported by a long tradition of prayer, doctrine and theology. The traditional claims are not untested in their history.

The various Christian traditions have all had their bouts with novelty. Some, after investigation of new or alternative proposals, have adopted them as a step in the right direction. Others have condemned them as heretical. Individuals have sometimes suffered severely for their ideas. I think of the fate of David Friedrich Strauss, who because of his book *The Life of Jesus Critically Examined* and his embrace of the historical–critical method, lost his academic position at Tübingen. Reference to this historical and historic case as an analogy is not inappropriate given the current climate, which even Hick admits has the character of "both religious fundamentalism and political nationalism".[27]

It would put many theologians and many faithful persons in direct conflict with their respective traditions and communities were they to subscribe to a pluralistic understanding of religion that ascribes salvific parity to the great world religions. Even if they find the evidence or argument compelling, they may think it politically rash to make the shift to a new paradigm. It is not just intellectual or emotional commitment that keeps people where they are theologically, but political considerations as well. Much is invested in the current paradigm, and many will not surrender that investment easily or be coerced to surrender it on rational grounds. In some communities there are severe consequences for what is judged to be disloyalty to the traditional or beliefs. Islam and Roman Catholicism are examples of two strongly traditional religions that do not accommodate doctrinal discontinuity. Those in Islam who would entertain the idea that the Qur'ān is not literally the word of God in a universally definitive way and those in Christianity who would cast doubt on Jesus as the Son of God and the definitive saviour for all would find their ideas (and themselves) unwelcome among many adherents of their respective faith groups. Fear for one's political fate can overpower one's intellectual convictions about what is true. This aspect of the issue will prevent many from embracing a pluralist vision as Hick understands it.

LASTING CONTRIBUTIONS

It may be premature to venture to assess the most lasting contributions of John Hick's work, but there are, to my mind, three that stand out as of prime significance. These are (1) his apologetic for faith, (2) his Irenaean theodicy, and (3) his pluralistic theory of salvation.

Faith as "experiencing-as"

The core of Hick's theology is his apologetic for faith. He believes in and attempts to demonstrate the rationality of belief. Unlike Anselm or Aquinas (or any revised version of their arguments), Hick does not think that it is possible to prove the existence of God. Yet he clearly believes that there is a God and that God (the Real) is not simply the sum of our impressions, hopes, intentions, or the like. This God exists independently and has an effect on human experience.

In his religious epistemology Hick argues that experience is never naked or uninterpreted. Relying upon Kant's noumenon/phenomenon distinction, Hick points out that we always "experience-as". We do not actually experience the noumenon, but we experience the phenomena of things. We in turn interpret that experience of phenomena. In the case of religion we interpret the whole of our experience in the world as religious – that is, as having to do with the infinite or the Real. Faith is a process of free interpretation. In the words of Gerard Manley Hopkins the believer believes (or interprets) that "The world is charged with the grandeur of God."

This epistemological justification of faith has been a consistent theme of Hick's work since the publication of *Faith and Knowledge* (1957). His idea of faith as a process of interpretation and "experiencing-as" (expanding upon Wittgenstein's "seeing-as") is a unique contribution. It is also, in my estimation, his most important one. It has been and will continue to be criticized, but it will outlive its author and its critics.

The Irenaean theodicy

Hick unfolded his Irenaean theodicy in his extensive study *Evil and the God of Love* (1966). The core of that work has been anthologized in numerous collections. What Hick has done is to use Irenaeus's ideas as a foundation for his own expanded theory on the problem of evil. The potential resolution to the problem implies theories of body–soul dualism, universal salvation, and a period of purification or growth for the soul after death. With Irenaeus as a patron saint, Hick has kept a foot in the tradition while stepping out on new and adventurous paths to address the problem of evil. Irenaeus's distinction between *imago dei* and *similitudo dei* in the creation narrative opens possibilities not available in the Augustinian conception of perfect creation. Thus, by interpreting creation as imperfect or immature, Hick has offered an alternative to the traditional Augustinian understanding of evil as a privation of good within a perfect creation. It is an alternative that I think will continue to be counted among the many possible options that address the problem of evil.

A pluralistic theory of salvation

Hick's so-called Copernican revolution and its consequent hypothesis of parity of salvation among the religions is without question at this moment his most celebrated theological proposal. He has brought as much attention to this area of inquiry as any contemporary author. The wide dissemination of his ideas makes his work central to the pluralistic hypothesis. The bold nature of his proposals makes his work controversial. It has also evoked much discussion and invited much criticism.

For these reasons his vision of soteriological pluralism is important. It is not, however, entirely new. In the last century Troeltsch offered similar, though less refined proposals. The difference is that Troeltsch's work in this area did not receive the attention that Hick's work is receiving. Perhaps it was not the right time in history to introduce such ideas and have them taken seriously by a wide audience. The time is right now. And it is as much for its timeliness as for its content that Hick's work is significant. This is not to suggest that his proposals are not significant also, for I think that they are important.

I also think that his work has marked a new openness on the part of religious thinkers, paving the way for future possibilities as yet unformulated. These new ideas may well be the consequence of the dialogue Hick has fostered. In that on-going dialogue Hick's ideas will be refined into a better pluralistic theory or even surpassed, but neither of these developments would be possible without his present contribution.

NOTES

1. *Philosophy of Religion*, p. 3.
2. *God and the Universe of Faiths*, p. 133.
3. Ibid., p. 141.
4. *Problems of Religious Pluralism*, p. 44.
5. *Interpretation of Religion*, p. xii.
6. Ibid., p. 28.
7. Ibid., pp. 307–8.
8. Ibid., pp. 3–5.
9. Ibid., p. 22.
10. Ibid., p. 143 n. 9.
11. Ibid., p. 167 n. 2.
12. For example, ibid., p. 170 n. 8, where he distinguishes his understanding of faith and perception from that of James Heaney.
13. Cf. ibid., p. 361 (D'Costa on eschatological verification).
14. For example, ibid., pp. 47, 52.
15. For example, ibid., p. 154.
16. Ibid., p. 52.
17. Ibid., p. 54.
18. Ibid., chs 17 and 18 (pp. 299–341).
19. Ibid., p. 309.
20. Ibid., p. 315 n. 13.
21. Ibid., pp. 326–7.
22. Ibid., p. 326.
23. Ibid., p. 178 ff.
24. Chester Gillis, *A Question of Final Belief: John Hick's Pluralistic Theology of Salvation* (London: Macmillan, 1989) pp. 59–66.
25. Hick, *Interpretation of Religion*, p. 351.
26. Ibid., p. 352.
27. Ibid., p. 377.

Critical Response

From Philosophy of Religion to History of Religion

CARL W. ERNST

The evolution of John Hick's thinking on religion testifies to a remarkable opening-up of the philosophy of religion toward the phenomena offered by the comparative study of religion, or history of religion. From its inception in the European Enlightenment, the modern philosophy of religion occasionally made bows in the directions of non-Christian religions, but philosophers from Hume and Kant onward tended to use such data only as part of a larger project, which was a rational critique of Christianity, mainly the Protestant variety. The philosophy of religion, relying exclusively on the concept of autonomous reason as a standard, treated thinkers from the Catholic tradition primarily in terms of logical consistency, and rarely let them off easily. More exotic doctrines were for the most part consigned to a kind of limbo or to places even more unkind.

The struggle to formulate a philosophy of religious pluralism, as we see it in the work of John Hick, or in that of theologians such as Hans Küng, is the sign of a major intellectual shift in the post-colonial era. I think Professor Gillis is right to warn us not to underestimate the difficulty of this transition, both in theological and in political terms. On the intellectual side, there are many substantive and methodological questions to be faced. One of these is the question of how philosophy of religion is to absorb the materials offered by the history of religion, and how it will itself be changed in the process. The following remarks are some suggestions from the viewpoint of a historian of religion, occasioned by Gillis's lucid critical review of Hick's *An Interpretation of Religion.*

At its worst, philosophy of religion's approach to the history of religion can be characterized as plunder. The theorist swoops down, snatches a likely-looking bauble, and carries it home gleefully to add to the collection. Various recondite terms from

Chinese, Algonquin or Arabic then eventually find their way to the open market, where eventually even freshmen will bandy them about. What is objected to here is not so much popularization, but the reductionist and tendentious use of religious symbolism and doctrine out of context. Such was the case in the *chinoiserie* fad in the eighteenth century, when Leibniz and Voltaire imagined Confucius as an enlightened deist. Twentieth-century philosophers have been considerably more subtle, but not much more successful. It is doubtful, for instance, that Karl Jaspers' friendly but superficial reflection on the Buddhist philosopher Nagarjuna will be long remembered. The main problem with these philosophical raids outside European territory is that they do not lead to any fundamental rethinking of the categories and methods of European rationalism. If the philosophy of religion aspires to go beyond a Eurocentric parochialism, it will be necessary to enlarge not only the scope of the religious data that are to be considered, but also the very concept of reason itself.

It is very encouraging to find that John Hick has recognized the new task facing the philosophy of religion, which he describes thus: "A philosopher of religion must today take account not only of the thought and experience of the tradition within which he or she happpens to work, but in principle of the religious experience and thought of the whole human race."[1] The potential burden imposed by this opening-up of the field to the entirety of human history is indeed vast, oppressively so. It is to Hick's great credit that for years he has actively and systematically engaged in the study of the panoply of world religions and in dialogue with representatives of different faiths. While no one can attempt to know all areas of religious history thoroughly, unless one makes a sustained effort as Hick has done, there is little hope of going beyond provincialism. Again, I do not underestimate the political difficulty of this task; as Chester Gillis observes, "much is invested in the current paradigm, and many will not surrender that investment easily or be coerced to surrender it on rational grounds".[2] Yet we are now offered a historically unparalleled opportunity to familiarize ourselves with the human religious universe, and I hope that Hick's example will stimulate others to continue in this effort.

The enlargement of the scope of philosophy of religion thus calls for an engagement with the various scriptural traditions (in the broadest sense, including oral as well as written traditions). The theorist needs to confront the manifold formulations in which the saints, prophets and buddhas of the world have expressed their experiences, and then imaginatively re-experience them.[3] It will not do if we simply accept the abstract textbook summaries of the world religions, which typically reduce religious teachings to simplified dogma or formula for action; we must think with the traditions, and see how the scriptural mandates are carried through historically, how the spirit of the law is conveyed and understood in society. For instance, in the question raised by Gillis of justice as a problem in cross-cultural ethics, if we push for a deeper understanding of political culture in the different religious traditions, the results will be more satisfactory than if we glance at them with the preconceptions of modern Western rationalism.[4] Thus, in looking at the Qur'ānic punishment of amputating a thief's hand, it is important to recognize that Qur'ānic demands for mercy make poverty an acceptable excuse for the crime.[5] The Hindu concept of *karma*, which to the Western mind may suggest a cynical justification of the *status quo*, is tempered with the ethical demands of *dharma* as a hierarchically ramified religious law.[6] The Buddhist tradition, far from lacking a concept of justice, conceives of the just ruler as implementing the ideal of the Buddha before his renunciation.[7] The apparently irrational excesses of the Iranian revolution need to be seen as the violent secularization of Shi'i authoritarianism through anti-colonial nationalism. And so on. It is not simply a question of "What sort of justice?"; in my view, it is a question of how our concept of justice may be extended by the history of religion.

As far as the concept of reason is concerned, I find myself in general agreement with Gillis's criticisms of Hick for conceding ground to positivism, for a reductive attitude toward myth, and for insufficiently dealing with issues of hermeneutics and the ambiguities within the various traditions. Yet I would go further in questioning the rationalist presuppositions that continue to direct phases of the inquiry. A doctrinal understanding of religion has dominated Christian theology ever since the term "religion" was adopted; Augustine's definition of religion as the acknowledgement, with piety, of God as the creator helped set in motion the perennial Western concept of a doctrinal and credal structuring of the relation between the human and the divine.[8]

The centrality of this rationalistic emphasis in Christian theology and, later, the European Enlightenment, is nearly unparalleled in other religious traditions. Thus Hick treats faith as primarily a cognitive issue, and describes religion's confrontation with naturalistic ideologies as a factual one subject to experiential verification. His argument then leads to the statement that, for those who participate in religious experience, "it is rational to believe in the reality of God".[9] I would suggest that this is to put the cart before the horse. Religious experience is fundamental; symbols, formulations, and doctrines are elaborated on the basis of experience.[10] The very origin of the concept of experience in Western thought attests to a struggle against dogmatism, whether religious, philosophical or scientific. In religion, it was primarily the Protestant reformers who invoked religious experience against the authority and doctrine of the Catholic Church, and this non-doctrinal usage continued down to William James's use of the term in his classic study.[11] In the scientific field, along with Baconianism, alchemy was another source of our concept of experience in its struggle against Aristotelian orthodoxy; alchemy, of course, had relgous implications as well. Here I would like to invoke an image from a seventeenth-century alchemical text, which allegorically depicts Experience as the Queen of Heaven before whom Philosophy bows down and worships.[12] So, with apologies to Philo, I would like to suggest that we think of philosophy as the handmaid of experience in the new context that we face today.

Faith needs rational justification only for those to whom reason is supreme. Philosophy can articulate through reason the fundamental experiences that have given the spiritual bases of the religious traditions. And reason itself, as articulated in ancient and medieval Western philosophy, was far more existential than its current reduction to propositional logic would allow. Rethinking the relationship of the Enlightenment to the rest of world history, and working through the scriptures and their philosophical interpreters from a global perspective, will give us a better foundation for describing the relationship between the intellect and the Real.[13]

The philosophy of religion has run a course from the beginnings of the Enlightenment to the post-modern age. It now has to break out of the self-imposed boundaries of the Eurocentric colonial period. The history of religion has much to offer to philosophers of religion as they rethink their task in the light of the world's religious traditions. The precise shape of a future philosophy of

religion that is based on a global awareness of religious experience
is something that we can not yet discern. Yet we can be sure that
the pioneering work of John Hick will stand as an important step
in this enterprise.

NOTES

1.   *An Interpretation of Religion*, p. xii.
2.   Chester Gillis, above, p. 42.
3.   Eric Voegelin, *The New Science of Politics: An Introduction* (Chicago:
       University of Chicago Press, 1952) p. 64.
4.   As Hick points out, the democratic concept of political equality has
       nothing to do with any of the world religions, but is an outcome of
       "the development of western science-based civilization" (*Interpre-
       tation of Religion*, p. 328).
5.   Marshal G. S. Hodgson, *The Venture of Islam*, I: *The Classical Age of
       Islam* (Chicago: University of Chicago Press, 1974) p. 336ff.
6.   Ariel Glucklich, *Religious Jurisprudence in the Dharmaśāstra* (New
       York: Macmillan, 1988) p. 39ff.
7.   Emanuel Sarkisyanz, *Buddhist Backgrounds of the Burmese Revolu-
       tion* (The Hague: Martinus Nijhoff, 1965) *passim*.
8.   Augustine, *On True Religion*, in *Earlier Writings*, tr. John H. S.
       Burleigh, Library of Christian Classics (Philadelphia: Westminster
       Press, 1953) p. 218ff.
9.   *Interpretation of Religion*, p. 211.
10.   I have argued the primacy of religious experience over language in
       the case of Islamic mysticism in "Mystical Language and the
       Teaching Context in the Early Sufi Lexicons", in Steven T. Katz
       (ed.), *Mysticism and Language* (Oxford: Oxford University Press,
       forthcoming).
11.   H. Pinard, "La théorie de l'expérience religieuse. Son évolution, de
       Luther á W. James", *Revue d'histoire ecclesiastique*, xvii (1921) 63–83,
       306–48, 547–74.
12.   "There with arose Phylosophy as one filled with grace, / Whose
       looks did shew that she had byne in some Heavenly place; / For oft
       she wipt her Eyes, / And oft she bowd her knees. / And oft she kist
       the Steps with dread, / Whereon Experience did tread; / And oft
       she cast her Head on high / And oft full low she cast her Eye /
       Experience for to espy, " – "Experience and Philosophy", in Elias
       Ashmole, *Theatrum Chemicum Britannicum* (1652; repr., Hildes-
       heim: Georg Olms, 1968) p. 341.
13.   David L. Hall and Roger T. Ames, *Thinking through Confucius*,
       SUNY Series in Systematic Philosophy (Albany, NY: State Uni-
       versity of New York Press, 1987), is an example of this kind of
       philosophizing.

Reply

JOHN HICK

Chester Gillis is a generous critic, both here and in his book *A Question of Final Truth*. Indeed, the fact that he sees so much to approve in the development of the *Interpretation of Religion* (IR) hypothesis gives added weight to his various points of criticism. Let me therefore turn immediately to those.

1 Gillis thinks that continued concern with the questions raised by the logical positivists two generations ago should long since have been abandoned; and many others would agree with him. However, it seems to me that discrimination is called for here. The logical-positivist movement is long dead, and it would be anachronistic to address in its terms the issues with which it was concerned. But some of those issues themselves are not dead. The basic empiricist principle that to exist is to make an in-principle experienceable difference was sound before positivism came on the scene and is still sound after it has departed. And its application to religion is inevitable. Hence the entirely proper question: what in-principle experienceable difference does it make whether or not God exists? If it makes no difference within actual or possible human experience (other than in our purely subjective states of mind) whether God exists, does it not follow that "God exists" is, for us human beings, factually empty, or pointless, or meaningless? (A like question can also be posed in non-theistic religious terms.) Does not this constitute a fundamental challenge to a realist use of religious language? And how is the challenge to be met, if not in terms of the contrasting accounts of the structure or character of the universe as religiously and as naturalistically understood; and of the consequent differences made within actual or possible human experience, according as one or the other of these understandings turns out to be basically correct? I should be more impressed by those who urge the abandonment of the idea of "eschatological verification" if they were to offer some alternative solution to the valid question which it seeks to answer.

Let me at this point respond also to Carl Ernst, with the thrust of whose remarks I wholly agree. As will be evident from *An*

Interpretation of Religion, I base religious belief emphatically in religious experience. As a Western philosopher I argue, in the empiricist mode, for the rationality of basing our beliefs upon our experience, including religious experience. This seems to me to be a legitimate and, indeed, in our Western society, a necessary exercise. But I join Ernst in hoping for a much greater openness on the part of Western philosophers of religion to the data of religion around the world.

2 Gillis gives an accurate summary of my concept of mythological truth as the practical truthfulness of stories and ideas that tend to evoke dispositional responses which are appropriate to the ultimate subject matter of the myth. Thus, for example, to picture the Real as a heavenly father who loves us tends to evoke an answering love, both upwards and also towards our neighbours, which is appropriate given the "cosmic optimism" of the great traditions. Gillis regards this as a non-cognitive account of myth. He is correct if he simply means that myth, so understood, does not make literally true propositional assertions. But, on the other hand, myth can be importantly truthful in orienting us rightly in relation to reality. In contrast to this, is not a purely propositional conception of truth excessively narrow and too much a function of Western rationalist modes of thought?

3 Gillis asks, "Could not the Real disclose itself in a definitive revelation?"[1] Such a question infringes the terms of the IR hypothesis in that it attributes the human concept of intentionality to that which lies beyond the scope of all such concepts. But, if we were to accept the question, the answer would presumably be "Yes, this is theoretically possible." What Gillis has in mind is, of course, that such a definitive revelation occurred in Jesus Christ, so that the Christian religion is the locus of final truth. But this is where we came in! Christians have traditionally made that claim; and Jews and Muslims and, in their different way, Buddhists and Hindus have made similar claims on behalf of their own religions. Hence the world-wide situation of conflicting claims to unique superiority that provokes the line of thought leading to the pluralistic hypothesis. It follows from that hypothesis that we must, within each tradition, learn to transcend our inherited claim to unique superiority and make whatever developments of our belief-systems this suggests.

I have to agree with Gillis that such a development will not be easy within Christianity. It may well even have to wait, as he hints, for a new generation of intellectual leadership. In the meantime, however, there is a growing movement in this direction. But Gillis is right again in pointing to the ecclesiastical–political pressures, particularly within the Roman Catholic Church today, against "a pluralistic understanding of religion that ascribes salvific parity to the great world religions".[2] I am aware of these ecclesiastical pressures even as a Protestant; but I am concious that they are much more powerful and threatening for a Catholic. It requires not only courage but also a certain independent standing in the theological world to be able to resist such pressures. I have sympathy with those Catholic theologians who are able publicly to espouse religious pluralism, and sympathy also with those who might wish to do so but for whom this is not politically feasible. It is enough for the present that, if thought on these issues is moving in the right direction, it will eventually bear good fruit.

NOTES

1. Chester Gillis, above, p. 40.
2. Gillis, above, p. 42.

3

Humanism and Hick's Interpretation of Religion

C. ROBERT MESLE

In the spirit of this occasion, I want to offer Professor Hick the salute of a friendly critic. Although we have not met before this conference, John Hick has been my teacher for the last four years. It is precisely at those points where I have disagreed with him that he has helped me to grow the most. His breadth of vision, depth of knowledge and persistence of effort have challenged me to ask ever-more basic questions, and so have lured me on toward a deeper struggle.

Hick's work is important on at least two grounds. First, he seems able to give clear, coherent expression to those vague but powerful intuitions shared by many people in the community of faith. This, I think, is what Tillich might have meant in saying that theologians must interpret the Christian symbols anew for each generation. Secondly, Hick works to pull the community of faith into a broader vision. He challenges the existing boundaries of the community's love and openness, reaching into the hearts of the people to show them that the love and truth they already know will reveal to them a larger experience of the Sacred if they will only open themselves to its transforming grace.

When I first set out to read papers challenging his soul-making theodicy and his notion of epistemic distance, I consistently found, to my dismay, that people were more persuaded by his ideas than mine! Even though I still disagree with both arguments, it is clear to me that in these ideas Hick has indeed touched and given systematic expression to a conviction rooted deeply in those members of the Christian community with whom I come into contact. Consequently, I was forced to ask myself anew why his ideas struck such deep chords in people, why I really disagreed with him, and, finally, what the whole discipline of theodicy is about. John Hick has been a valuable teacher for me.

Furthermore, there is no question in my mind that Hick has offered ideas which can help both Christians and non-Christians to broaden the boundaries of their concern and vision. Surely we must credit him with being among those who have most vigo-rously argued against the idea of hell as an expression of a loving deity. His affirmation that an infinitely loving God would never abandon us provides a view of divine ethics far superior to more traditional models. And, especially, who can deny that Hick's work in religious pluralism puts him among the leaders in calling Christians and others to move beyond the unloving game of dividing the world like bridge teams into "we the saved" and "they the damned"? I thank John Hick and all those who battle against hateful visions of love. So, while I continue to disagree with him at many points, my admiration for him continues to grow.

THE PLACE OF NATURALISM IN HICK'S INTERPRETATION OF RELIGION

Hick's work in religious pluralism seems directed in large part toward enabling us all to treat each other with respect. He seeks this goal by outlining a vision of both ultimate reality and particular religions which allows us to see each major religion as an authentic, honest, intelligent and ethically sound response to reality. We need not see other religions as revolving, even anony-mously, around ours. And we are freed from any need to condemn others *a priori* (as the apostle Paul seems to do in Romans 1:18ff) for wilfully turning away from plain truth in preference for a pleasant lie. All of this has been clear in Hick's work.

What has been unclear in the past, and remains unclear now, is how humanistic naturalism fits into Hick's philosophy of religious pluralism. My basic thesis is that in *An Interpretation of Religion* Hick has made significant strides toward affording naturalism philosophic respect, but has not yet made that respect systema-tically coherent. My goal is to illustrate this unresolved progress, and raise questions which may help us move toward a more complete solution.

A brief definition of humanistic naturalism seems in order. For naturalists, nature is what there is: nothing less and nothing more. There is nothing transcendent to the natural universe. Humanists,

as meant here, are naturalists with an overarching ethical commitment to the human community. Further, most humanists have an
appreciation for nature at large and especially for non-human life
which might involve enjoyment and suffering.

On these minimal terms, there are many kinds of humanistic
naturalists. Some are Marxist or Maoist; many are not. Some are
reductive materialists; some, like process philosophers, are not.
Some have hostile attitudes toward theistic religions; some do not.
While it has historically been the case that humanistic naturalists
have been forced to invest much energy in arguing against theism
and other religious ideas, fairness demands the acknowledgement
that humanism is a positive vision of reality, not merely a negative
rejection of God or religion. But the key issue for the current
discussion is that humanistic naturalism is a way of experiencing
and conceiving of reality without reference to anything beyond
nature – without Hick's transcendent "Real". With this explanation, I hope it will be acceptable for me to speak of either
humanism or naturalism interchangeably.

Most of the time, Hick's philosophy of religious pluralism
proposes a common ground for all the great religious traditions by
placing them on the same side of a dividing-line betweeen two
broad categories of people – the religious and the naturalists.
Using the family-traits method of definition, Hick is certainly
willing to share the honorific term "religion" with Marxists and
other humanists. But, both philosophically and textually, there
remains a fundamental division between religious people who
acknowledge transcendence, and non-religious people who do
not. As a linguistic distinction this is no problem. The question is
whether Hick's philosophy enables us to treat humanism with the
same respect afforded the religious.

POSITIVE STANCES TOWARD HUMANISM

There are three very important ways in which Hick's philosophy
treats humanism with a respect rarely afforded it by other non-
humanists.

First, it has been fundamental, explicit and pervasive in Hick's
work for many years that the world can be interpreted coherently
on naturalistic terms. Indeed, Hick's theodicy, his concept of faith
and his philosophy of religious pluralism have all hinged, in

different ways, upon this very claim. So humanists can hardly accuse Hick of not fully appreciating or treating respectfully the naturalistic accounts of the world.

Secondly, in *An Interpretation of Religion*, Hick points to vital common ground between religious realists and non-realists. (It seems clear that by "religious non-realists" Hick simply means those naturalists who take an appreciative and positive stance toward religious language, images and symbols, as contrasted with those who have more hostile critiques of religion.) Hick sees common ground at four key points: (1) both can agree on the intrinsic goodness of love or compassion as a transcending of the self-centred point of view, whether or not a divine Reality exists;[1] (2) both can agree that "the forms of religious belief, experience and practice have always been culturally conditioned";[2] (3) both can agree that religious faith can evoke appreciation of "new dimensions of meaning and value in the natural world and human life";[3] and (4) both can agree on the autonomy of moral values.[4] The acknowledgement by Hick of this wide range of agreements certainly reflects his respectful openness toward the insights and values of humanism.

Thirdly, where some others might be tempted to argue that whatever good there is in humanism comes from its Judaeo-Christian roots, Hick argues that Christianity cannot claim credit for the basic positive values of humanism. In *An Interpretation of Religion*[5] he offers two major arguments to this effect. Christianity cannot, he says, claim credit for the birth of modern science. It may be argued that the medieval Christian concept of an orderly, rational universe provided a necessary condition for science. But Hick notes that this world view dominated Western Europe for a full millennium without producing any significant science. It was only under the stimulation "of the Greek spirit of free enquiry" that science arose. And, when it did, the Church was its primary foe.

He also argues that we cannot see the modern humanist values of equality, dignity and liberation as mere flowerings of the Christian love ethic. "The love commandment of the Sermon on the Mount by itself, without the insistent promptings of humanist and rationalist voices, did not end slavery and has not ended exploitation. Nor did it even, by itself, bring the perception that freedom and equality are ideas to be sought after."[6] The sexism of the Judaeo-Christian religion is a conspicuous example. Again, "it was the fertilisation of the medieval Christian ethos by the humanistic ideals of ancient Greece, recovered in the Renaissance . . . that produced the contemporary liberal moral outlook".[7] Furthermore, it is the rise of modern social sciences which has made it possible for us to become aware of social and political *structures* as sources of oppression. Here again, Christianity cannot claim to have originated this insight.

Of course, Hick reminds us that humanists must share responsibility for the dark side of modern technology as well as its virtues. Nevertheless, he deserves substantial thanks from naturalistic humanists for the respect he has offered their perspective in these arguments.

NEGATIVE STANCES: ELITISM

Hick's defence of humanism as the source of the modern liberal values of equality and liberation makes it ironic that his most clear and persistent criticism of humanism is that it is elitist. This charge can be found, for example, in *Death and Eternal Life*, in *Why Believe in God?*[8] and also in *An Interpretation of Religion*.

In *An Interpretation of Religion* the charge occurs at the end of the section in chapter 6 comparing realist and non-realist interpretations of religion. After identifying the issues on which these positions can find agreement he identifies elitism as the ultimate and fundamental issue between religious and humanistic perspectives. His reasoning is clear. In this life, most people get a bad deal. Poverty, disease, injury, oppression and other evils prey upon us all, and prevent most people from finding salvation in this life. The great religious traditions, he says, have all allowed for some sort of immortality which makes the limitlessly better life of salvation available to all. Humanism denies this immortality and thus restricts salvation to an elite few who are able, by good fortune or extraordinary character, to find salvific peace in this life. Thus humanism involves "an unintended elitism".[9]

Hick acknowledges that religious ideas such as hell may also be elitist, but sees these as mere aberrations. On the whole, he maintains, religious perspectives are good news for all rather than for a fortunate few. Through this elitism, humanism "would negate any notion of the ultimate goodness of the universe".[10]

Hick offers two analogies of interest. First, he considers that branch of Buddhism which denies immortality. It still allows, Hick notes, that theoretically anyone can achieve *nirvāṇa* in this life. But, practically, this is like saying that in a desperately poor country anyone is allowed to become a millionaire.[11] The second "unflattering" analogy is a comparison of humanist elitism with Calvinistic predestination, which condemns all but a fortunate few to eternal damnation.

Hick may be correct that on the point of immortality humanism cannot "credibly claim to represent the message of the great spiritual traditions".[12] But the charge of elitism is troubling. I want to propose a number of objections to his position.

First, "elitism" is a highly prejudicial term, and seems entirely misplaced here. In my understanding, elitism involves a moral claim that one's group is somehow *deserving* of a better life than others. "We *should* be better fed because we are smarter or richer or white or favoured by God." Consider the analogy with the claim that in a desperately poor country it is still theoretically possible for anyone to become a millionaire. Such a claim is surely one we would associate with the wealthy elite trying to justify their wealth in the midst of poverty. Humanists are not trying to offer any such justification or defence of their spiritual "wealth" from others. There is nothing about the humanist perspective which defends elitist rights or pleasures.

This mistaken analogy has deeper roots, I believe, which can be seen by examining Hick's argument against humanism in *Death and Eternal Life*. There too he asserts that humanism offers hope only as an "elitist doctrine for the fortunate few".[13] His reason is revealing. In a discussion of humanism and the problem of evil, he presents humanism, like theism, as trying to justify the suffering of this life.[14] Any "solution" to the problem of suffering, Hick says, "must consist, not in denying the reality of suffering, but in showing how it is to be justified or redeemed".[15] In Hick's view, this can be achieved only through a doctrine of immortality.

> Attempted justifications which refuse to take this step fail under the criterion of universal love: only a fortunate few are regarded as ends in themselves, the less fortunate mass being treated as involuntary means to an end of which they are not aware and in which they do not participate.[16]

But, as he understands it, humanists offer this justification by seeing the struggles of the human race as leading to a future "super-humanity". This is morally objectionable to Hick for the common-sense reason that those who pay the price don't collect the goods.

This argument is revealing, and connects to the analogy with Calvinism. For it is crucial to recognize that Hick continues in *An Interpretation of Religion* to compare humanism with religious perspectives which seek to *justify* the reality of suffering. Since in Calvinism it is *God* who predestines people to hell, Calvinism must hold that it is ultimately good for this to happen. That is elitism. But humanism makes no such claim. It may also be worth noting that in the third edition of *Philosophy of Religion*[17] Hick levels the same charge of elitism against process theists, who usually deny subjective immortality. But he overlooks the crucial fact that neither humanism nor process theism makes any claim to *justify* suffering in this life. Neither implies that it is morally *right* that people suffer, since both deny that there is a God capable of preventing it.

My suggestion, then, is that Hick has made the very natural error of carrying over into the position of others a basic assumption foundational to his own theology but alien to theirs – the assumption that we must believe that suffering is justified because otherwise God would prevent it. If that is not the explanation, Hick's criticism of humanism seems very peculiar indeed. In that case Hick would seem to mean that elitism is simply the act of acknowledging the injustices of the world. Some people get cancer and some don't, some are poor and hungry and some are not, and there is no fair compensation for those should suffer. Do humanists claim that the people who get cancer *deserve* it? Of course not. And there are surely many poor, hungry, war-ravaged people in the world who don't believe in God or an afterlife to set things straight. Are they, too, elitist because they don't see the universe offering them guarantees for a better future?

My second objection is that this alleged elitism is not nearly so clear a point of distinction between religious and non-religious ideas as Hick suggests. Hick glosses over crucial exceptions.

(a) *Buddhism.* Hick himself observes that by his standards a similar elitism has held a "dominant place within the long Buddhist tradition as a whole".[18]

(b) *Judaism*. The bulk of the Hebrew Scriptures would have to be judged elitist by Hick's standards. God chose Israel and no one else. That is surely elitism at its strongest. But, more fundamentally, the idea of Sheol is not a "saving" immortality. Jeremiah and Job both make this very clear. Apart from punishing the living "to the third and fourth generation", Hebrew theology allowed no way in which Yahweh could correct the fundamental injustice that the righteous suffer while the wicked prosper.

(c) *Christianity*. Although Hick and many other contemporary Christians reject the doctrine of eternal damnation, he himself has frequently objected to the fact that the bulk of the Christian tradition has condemned the majority of humankind to hell for eternity. His Irenaean theodicy of universal salvation, after all, is "the minority report" in the Christian soteriological tradition.

Also, many Christian theologians in this century, including most process theologians, have not affirmed doctrines of immortality which would satisfy Hick's standard of non-elitism.

(d) *Hinduism*. The caste system of Hinduism may not be for eternity, but in many eyes it is surely elitist in a far more objectionable way than is humanism. As Hick himself argues, the modern opposition to it is probably more indebted to secular, humanist values of individual dignity than to religious roots.

I conclude that it is simply misguided of Hick to condemn humanism as elitist. First, the charge of elitism is inaccurate and unfair. It implies that humanists somehow approve of the world's injustices. Secondly, it is not really a distinction between religious and non-religious perspectives. Thirdly, the elitism of many religious perspectives is morally reprehensible in a way in which humanism is not. What he ignores is the crucial distinction between most religious perspectives, which see the misery of the world as somehow morally sanctioned by Reality, and humanism (and process theism), which sees misery and injustice as *unequivocally* repugnant since there is no implication that a divinity intends, approves of or otherwise sanctions the injustice. Humanists are free to oppose the cruel realities of human and animal suffering precisely because no greater moral Reality supports it.

THE NOTORIOUS PASCAL QUOTATION

In *An Interpretation of Religion* Hick allows that humanism can be a response to the divine. While, within Hick's framework, this is a major step forward, there is reason to doubt that this shift, standing in its present context, is sufficient to avoid a deep systematic problem.

The second major problem in Hick's approach toward humanism can be most clearly introduced by examining what I have come to think of as the "notorious Pascal quotation". So far, I have found this quotation in seven of Hick's books.[19] It has served as a central passage in explaining his concept of the "epistemic distance" which he claims that God has created to allow us room for a free faith response. Consider how this quotation subtly but decisively draws a line between the faithful and the infidel:

It was not then right that He should appear in a manner manifestly divine, and completely capable of convincing all men; but it was also not right that He should come in so hidden a manner that He could not be known by those who should sincerely seek him. He has willed to make himself quite recognizable by those; and thus, willing to appear openly to those who seek Him with all their heart, and hidden from those who flee from Him with all their heart, He so regulates the knowledge of Himself that He has given signs of Himself, visible to those who seek Him, and not to those who seek Him not. There is enough light for those who only desire to see, and enough obscurity for those who have a contrary disposition.[20]

It is worth noting that Pascal was originally speaking of the classic Christian doctrine of incarnation, a position Hick now rejects. Over the years, presumably as Hick's own vision has grown, he has applied it more broadly to the Christian concept of God *per se*, and finally, at least by implication, to his ultimate Reality.

Notice the failure to distinguish between philosophical disagreement and moral infidelity. How can humanistic naturalists, who do not experience or conceive of the world as grounded in a divine, transcendent Reality, avoid the conclusion that the notorious Pascal quotation judges us as dishonest and insincere, fleeing from God or Reality with all our heart, and not even desiring to see the light? This interpretation seems confirmed by Hick's comments to the effect that human responses to the ultimate divine Reality range "from the negative response of a self-enclosed consciousness which is blind to the divine presence, whether beyond us or in the depths of our own being, to a positive openness to the Divine which gradually transforms us and which is called salvation or liberation or enlightenment".[21] Doesn't all this drive us to see humanists as belonging to the "negative" group rather than to those with "positive openness to the divine"?

These problems are compounded by the fact that, with reference to belief in the transcendent Real, Hick consistently distinguishes between those who are "Reality-centred" and those who are "self-centred". The implications for humanism seem clear.

Given Hick's meaning of "Reality", naturalists could probably tolerate – though not happily – being classified as not "Reality-centred" if that were not connected to self-centredness and to Hick's doctrine of faith as cognitive freedom. *God Has Many Names* illustrates the problems well. After explaining the idea of "seeing-as" as an interpretative act, he presents his usual argument that we have little cognitive freedom in interpreting the physical world but much more in interpreting the moral world. "If we do not want to be conscious of a moral obligation, we are able to rethink the situation and so come to see it in a different light. This is the way in which human wickedness normally operates, namely by self-deception."[22]

Then Hick claims that the field of religious awareness offers us an even greater degree of cognitive freedom. The Eternal One is always "pressing in upon the human spirit, seeking to be known and responded to".[23] But, having created us at an epistemic distance, the Eternal One assures that

faith is an act of cognitive freedom and responsibility. It reflects the extent to which we are willing, and ready, to exist consciously in the presence of the infinite reality in which being and value are one. . . . [The knower] is able to shut out what he does not want, or is not ready, to let in.[24]

Now, if choosing not to see moral obligations is an act of self-deception, and if our freedom to interpret the world so as to acknowledge or deny the true foundation of value is even greater, isn't it implied that the humanist is guilty of an even more vile act of self-deception than is the one who refuses to acknowledge a moral obligation? As with the Pascal quotation, it seems that a humanist "does not want, or is not ready" to acknowledge God or the value-grounding Reality. Although Hick never, to my knowledge, explicitly links this argument to humanism, the whole argument, I believe, has systematically placed humanists among the self-deceiving and self-centred.

The same basic argument can be found easily in many of Hick's major works, up to and including *An Interpretation of Religion*. There he develops essentially the same logic, saying that "at the religious level we have a much more comprehensive capacity to shut out of consciousness that which we are not ready to face".[25] And, since, in Hick's view, "the Real is the ultimate ground not only of the human life that has generated our moral categories but also of the religious invitation or claim or challenge to a radical self-transcendence",[26] we must wonder again how to avoid grouping humanists among those who have freely chosen to filter out that challenge to self-transcendence. And, since Hick consistently charges humanists with being elitist, the logical implication that humanists are self-centred is all the more disturbing.

If the notorious Pascal quotation stood in philosophical isolation we might ignore it, despite its persistent use. But that passage has in fact intentionally been set forth by Hick as the paradigmatic expression of his whole concept of epistemic distance, which itself has been systematically integrated with his doctrine of faith as "seeing-as" which includes cognitive freedom, his arguments for the world's ambiguity, his rejection of theistic arguments and, indeed, his entire theodicy of soul-making. The Pascal quotation has been as central to Hick's entire theological framework as any single passage could be.

I shall consider below the extent to which Hick has taken steps to escape these problems. To maintain fairness, however, let me again acknowledge that Hick clearly believes, and has invested much of his life in defending, the idea that all of the major religions reflect honest visions of Reality. Surely he treats humanists with the same respect, personally. The question here is whether his philosophy of religious pluralism is as generous of spirit as is Hick himself. At the point of the notorious Pascal quotation, and all it systematically implies, I believe it is not.

PROBLEMS REMAINING

I have identified two major problems with Hick's approach to humanism. The first problem might largely be solved if we simply said, "You're right. The elitism charge is mistaken." Whether Hick would be persuaded of this is for him to say.

What of the second problem? Has Hick already resolved it? Or, at least, can it be resolved (within Hick's current system) as easily as the first simply by saying, "Being a philosophical humanist doesn't make someone self-centred", or "We can agree that humanists are also Reality-centred"? I don't think it will be so easy.

Hick has indeed decided that humanists are responding to the Real.[27] In effect, they are (to coin an ugly phrase) "anonymous religionists", analogous to Rahner's anonymous Christians. If we agree with Hick that Rahner's Ptolemaic epicycle is patronizing and exclusivist, why isn't Hick's? But, much more important, there are major systematic problems remaining, and it is not obvious what they imply or how they can be resolved.

The parallel distinctions between Reality-centred and self-centred people on one side, and people who interpret the universe religiously or naturalistically on the other, remain central and troubling. There is no doubt that "Reality-centred" is the corollary of "religious". So how much systematic pressure is there to connect "self-centred" with "naturalistic"? My concern is that the pressure is considerable. In *An Interpretation of Religion* Hick does not argue directly for the idea of "epistemic distance". Nor does he use the Pascal quotation in its usual context. But he has indicated verbally that he still affirms the epistemic-distance idea. How much has the place of humanists in his system really changed?

Hick continues to affirm that,

If the question is whether, from a religious standpoint, the universe can properly be seen as a creation or emanation or expression of the divine, the answer has to be Yes. There are two broad alternative views of the relation between the material universe and the supposed transcendent Reality of which religion speaks. One is the naturalistic conception . . . the other is the religious conception of the divine as ontologically prior and the physical universe as secondary and derivative. This religious option entails that the material universe, with its actual structure and history, stands in some kind of instrumental or expressive relationship to the divine: the fact that the universe exists and has the character that it has, including its liability to produce human life, is ultimately to be attributed to the divine Reality.[28]

With this in mind, we need to consider the connection between several systematically basic components of Hick's philosophy. First, combine the claim that the universe's actual structure and history is created by and is instrumental for the Divine with the systematic claim that the world is religiously ambiguous: that is, it can be interpreted either religiously or naturalistically. Then connect this with Hick's doctrine of faith as "seeing-as", involving free cognitive choice. Isn't the free faith decision precisely that between religion ("Reality-centredness") and naturalism (. . . ?). Hick's system is still presenting the world as created by the Real so as to allow people to make this basic faith decision. So, despite Hick's willingness to see humanists as responding to the Real, all of the old context remains which powerfully presents humanists as wilfully hiding from the divine Reality.

That is the frustrating part of good system-building, isn't it? If you do a good job, it is awfully hard to change one or two pieces without disrupting the whole system. Hick obviously has recognized that, since naturalists are good people, his system says they must be responding to the Real. So he simply "converts" them in one or two sentences. But is it really so easy? No. The system remains.

Indeed, the problems confronting Hick with regard to humanism are not isolated. In his efforts to avoid a "Ptolemaic" view of world religions he took the strategy of gradually denying to the divine Reality any feature which might make it offensive to any particular religion. It is hardly surprising that he has not been entirely successful in maintaining a fully integrated system. Consider the following problems.

In a single paragraph [29] Hick indicates his position that the Real *an sich* is impersonal. In a separate single sentence, he informs us that language about the Real, "as a personal being carrying out intentions through time, cannot apply to the ultimate transcendent Reality in itself".[30] On this ground, he now views his entire theodicy as "mythically true" but not "literally true". Yet he still claims that there is that "assurance" that "all shall be well".[31] How

can there be such an assurance? How can immortality be mythically true if not literally true?

Hick develops the noumenal/phenomenal-projection strategy to
address diversity *within* the religious interpretation. But it is not
clear that this can account for the ambiguity of the world as
interpretable both religiously and naturalistically. If the Real
cannot act in time to carry out intentions, how can it be the cause
of the universe being ambiguous, or indeed the cause of anything?
(Remember Hick's former arguments that God created the universe through the very temporal process of evolution to bring
about this ambiguity.)

What is the difference between nature alone and nature plus the
Real? The Real does not love, forgive, create, act, or even save, so
far as I can see. All of these imply a personal being carrying out
intentions over time. And, if there is no immortality, what
happens to eschatological verification?

How does the Real reveal itself? Is there any way for Hick to say
that the distinction between a religious and a naturalistic interpretation of the origin and nature of the world is not purely arbitrary?
In what way, if at all, is the religious person more open to some
revelation of the Real than is the naturalist?

What happens to the ability of the religious traditions to offer
salvation to all if immortality itself is only mythically true and not
literally true? Does Hick's system hereby become elitist?

And, of course, how can he deny literal action to the Real and
still say that the Real creates the world?

Hick's problem could also be seen as a dilemma regarding his
approach to the Real. By accepting humanism as a legitimate
religious response to the Real, Hick seems finally able to treat
humanism with full respect. In so doing he effectively abandons
his fundamental ontological distinction between religion and
non-religion.

But how can he avoid abolishing the distinction between
religion and naturalism? If all particular religious visions are
phenomenal projections anyway, and we take the *via negativa* of
denying all positive qualities to the real, how can we draw any
distinction between those who do and those who don't affirm its
Reality? If the naturalistic rejection of all specific religious projections is now seen by Hick as itself a response to the Real, what is
the difference between affirming and denying the Real? If any
moral human perspective must be interpreted as a response to the

Real, "Reality-centredness" becomes a moral rather than an onto-logical category.

SOME PROPOSALS FOR CONSIDERATION

A major overhaul of Hick's system to resolve these problems is obviously beyond the scope of this paper. But I would like to offer three constructive proposals.

Other-centredness

Hick could elevate the category of "other-centred" life-paths as the proper contrary of "self-centred" ones. This would be entirely consistent with his focus on salvation over specific beliefs. Then we could simply acknowledge broad kinds of paths away from self-centredness toward other-centredness. Within the category of other-centredness we can easily and non-judgementally distin-guish naturalistic and transcendence-oriented paths. The dis-agreements between the broad paths would be accepted as part of our on-going exploration and dialogue.

Shifting away from the concept of "Reality-centredness" to "Other-centredness" might involve a shift away from the analogy of a Copernican revolution, since we could not describe all of the traditions as revolving around a common transcendent reality. But perhaps the movement beyond Copernicus is as necessary and appropriate in religious pluralism as it is in astronomy. The plurality of human struggles seem to push beyond having one clear centre, even though we can see them as growing out of some common origins in biological and psychological evolution and the common human experiences of suffering, love and death.

Naturalism

I cannot resist the feeling that in his pursuit of a universal vision which treats everyone with respect, gradually tending to treat religion as a moral category, Hick has driven himself toward a position which differs from naturalism in name and feeling, but not in substance. By stripping the Real of all positive qualities Hick collapses the difference between nature alone and nature plus the "Real". Furthermore, Hick's doctrine of faith as "seeing-as" (especially if there is no eschatological verification) simply confirms that there is no "literal" difference between the world with the Real and the world without it. The difference, despite his intentions, sees to be reduced to a purely subjective stance.

It may, then, be worth considering a naturalistic proposal for addressing the problem of religious pluralism.

From a naturalistic perspective, we could simply affirm nature as the Real, and say that the many religions, including human-isms, are responses to that vast, confusing ambiguous reality. Are religious experiences delusions? No more so than they are in Hick's system. He, too, sees them as projections, but claims that they are projections rooted in Reality. Naturalists can just as well say that these projections are rooted in natural reality, the reality of human consciousness interacting with the world around us. Why is that any more a delusion that what Hick proposes?

Similarly, we may ask, "Is nature the reality in which being and value are one?" Yes and no. But then Hick must give the same answer about his Reality. Hick is careful to say that his noumenal Real is beyond the categories of good and evil. That says nothing very helpful to me, but it certainly seems to be a "yes and no" kind of answer to the question above. Is nature the ground of both being and value? Well, it is not itself loving or morally good, but it is certainly the foundation of whatever love or moral goodness there is, in a manner far clearer than that of Hick's noumenal Real.

Naturalists can agree that the world is ambiguous. But this is an empirical observation, not an *a priori* axiom arising from a theodicy. The world is ambiguous because it is vast, complex and confusing, and because each person sees only a small piece of the puzzle. So there is no philosophical reason to prejudge a particular position as inherently dishonest. And, since the ambiguity arises primarily from our ignorance, there is no reason why we cannot share our experiences and arguments in the hope of gradually producing a more adequate, less ambiguous picture. There is no God to rig the rules, condemning exploration to failure.

Process theism

A final option I intend to develop elsewhere would be through process theism. The process vision of God is extremely relevant to much of Hick's work, I believe. Of primary significance is the fact that process theism very clearly accounts for the ambiguity of the world because God's power is always, inescapably interwoven with the causal forces of the world. So the world is indeed ambiguous. But this ambiguity is not a test carefully designed by God which neatly separates the religiously open from the religiously closed. Instead, the ambiguity of the world is that veil through which God is exerting every effort to reach us. God is self-revealing in every moment, but in a situation God cannot unilaterally manipulate.

Using the categories of process theism we could very easily adapt Hick's use of the concept of projections. We could see a genuine, positive, divine Reality, "as pressing in upon the human spirit, seeking to be known and responded to",[32] to which the many human visions are, indeed, all responses. But, since that divine self-revelation is always in and through a world with its own agency, its own history, and so on, Hick's recognition that we perceive the world in a context makes perfect sense. (Indeed, Hick does say at one point that, "Because the universe has its own autonomy it is religiously ambiguous."[33] But he never develops the idea.) The many phenomena of the world religions – and even of humanism – could be accepted as honest efforts to interpret and make sense of the world and values.

Rather than try to pre-empt disputes or progress in understanding by denying any positive character to the Real, or saying that God omnipotently plans the world's ambiguity, however, process theology would still affirm that there is a positive reality there which some may perceive and describe better than others. The adventure and dialogue among those searching for the truth would remain meaningful.

CONCLUSION

The purpose of my analysis, questions and brief proposals has been to help us avoid pitfalls and explore possibilities toward what I take to be Hick's noble goal: an interpretation of religion – including humanism – which leads us toward a world of mutual respect.

NOTES

1. *Interpretation of Religion*, pp. 201–2.
2. Ibid., p. 202.
3. Ibid., p. 203.
4. Ibid.
5. Ibid., pp. 328–31.
6. Ibid., p. 330.
7. Ibid.
8. John Hick and Michael Goulder, *Why Believe in God?* (London: SCM, 1983) ch. 6.
9. *Interpretation of Religion*, p. 207.
10. Ibid.
11. Ibid., p. 206.
12. Ibid., p. 208.
13. *Death and Eternal Life*, p. 152.
14. Ibid., p. 156ff.
15. Ibid., p. 157.
16. Ibid., pp. 160–1.
17. *Philosophy of Religion*, 3rd edn, pp. 49–56.
18. *Interpretation of Religion*, pp. 184–5.
19. Ibid., pp. 156–7; *Problems of Religious Pluralism*, p. 25; *Faith and Knowledge*, 2nd edn, pp. 3–4; *Faith and the Philosophers* (New York: St Martin's Press, 1964) p. 248; *The Existence of God* (New York: Macmillan, 1964); *Arguments for the Existence of God* (New York: Macmillan, 1970).
20. *Faith and Knowledge*, 2nd edn, p. 141.
21. *Problems of Religious Pluralism*, p. 29.
22. *God Has Many Names*, p. 49.
23. Ibid., p. 48.
24. Ibid., p. 50.
25. *Interpretation of Religion*, p. 161.
26. Ibid.
27. "From a religious point of view the basic intent of the Marxist –Leninist, Trotskyist, Maoist, and broader socialist movements, as also of 'liberation theology' and the contemporary drive for racial and gender equality, has to be interpreted as a dispositional response of the modern sociologically conditioned consciousness to the Real," (*Interpretation of Religion*, p. 306).
28. Ibid., pp. 85–6.
29. Ibid., p. 264.
30. Ibid., p. 359.
31. Ibid., p. 360.
32.. *God Has Many Names*, p. 48.
33. Ibid., p. 50.

Critical Response

Sin and Salvation from a Feminist Perspective

JUNE O'CONNOR

My response to C. Robert Mesle's paper is one of imitation rather than criticism. Mesle has taken Hick seriously, on the one hand praising and thanking him for his rich and admirable Gifford Lectures, and, on the other, highlighting and illustrating "unresolved progress" with respect to the place of humanistic naturalism in Hick's philosophy of religious pluralism. Voicing the views, values and sensibilities of a humanistic naturalist, Mesle cites ways in which this world view has been misrepresented and, he claims, unfairly excluded from the other major world views and religions on the grounds of elitism, moral failure, self-deception and self-centredness. Mesle sketches two constructive proposals: (1) employing other-centredness as a more useful category than Reality-centredness; and (2) affirming *nature* as the Real and seeing the numerous religions and humanisms as responses to that vast, complex, confusing, ambiguous reality of nature. He offers intimations of a third, regarding the relevance of process theism, which he promises to develop elsewhere.

My imitation of Mesle lies in this: I, too, wish to thank and praise John Hick for a richly researched and provocative pluralistic interpretation of religion; and I, too, wish to probe, expose and explore a perspective which is inadequately addressed in his theory, namely feminism. Although feminism is discussed briefly in *An Interpretation of Religion*,[1] it is inadequately represented and what is cited is largely dismissed. Much remains to be said, if genuine dialogue is to take place in which both partners recognize their own positions.

AN OPEN LETTER TO PROFESSOR JOHN HICK

Dear John,
  Your attention to feminism, focused on the now classic essay of

Valerie Saiving Goldstein, "The Human Situation: A Feminine View,"[2] is an appropriate starting-point for understanding a feminist critique of prevailing Christian theological views about sin and salvation. In this essay, as you note, Saiving looks at the Christian concept of sin as pride from the point of view of gender, suggesting that, while for men pride may be the appropriate designation for sin, for many, perhaps most women, pride is not the problem. Sin for a woman more likely consists in dissipation, diffuseness, and dependence on others, and also acceptance of others at the expense of standards of excellence.

Basing much of her thought on the observations of anthropologists Ruth Benedict and Margaret Mead, Saiving reflects on the feminine experiences of pregnancy, childbirth and lactation, pointing out that the movement of a child from dependence within a woman's body to dependence outside of her body moves a woman's attention in powerful and profound ways. She is called again and again to transcend her own patterns of thought, feeling and physical need as she nourishes this other. She thereby becomes practised in the art of empathy. By listening, inviting and identifying with, she comes to know well the demands, the feelings and the possibilities of self-transcending love.[3] This poises her for the possibility of exaggerated attention outward and makes her vulnerable to the temptations and sins of dissipation, diffuseness and dependence.

You add to Saiving's observations that pervasive cultural and social forces cause this sensibility of reticence, inferiority and unworthiness in many men as well, particularly males of minority cultures who have internalized racist views of their derivative standing and value. Committed to your theory that salvation or liberation, the heart of the many religions of the world, consists in the transformation from self-centredness to Reality-centredness, you judge that,

> In so far as anyone, female or male, lacks the ego-development and fulfilment necessary for a voluntary self-transcendence, the prior achievement of self-fulfilled ego may well be necessary for a true relationship to the Real. For in order to move beyond the self one has first to *be* a self.[4]

I wish to question this. You interpret Saiving's comments about women to imply that this tendency to selflessness that characterizes many women (and some men certainly) means that there is no self, or at least that such selves are insufficiently developed for salvation or liberation to take place (namely, transformation from self-centredness to Reality-centredness). But Saiving's discussion rests on a metaphor of balance rather than sequential development and I think we need to linger over this image, for it is central to understanding her point.

She writes that the woman given to self-transcending love knows also that it is not the whole of life and that it can be deadly: "The moments, hours, and days of self-giving must be *balanced* by moments, hours, and days of withdrawal into, and enrichment of, her individual selfhood if she is to remain a whole person" (emphasis added).[5] The woman with a sense of balance knows that life challenges her to value and to live both aspects of love: love of other and love of self. The temptation is to abandon the dialectic and surrender totally in one direction or the other, committing the "sin of alterity"[6] or the sin of self-absorption and self-indulgence.

Since self-transcending love can be construed as a virtue opposed to the vice of selfishness, let me be explicit that I am using it here (as Saiving does by implication) as excessive attention outward such that one avoids or abdicates responsibility. By that I mean the responsibility one has to activate one's intelligence, creativity and conscientious judgement, and responsibly to probe the fundamental religious questions about origin, value, purpose and destiny. Thus the critique is not psychological in focus (I leave that task to the psychologists). My support of Saiving's basic insight rests on theological and ethical grounds which are rooted in a basically religious view of life.

The woman who commits her life in love to others (in physical motherhood, "spiritual motherhood", or various other forms of committed giving and radical service to others) is trained, called, exhorted, indeed required, to transcend the self regularly. What she needs to be reminded about by theologians, Saiving suggests, is the equal importance of disciplining the self to come home to itself, and there to notice, nourish and enrich the resources of that self which she is called to "transcend" in love and service to others.[7] The self is there; there is no no-self in Saiving's essay. For Saiving, woman's self is a given which is given to others *and* must also be withdrawn periodically in order to be nurtured and enriched.

And so I invite you to take another look at Saiving's essay, John, because your response (namely, that the absence of self and fulfilled ego development may render transformation from self-centredness to Reality-centredness impossible or unlikely) does not grapple with her root metaphor of balance. The different images with which you and Saiving think are noteworthy and significant for the different interpretations they stimulate. You work within a sequential and developmental root metaphor for understanding salvation and liberation (transformation from and to), thereby requiring one without a self-fulfilled ego or sufficient ego development to achieve that ego in order to move beyond it.

Saiving's root metaphor of balance suggests this: if sin consists in giving to the point of dissipation of self and dependence on others for a sense of self, grace consists in the recovery of self combined with the giving of self, so that there is a unique self with talents and gifts to be shared – and replenished – and shared – but also nurtured – and shared – then enriched – and shared. Neither the movement of withdrawal and self-nurture nor the movement of generous love has the final say. Both are necessary to a graced life. Moving in and out of each with some measure of grace and rhythm can be an illuminating model of salvation for a woman who, from time to time, catches herself longing for rest at one pole or the other, notices that she is tempted by the hope of rest in self-indulgence or alterity. This, I think, is the real insight of Saiving's essay. Salvation is a movement of balance, to and fro, in and out, being with and being alone – a movement without ceasing, for each term of the movement (self and other), each pole of the dialectic is valuable and can provide access to, can mediate, the Real.

Your sequential, developmental view, based on a linear root metaphor, may be less gripping to those folk who find religious and spiritual resources in the self (i.e. God in and through the self or Real within) and those who think in more communitarian terms. Your judgement that, for "anyone [who] lacks the ego-development and fulfilment necessary for a voluntary self-transcendence, the prior achievement of self-fulfilled ego may well be necessary for a true relationship to the Real", and that "in order to move beyond the self one has first to *be* a self",[8] gives a formula for salvation that is more rigid than human experience warrants. It carries the added disadvantage of echoing the ancient (apocryphal) gospel of Thomas, which claims that "every woman who will make herself male will enter the Kingdom of Heaven".[9] (One thinks also of a more recent analogue: Henry Higgins's musical refrain "Why Can't a Woman Be More Like a Man?")

And yet I see no need to reject your basic metaphor. What I wish to do is relativize your metaphor, place it as one metaphor alongside others. I believe that your theory would be strengthened and improved by relaxing and expanding your view of salvation/ liberation. Instead of seeing this as the transformation from self-centredness to Reality-centredness, I recommend that you describe it, rather, as a process of movement and improvement (both ontologically and morally considered) which is differently defined not only by the different traditions, but also by religious persons within the same tradition. The cluster concept of movement and improvement could then incorporate both a developmental model that esteems movement forward, as your thought suggests, and a dialectical model that reveres a dynamic (not static) sense of balance in which opposites or complementarities are explored interactively.

To modify the meaning of sin and salvation on the basis of Saiving's single-voiced protest can be a first step in taking seriously a variety of descriptions about how temptation is experienced, what sin is, and how salvation is to be understood and achieved. Her essay requires and enables us to think more broadly about these questions and the root metaphors we think with as we search for insight. While affirming her contribution to our thinking on this matter, however, I wish also to recognize some limits. For this (thirty-year-old) essay has been supplemented and helpfully contextualized by a multitude of more recent historical, philosophical, theological, phenomenological, ethical and constructive feminist studies.[10] Indeed, in light of the insights unearthed in the past three decades of research, I notice that Saiving does not give attention to the ways in which differences of class and race, as well as gender, shape, enable and limit experiences.[11] While reading Saiving's portrait of "feminine experience",[12] one might justly wonder if women in the barrio and ghetto, in the factory and on family farms, in US unemployment lines and on welfare rolls, and in the villages of Ghana and Guatemala would recognize themselves in the language of this essay. Also, one might ask, what about women who are, for whatever myriad reasons, abusive to their children rather than empathetic, selfish and greedy rather than self-transcending? It is important to recognize that, although we must listen to women's experience, we must continually feed our understanding with the particularities of women in specific and highly variegated socioeconomic, cultural, and geo-political settings. Differences *among* women must also be accounted for as we seek to generalize about "women's experience" or the "feminine experience".

Studies about men as well as women with race or class as a lens for understanding further complicate the data base from which we must construct our theories. They alert us to the tremendous variety and complexity of human experiencing, symbol-making, myth-making and ritual enactment that characterize the religious lives of human beings around the world. Our theologizing and philosophizing are thereby challenged anew to notice the complexity, listen to the complexity, probe the complexity, account for the complexity. This makes the job of the philosopher of religion much more difficult. A good bit of relevant data is only now coming in, in light of these emerging sensibilities, and much more invites attention.

It does seem to me, however, that such work can be integrated into a revised version of your interpretations. Three examples come to mind.

1   Just as you understand "religion" according to the categories of family resemblances and cluster concepts,[13] could you not also understand sin and salvation/liberation in terms of family resemblances and cluster concepts? Would it not be fruitful to be as "loose" with your views of sin and salvation/liberation as you are with your views of religion? Just as you see the quality of importance as pervading the field of religious phenomena and so of providing a context for looking and understanding, could you not name the quality of movement and the desire for improvement as the context for understanding the sense of process that we find in religion (both ontologically and morally considered)? As a cluster concept, this sense of movement and improvement could account for the widespread religious sense of discontent with what is and hope for what might be, aspirations for moving from less aliveness to greater aliveness, ignorance to knowledge, imperfection to perfection, but could also allow for a dialectical model of movement (back and forth, giving and receiving, spending and recovering, being with and being alone) that searches to affirm and to explore alternative, mutually enhancing goods.

The advantage of highlighting this sense of movement and improvement as a feature of religious phenomena would leave open the precise selection of metaphor, image and concept used to describe and give access to the experience commonly known as salvation or liberation. For there are many ways in which humans express, symbolize and interpret such aspirations. If women's voices are accepted as valid and valuable resources for understanding temptation, sin, hope and salvation/liberation, which I think we must grant, your pluralistic hypothesis about religion could be strengthened by voicing a pluralistic hypothesis about sin and salvation which is seen to consist not in the transformation from self-centredness to Reality-centredness, but simply in a sense of movement and improvement both ontologically and morally considered. In this context, transformation from self-centredness to Reality-centredness is an acceptable description of salvation or liberation, but is not sufficiently universal to merit the central place you afford it.

2   Another way in which this broader hypothesis can be integrated within the terms you have already outlined pertains to your description of the Real. Just as you have written that the Real "is differently conceived, experienced and responded to from within the different cultural ways of being human",[14] so, too, you could argue that the apparently universally felt need for movement and improvement is differently conceived, experienced and responded to from within the different geographical, cultural, social, racial, feminine and masculine ways of being human. This shift would then permit both a pride-based notion of self/temptation/ sin and a diffidence-based notion of self/temptation/sin, as well as many other images and descriptions.

3   Your view of myths could also support this change. "Myths", you write, "are capable of being in varying degrees true or false according as they serve to relate us appropriately or inappropriately to the Real."[15] The criterion of truthfulness for testing your own philosophical myth, then, is its ability to relate its hearers appropriately or not to the Real. Valerie Saiving and other feminist thinkers are saying that some of the categories used by scholars of religion are inappropriate because they do not correspond to experience, they do not catch the struggle, name the balancing-act, resonate with the reader where and how she lives. They fail to name her experience and thus may fail to relate her to the Real. The myth speaks neither to her nor of her.

The language of recovering, reclaiming and consciously reappropriating individual and communal spiritual resources and forgotten or suppressed visions does seem to resonate with many women today, suggesting a fruitful direction in the formulation of contemporary soteriology.[16] Within this context of recovery and reappropriation, the dangers of self-transcending love can themselves be redeemed and transformed. The virtue of self-transcending love can be recovered when both giving and receiving, spending and restoring become part of its definition. Seen this way, self-transcending love can serve as a model for responsible living that values both generous love for others and appreciative acceptance of self, for men and women alike, in any variety of geographical and social locations.

One final point which requires more discussion than I have room for here: I find that C. Robert Mesle's suggestion that you replace "the Real" with "the other" resonates with my own Western, Christian, feminist sensibilities. As a Christian humanist–feminist, I link the Other who is God (the Real) with the other which is nature, which other includes many others – children, spouses, friends and colleagues, enemies and adversaries, animals, plants, inanimate things, and the energy that comprises us all. In a word, I would be inclined to use "other"/"Other" here to refer to all personal, impersonal and transpersonal reality which is not identical to, but is intimately related to, my self. In fact, one of the ways in which I see and understand my self, my responsibilities and possibilities, is precisely in relation to these others. For many of us, I think, it is with these others and through these others and in these others that we find "the Other" (in Christian terms, the divine; in your philosophy, the Real). (This notion of "other" pertains to ourselves as well, of course, for we are "other" to our others. We live and we learn in relation.) The category of "Other"/"other" highlights for me, in a way "the Real" does not, the communal, collective context in which the relationship of self to other takes place and through which it is mediated. I suspect, though, that this might not resonate with the religions of the East. It may well be a characteristically Western category and thus not universalizable. A more inclusive concept with rich communitarian connotations may have to be discovered elsewhere. Surely this exchange needs to be continued.

In closing, I wish publicly to thank you, John, for the energy, love and insight which you have poured into this work. You have enabled us to understand better the many worlds of religion, and you have invited us all to do our own thinking as we consider these important questions.

NOTES

1. *Interpretation of Religion*, pp. 52–4.
2. Valerie Saiving Goldstein, "The Human Situation: A Feminine View", *Journal of Religion*, 40, no. 2 (Apr 1960); repr., under the name Valerie Saiving, in Carol P. Christ and Judith Plaskow (eds), *Womanspirit Rising: A Feminist Reader in Religion* (San Francisco: Harper and Row, 1979) pp. 25–42.
    Since "feminism" is a charged word, I wish to be clear about what I mean by it here. By "feminism" I mean a mode of inquiry driven by questions about women in the religious traditions of the world: questions about women's presence and absence, words and silences, convictions, concerns and critical judgements. Although a feminist perspective implies commitment to women's well-being and equality with men, what constitutes women's well-being and how equality is to be understood are not settled in advance but become issues for debate.
3. Although Saiving focuses on the experience of motherhood as her central example, other experiences of commitment could appropriately be used as well, given the training and expectations placed on women and given the types of employment traditionally open to women (teaching, nursing, domestic work and child-care). The other may be a child, but may equally be a spouse, friend, student, neighbour, co-worker, the poor and the needy, and so on.
4. *Interpretation of Religion*, p. 54.
5. Saiving, "The Human Situation: A Feminine View", in Christ and Plaskow (eds), *Womanspirit Rising*, p. 37.
6. Sandra MacNevin-Xu, personal conversation, 30 Mar 1989. Another response to John Hick's discussion of feminism can be found in Maura O'Neill, "A World of Differences: Examining Gender Issues in Interreligious Dialogue" (Claremont Graduate School Dissertation, 1989) pp. 62–7.
7. Nelle Morton's *The Journey is Home* (Boston, Mass: Beacon, 1985) develops this image in a feminist exploration of the power of word, image and metaphor.
8. *Interpretation of Religion*, p. 54.
9. Log. 114, tr. Thomas O. Lambdin in *The Nag Hammadi Library in English*, 3rd, rev. edn, ed. James M. Robinson (San Francisco: Harper and Row, 1988) p. 138.
10. Bibliographical review essays that survey this research include the following: Anne E. Patrick, "Women and Religion: A Survey of Significant Literature, 1965–1974", *Theological Studies*, 36, no. 4 (Dec 1975) 737–65; Anne Barstow Driver, "Review Essay: Reli-

gion", *Signs: Journal of Women in Culture and Society*, 2 (Winter 1976) 434–42; Carol´P. Christ, "The New Feminist Theology: A Review of the Literature", *Religious Studies Review*, 3, no. 4 (Oct 1977) 203–10; Gayle Graham Yates, "Spirituality and the American Feminist Experience", *Signs: Journal of Women in Culture and Society*, 9, no. 1 (Aug 1983) 59–72; Barbara H. Andolsen, "Gender and Sex Roles in Recent Religious Ethics Literature", *Religious Studies Review*, 11, no. 3 (July 1985) 217–23; and June O'Connor, "Re-reading, Reconceiving, and Reconstructing Traditions: Feminist Research in Religion", *Women's Studies: An Interdisciplinary Journal*, 17, nos 1–2 (1989), 101–23.

11.   Kathryn Allen Rabuzzi's *The Sacred and the Feminine: Toward a Theology of Housework* (New York: Seabury, 1982), for example, probes the experience of white, middle-class, educated women shaped by the myth of "happily ever after"; Cherrie Moraga and Gloria Anzaldua present perspectives from Native American, Asian, Hispanic and black women in the United States in *This Bridge Called My Back: Writings by Radical Women of Color* (Watertown, Mass.: Persephone Press, 1981). Proceedings from a February 1987 conference on gender, class and race sponsored by the UCLA Center for the Study of Women are available in *Women's Studies: An Interdisciplinary Journal* (see note 10).

12.   In order to avoid a false split between male and female experience, in order to avoid perpetuating stereotypes, Saiving makes this importantly nuanced observation early in her essay: "It is my contention that there are significant differences between masculine and feminine experience and that feminine experience reveals in a more emphatic fashion certain aspects of the human situation which are present but less obvious in the experience of men" – Saiving, "The Human Situation: A Feminine View", in Christ and Plaskow (eds), *Womanspirit Rising*, p. 27.

13.   *Interpretation of Religion*, pp. 3–4.

14.   Ibid., p. 14.

15.   Ibid., p. 176.

16.   Elisabeth Schussler Fiorenza's work is a sterling illustration of this in Christian studies. See *In Memory of Her: A Feminist Theological Reconstruction of Christian Origins* (New York: Crossroad, 1983); also Rosemary Radford Ruether, *Sexism and God-Talk: Toward a Feminist Theology* (Boston, Mass.: Beacon, 1983).

Reply

JOHN HICK

I have received two salutary shocks from Robert Mesle's paper—
The first concerns the question of elitism. As a result of his protest
I realize that it would probably have been better not to have used
the world "elitist" in the discussion of humanism, in that the point
that I was making in each of the writings to which he refers could
better have been made without it. This is that, whereas the
religions offer a picture of the universe which, if true, constitutes
good news for all humanity, the humanist picture, if true, constitutes bad news for all except a small and exceptionally fortunate
minority. I did not in fact suggest that this makes humanists, as
such, elitist. But I did suggest that those humanists who express
satisfaction with the lot of the fortunate few who are happily able
to attain to inner serenity and self-transcendence, whilst ignoring
the harsh pressures under which the large majority of human
beings live, are guilty of an unintended elitism; and I have quoted
some such humanists. But, since it is regrettably easy for a kind of
guilt by association to spread to humanism as such, it would have
been better not to have used the word at all. I am grateful to Mesle
for making this clear.

I cannot, however, include here the process theodicy which
Mesle links with humanism. He rightly points out that humanism
does not seek to justify the sufferings and injustices of life. But the
process theodicy which I have discussed, that of my colleague
David Griffin in *God, Power and Evil*, does seek to justify this. This
is clear from Griffin's statement that the "question as to whether
God is indictable is to be answered in terms of the question as to
whether the positive values that are possible in our world are
valuable enough to be worth the risk of the negative experiences
which have occurred".[1] Griffin argues that the good that has been
realized in a fortunate few *does* justify the evil suffered by the rest
of humanity; and it is this argument that provokes the charge – to
my mind, the justified charge – of an implicit elitism. But I accept
that, as Mesle points out, humanism as such does not seek to
justify the evils of this life and cannot therefore be described as
elitist.

The other salutary shock concerns what Mesle calls "the notorious Pascal quotation". I am afraid that I had not realized how
hostile this can seem to a humanist. I had used it simply as a vivid
expression, by a great thinker, of the idea of the religious ambiguity of the universe and of the fact that to experience life religiously
requires a free cognitive choice, which I call faith. But in so using
it I ought to have made it clear that I do not want to launch the
chain of reasoning which Mesle spells out, leading to a condemnation of humanists as self-centred and as guilty of a morally
reprehensible self-deception. That I have not intended this is, I
hope, indicated by the suggestion that, whereas in traditional
societies the religions have functioned as cognitive filters shield-
ing humanity from the direct presence of the Real, in the modern
West "our human freedom in relation to the Real has come to be
typically maintained in a new way, namely by a radical scepticism
which rejects transcendence as such. This is expressed in the
characteristic atheism, humanism, secularism and theoretical
materialism of the modern period."[2]

It is true that Western secular humanism is overshadowed in *An
Interpretation of Religion* by the much larger phenomenon of
Marxism, and more broadly by the many-sided struggle today for
human liberation. Concerning this I say that

> from a religious point of view the basic intent of the Marxist–
> Leninist, Trotskyist, Maoist, and broader socialist movements,
> as also of "liberation theology" and the contemporary drive for
> racial and gender equality, has to be interpreted as a disposi-
> tional response of the modern sociologically conditioned con-
> sciousness to the Real.[3]

This does indeed amount, as Mesle points out, to a kind of
inclusivism, in that it says that humanists and Marxists may be
responding to the Real without knowing that they are doing so. I
see no way of avoiding this. It is, indeed, from a religious
standpoint, an entirely appropriate inclusivism.

But of course the radical intellectual difference between, on the
one hand, a religious and, on the other hand, a naturalistic or
humanist interpretation of the universe remains, and I do not
wish to diminish it. Respect for humanists does not entail thinking that their belief system is true. It is here that I want to add that
the difference between a naturalistic and a religious interpretation

of the universe being true will show itself eschatologically. If after bodily death we find ourselves in existence and moving – perhaps over a long period of time – towards a limitlessly good fulfilment of the human potential, then, even if all our mythological pictures of that eschaton prove to be inadequate, it will nevertheless be evident that the naturalistic belief system was mistaken and that the religious belief systems were on the right lines.

Turning to June O'Connor's response to Mesle: this introduces an important new dimension into our discussions. I must accept her correction of my reading of Valerie Saiving. I had taken Saiving to be saying that, whereas men (generally speaking) have to overcome their tendency to self-centredness and self-assertion in order to become re-centred in the divine, women (generally speaking) have to overcome an opposite tendency to self abnegation and dependence. I thus saw her as implying that the conception of salvation/liberation as the transformation of human existence from self-centredness to Reality-centredness applies (generally) to men but not (generally) to women; and I responded with the suggestion that it applies to women also, but that, in so far as they (and also in so far as any men) lack a strong ego, they have to develop one before they can transcend it. This leads to the unwelcome conclusion that many women have to go through two stages to salvation, but many men only one!

June O'Connor offers a more nuanced interpretation of Saiving as saying that women (more than men) have to maintain a balance between the temptation to "alterity" (typically, in self-giving to her family), and the temptation, shared with men, to self-assertion. Her special temptation, as woman, is to overdevelop her alterity at the expense of her egoity; whereas a man's characteristic temptation is the contrary one. I accept gratefully this more rounded understanding of Saiving.

I do, however, have reservations about O'Connor's further suggestion concerning the nature of salvation/liberation as consisting in "a sense of movement and improvement (both ontologically and morally considered)".[4] Much may perhaps depend upon what is meant here by "ontologically". But the notion of a "sense of movement and improvement" sounds too purely psychological. It sounds as though to be in process of salvation is to have a sense that one is changing and improving. No doubt, if one is in process of salvation one does have such a sense. But does salvation *consist in* this? There is no reference here to the distinctively religious concept of the divine, the transcendent, the Real. But if we are interested in a religious interpretation of religion, will not salvation have to be defined in terms of relationship to the ultimately Real as well as in terms of its fruits in moral and other forms of improvement?

Within a generic concept of salvation/liberation as the movement to a new centring in the Real there must of course be room for the different ways in which this relationship is conceptualized within the different traditions, and also for the different psychological patterns formed by gender as well as by cultural differences. June O'Connor has written illuminatingly about the differences that gender makes; and we males need continually to hear this kind of reminder and correction from the other half of the human race. In the light of it I want to retain my generic concept of salvation/liberation, but to learn to recognize more fully and consistently that the range of which it is a generalization includes the distinctively female and male, as well as Eastern, Western and other paths of human transformation.

NOTES

1. David Griffin, *God, Power and Evil* (Philadelphia: Westminster Press, 1976), p. 309.
2. *Interpretation of Religion*, p. 163.
3. Ibid., p. 306.
4. June O'Connor, above, p. 76.

4

John Hick's *An Interpretation of Religion*

PAUL BADHAM

Lord Gifford would have been delighted by this book. It is hard to think of any previous Gifford Lectures which more precisely fulfilled the terms of his will. John Hick certainly fits the specification of an "able and reverent man, a true thinker, a sincere lover of and earnest inquirer after truth". His book looks into "all questions about man's conceptions of God or the Infinite, their origin, nature and truth, whether he can have such conceptions . . ." and so on. His study is of "Natural Theology in the widest sense of that term", in that he does not confine himself simply to personal concepts of God but also explores impersonal understandings of "the Infinite, the All . . . the Sole Reality". In one respect Hick seems at first sight to depart from Lord Gifford's requirements in that he explicitly puts forward a religious, rather than a naturalistic, interpretation of religion, and this might seem to clash with the clause in the will which specifies that natural theology be treated as a "strictly natural science". However, Lord Gifford clarified this to mean that the lecturer should make no "reliance upon any supposed special, exceptional or so-called miraculous revelation", but instead should see the foundation for a religious perspective in "the true and felt knowledge (not mere nominal knowledge) of the relations of man and the universe" to God or Reality.[1] This is precisely what John Hick seeks to do in *An Interpretation of Religion*. It is an interpretation of religion which is at every point focused on living human experience, and which insists that all our speculations and theories must be rooted in, and true to, the diverse human responses to what believers experience as divine Reality. The book has two central concerns: first, to establish the validity of a religious world view as one possible way of interpreting a systematically ambiguous cosmos; and, second, to justify a religiously pluralist understanding of religion.

John Hick believes that in our present state of knowledge it is impossible either to establish or to refute the existence of a transcendent Reality. He thinks this ambiguity is religiously important since it enables faith to be a free, rather than a forced, response. The arguments for God's existence are sufficient neither to establish belief nor even to make it strictly probable, since there is no agreed consensus as to how to weight the significance of the various factors which can be argued for and against on either side. However, Hick thinks that the rationale for believing in God is at least adequate to make the option of such belief intellectually defensible for those who experience themselves as living in the presence of God.

If faith is ultimately based on experiencing, this does raise the issue of the plurality of religious experience. For authentic religious experience is in no sense confined to one tradition in the way that traditional Christianity has tended to suppose. John Hick himself found it necessary to abandon the Christocentric exclusivist position in which he had first come to faith, because he found it impossible to reconcile this position with his subsequent experiences. There seemed to him no grounds to doubt that the theistic worship he observed in the temples, mosques, gurdwaras and synagogues of Birmingham derived from, and bore witness to, genuine human responses to the same transcendent reality as he had encountered in Christian worship. Subsequent knowledge of persons in the Advaitic Vedanta and Theravāda Buddhist traditions convinced him that the same Reality was also encountered in those traditions, although there described in non-personal terms. To suggest that all such experiences should be attributed to a Christianly described divine Logos seemed to him a form of Christian cultural imperialism which failed to do justice to the distinctive insights of other world faiths. A genuinely pluralistic interpretation of religion seemed to him to be required by sensitive experience of life in a religiously plural world. That insight is what has led to the hypothesis offered by *An Interpretation of Religion*.

John Hick argues that religion can essentially be described in two ways: as a purely human phenomenon to be accounted for in wholly naturalistic terms, or as a human response to a transcendent reality. Because of the "pervasive ambiguity of the Universe", it is not possible to refute either description.[2] And indeed the two hypotheses are not mutually exclusive, because, even when religion is deemed to be a human response to a divine Reality, the mode of that response remains embedded in the cultural, social and intellectual world of the believer. This latter consideration is of crucial importance to Hick's thesis, because he seeks to account for the differences between the various concepts of the divine Reality to be found in the religions of the world as the product of these factors.

The problem for a pluralist understanding of religion has always been the need to reconcile the notion that each religion is in some sense an authentic response to the one divine Reality while at the same time facing up to the immense diversity of ways in which that Reality is pictured. Hick's solution is to emphasize the way in which each of the world's religions has drawn a distinction between the Real as such, and the Real as perceived by us. He is able to show that leading thinkers in each of the world's traditions, whether Jewish, Christian, Islamic, Buddhist, Taoist or Hindu, have all been vividly conscious of this, and have insisted that all the ways we image God, Brahman or the *dharmakāya* are ultimately misleading.[3] He suggests that the distinction Kant drew between things as they really are in themselves, and things as we perceive them within the categories of our thought structures, might be a useful analogy to help us to appreciate this distinction.

What Hick is claiming is that the world religions are a response to a single divine Reality, and that their differences in describing that which they claim to encounter are culturally conditioned human projections which seek to image that reality. Each "name of God" represents a different persona of the divine Reality as responded to in human history. Hick takes as examples of his thesis the character of Krishna as worshipped in the Vaiṣnavite tradition of India, and the character of Yahweh as believed to be disclosed in the life and experience of ancient Israel. Although these are perceived as quite distinct personae, they are both experienced as the focus of religious experience within the cultural and historical traditions to which they belong. Hick believes the same to be true of "the heavenly Father of Christian faith, known through the distinctively Christian response to Jesus of Nazareth; the Allah of Islamic faith, known as self-revealed in the Qur'ān through the prophet Muhammed; and Shiva known and intensely experienced within the Śaivite cults of India".[4]

What is the ontological status of these personae? Hick believes it is not really plausible to suppose that they all separately exist as literally distinct entities: as rival gods in some polytheistic pantheon. Nor is it justifiable to say that only one corresponds to Reality and that the rest are *simply* human projections, for there are no adequate criteria to make such a distinction. From a phenomenological perspective each appears equally "real" to its believers. Hick's conclusion, therefore, is that the one God is differently described, because experience of God, like all other human experience, is necessarily coloured by the differing cultural traditions and historical experiences of particular human groups. Hick believes that this perspective also applies to those religious traditions which reject the notion of a personal deity and think of the Real in impersonal terms as the Absolute. This Absolute is also differently signified in different cultures as Brahman, *nirvāṇa* or *śūnyatā*. Once again these should not be perceived as descriptive of different realities, but rather as alternative culturally conditioned apprehensions of the one supreme Reality.

One significant reason why Hick believes that the experiential claims of each of the great post-axial religions should be treated on a par is his view that they are equally efficacious in bringing about human transformation, experience of salvation/liberation and a sense of cosmic optimism and well-being. All teach in different ways the importance of dying to self and the moral ideal of generous goodwill, love and compassion. All religious traditions have, as a matter of history, much to be ashamed of in the way their members have fallen short of the highest ideals of their community. But, on the other hand, all also have made immense contributions to human welfare. Hick concludes that, on applying the moral criterion of evaluating religions by their fruits, it is impossible in our present state of knowledge to give the palm to any one tradition. As Hick says,

It may be the case that from the point of view of omniscience, one tradition stands out as morally superior to all others. But if so this is not evident from our partial human perspective. It is not possible, as an unbiased judgement with which all rational persons could be expected to agree, to assert the overall moral superiority of any one of the great religious traditions of the world.[5]

One problem which faces the pluralist position is that the world religions disagree on a number of factual propositions. Since these propositions are characteristically incorporated into what is affirmed about God or the nature of ultimate Reality, and since they are often associated with what is believed about the ultimate destiny of human persons, these disagreements are significant. Hick finds the approach of the Buddha helpful. The Buddha insisted that there are many questions concerning the eternity or otherwise of the cosmos, the relation between soul and body, and the nature of life after death which are unanswerable in the context of our present knowledge and the categories of our present thinking. However, Buddha believed that such unanswered questions do not and should not affect our quest for liberation in the present. This is essentially the position John Hick also adopts. He argues that the fact that world religions differ on such points in no way affects their ability to help people to find salvation/liberation and that there is at present no way to resolve these differences of opinion. Hick also believes that in practice differences of viewpoint characteristically exist within, as well as between, the various religious traditions, and that many people are coming to see some of the disputed claims, such as the Christian claim that Jesus is God the Son Incarnate, as religious myths rather than as factual claims.

John Hick's thesis raises many important issues for discussion both for Christian theology and for religious studies. Let me start on a relatively minor point, that of terminology. Hick uses the phrase "the Real" to describe that to which the world religions respond. He rightly points out that each of the main traditions already makes use of this expression and hence the term has the advantage that "without being the exclusive property of any one tradition it is nevertheless familiar within all of them".[6] I suspect that the term is also attractive to Hick because, as is clear from his discussion in chapters 11 and 12 of *An Interpretation of Religion*, he is opposed to "non-realist" accounts of the most central religious claims. But, while the term is indeed useful in certain contexts, I do not believe it can carry the full weight of inter-religious discussion. The reason why the expression "the Real" is without negative overtones in any religious tradition is that it is not often used in any of them. It is a relatively specialist term, and while understandable to scholars it would not be so readily recognized by the wider religious community. This is especially true in the Western world, where the situation is complicated by the fact that the word "real" has a very well-established secular and naturalistic meaning as referring to what is in fact the case. When a Western speaker urges us to "face reality", he or she is not characteristically inviting us to contemplate the divine. Hence, to use the expression "the Real" to refer to the transcendent is likely to confine the discussion to specialists in the field of religious dialogue, when the greatest need in an increasingly pluralist society is to aid interfaith understanding at a grass-roots level. In this context I suggest it is better to continue to use the mainstream religious words, such as "God", "Allah", "Brahman" or *dharmakāya,* and then to stimulate further reflection by using less specific terms such as "the Real" or "the Transcendent" or "the Ground of Being". Prolonged discussions prior to the launch of the interfaith series of "God conferences" suggested that "God" was the most widely accepted term for the Ultimate, and that it was widely regarded as appropriate in both personal and impersonal understandings. On the explicit point Hick makes about "God" being too identified with a personal theistic understanding,[7] I believe it would be positively helpful to interfaith dialogue if contemporary Christians were reminded how modern the dominance of such a personal understanding of the term is within their own tradition. The essentially impassible God of the Christian Fathers, with his aseity, incomprehensibility and infinity, would seem much closer to the concept of the *dharmakāya* than the anthropomorphically conceived divinity of much contemporary Christian devotion. Hence using the term "God" in non-personal contexts in interfaith dialogue might help Christians to rediscover that awareness of the complexity of talking about God which was so strong an element in the apophatic and mystical traditions of both Eastern and Western Christianity.

From the perspective of religious studies, one of the most fascinating features of *An Interpretation of Religion* is its discussion of Buddhism. Many Western scholars have come to identify Buddhism with a very narrow philosophical tradition, which does little justice to the religious depths and richness of the Buddhist inheritance. This is not true of Hick's work, and his book opens up in a way accessible to all the immense range and variety of Buddhist thought in a treatment which has already brought the warm endorsement of one of Japan's leading scholars. Islamic specialists may, however, be more reserved about the book, because Hick draws frequently on the Sufi tradition to illustrate trends in Islam which open up real possibilities for interfaith exploration. To some Muslims this tradition is simply not acceptable. Yet there is no doubt that it is part of the broader Islamic inheritance, and that experientially it represents a living and dynamic dimension. However, the ambiguity of its status raises one of the problems which must constantly face a person seeking, as Hick is, to find common ground within the world religions. Such common ground is always essentially experiential, based on what Lord Gifford referred to as "true and felt knowledge" of the divine, rather than the often "nominal knowledge" of those who build their faith on the sole foundation of what they learn from ancient documents.

Conservative evangelical Christians will find their worst suspicions of Hick confirmed by his book. For it is axiomatic to the understanding of Christianity here presented that Jesus was esentially concerned to proclaim good news concerning God, and that he had no conception of his own supposed deity. In taking this view Hick is, of course, only spelling out what the overwhelming consensus of New Testament scholarship implicitly shows, even though many scholars are reticent about facing as openly as Hick does the implication of their findings. More significantly, the experiential awareness of the reality of a divine encounter which Hick has witnessed in other faiths makes exclusivist Christianity the one form of that religion which is wholly unacceptable to his pluralist vision.

A more fundamental critique of Hick's position might come from the perspective of the philosophy of religion. This relates to Hick's implicit assumption that authentic knowledge must be restricted to what all would recognize as indisputably true. This assumption is made with regard to three important elements in Hick's thesis: first, his view that the universe is systematically ambiguous, and that religious faith and naturalistic faith are therefore equally plausible interpretations of it;[8] secondly, his view that it is unreasonable to claim moral superiority for any one of the great religions of the world;[9] and, thirdly, his belief that it is impossible to adjudicate conclusively between their conflicting truth-claims.[10] I would not for one minute deny the great practical difficulty of coming to justifiable evaluations on such issues, and I concede at once that unanimity of judgement is out of the question. Nevertheless I do wish to claim that well-justified assessments should be considered to be at least possible in principle.

My basic point is the one argued for at length by Basil Mitchell in *The Justification of Religious Belief:* namely, that in many, perhaps most, academic disciplines we commonly and justifiably make use of rational arguments other than those of proof or strict probability; and that, typically, theological arguments are of this kind.[11] Mitchell shows how in literary criticism, historical inquiry, philosophical debate, and even paradigm shifts in scientific theory we commonly make use of arguments which fall short of proof, and arrive at conclusions which we believe to be rationally defensible even though no universal agreement exists and refutation of alternative views is impossible. Mitchell's argument can be widely extended and I suggest that in most matters of political and economic theory, most matters of law and social policy, and almost all ethical and aesthetic judgement genuine knowledge is to be found, even though universal consensus is very rarely to be obtained.

Hick, as the editor of Mitchell's work, is of course well aware of such arguments, and his own general approach to theological and religious issues exemplifies the virtues of such a position. *An Interpretation of Religion* is for the most part a model of how to present rational arguments which fall short of proof, but which nevertheless develop a sustained and cumulative rational case for the position being defended while always being aware of, and fair to, the factors which count against his position. It is therefore at first sight surprising that at such crucial points in his argument he should relapse into a kind of positivism which says that, since alternative views are possible, no justifiable conclusion can be drawn.

The first instance I wish to explore is on p. 123 of *An Interpretation of Religion,* where, having set out very clearly the factors which count for, and the factors which count against, a theistic world view, Hick says,

The question is whether having thus set them out in two opposed columns we can conclude that one list outweighs the other. It appears to me that no such outcome is possible. For it would require us to quantify the values of the different items of evidence. . . . But any such relative quantifications could only be arbitrary and subjective. It is questionable whether we can even, with any hope of consensus, arrange the items within the same list in an order of relative importance . . . it seems then that the universe maintains its inscrutable ambiguity.

In defence of what Hick says we must at once concede that consensus is quite out of the question. Equally well-informed, rational and sensitive persons constantly make different judgements on such issues. I frequently ask my students to write essays evaluating the arguments for and against belief in God. It would be utterly intolerable if my assessment of such essays were in any way influenced by the conclusions they arrive at, rather than by their critical evaluation of the issues. Theology, like most humane disciplines, differs from the natural sciences precisely in that it offers no "right answers"! But this does not mean that agnosticism (in the strict and correct meaning of the term as a total suspension of belief either way) is the only rational response to the data. Rather, I suggest a reasonable person should attempt to do precisely what Hick says cannot be done, and seek to evaluate the relative weight of the various factors he lists.

There is no other area of human concern where all rational people would not admit the duty to attempt to make an informed judgement on the pros and cons. Take the issue of Marxism *versus* liberal democracy. The advantages of each could comparably be set out in parallel columns, but, once more, there would be no agreed consensus as to which factors to give the greatest weight. Equally intelligent and informed persons would come to different conclusions, but few would be willing to accept that no reasoned choice could be made. The same would be true of such issues as the legitimacy of abortion, the use or otherwise of nuclear power, or any other controverted issue one cares to name. They are controversial precisely because there is no consensus about how to quantify or weight the considerations put forward in argument on either side.

A comparable issue arises with John Hick's evaluation of the great religions of the world. He carefully documents his belief that

> the ethical principles of the great traditions express essentially the same ideal of love, compassion, forgiveness. But their applications of this ideal to the concrete circumstances of life have varied greatly . . . we can point to good and evil within each tradition. . . .But it is virtually impossible to weigh up the overall moral value . . . of one tradition as compared with another.[12]

As a matter of general policy I agree with Hick's basic point. It is not our place to sit in judgement one over another. "Comparisons are odious", and, rather than seek to establish an order of merit among the world's religions as totalities, it is almost certainly more beneficial to see what we can learn from the values of other traditions and to work within our own tradition to put right the evils present within it. For example, rather than criticize what I perceive as the Islamic attitude towards women, I should work for reform within the Anglican Church in England and Wales on attitudes to women and their role in the Church.

However, although I see the strength of what Hick is saying, I am not entirely convinced that comparisons are always out of place, and still less am I convinced that such comparisons can not be made. I am glad that Christianity replaced the religion of the Aztecs, and I suspect that historians of the future may conclude that the missionary movement of the nineteenth century did more good than harm to the human race. If today we are able to see the great Hindu tradition as on a par with our highest ethical ideas, it is at least in part due to a renaissance within Hinduism during the nineteenth century prompted by self-comparison with Christian mission, and an awakening of concern about such formerly accepted customs as suttee, temple prostitution and a rigid caste system. It is possible today that Christians may comparably relearn from contemporary Hindus about the values of family life, a supportive community, the disciplines of hard work and saving, and the importance of cultivating habits of meditation and mystical awareness. The negative side of arguing that comparisons are impossible is that opportunities for learning and growth may be denied.

On a strictly academic point I believe that Hick is wrong to suggest that comparisons are impossible on the grounds that we lack omniscience, and that any such judgement would be partial in both senses of the term. Yet sociologists, political scientists, economists, students of comparative literature and culture all continually make comparative studies of human societies from a variety of perspectives. Such studies are rarely free from all bias, or from overtones of cultural imperialism one way or the other, but they do contribute to the sum of human knowledge.

Although unanimity may be elusive, I do not think that total relativism emerges as the general consensus. If a political scientist were to write a book saying that, after studying all the different political systems in the world he had concluded that they were all equally good in providing for the well-being, health and happiness of their people, I think people would be surprised. Inasmuch as religious totalities are also, at least in part, human institutions, I think the total relativism implied in Hick's assessment is open to serious question.

Finally I turn to the question of conflicting truth-claims in the world's religions. Once more I would criticize the "positivism" implicit in Hick's insistence that the criterion for truth is that issues be "definitively settled so as to become matters of agreed public knowledge", or, as Hick also puts it, that claims become recognized as "indubitable knowledge", as against "strong belief backed by evidence and arguments".[13] For the very reasons Hick himself sets out in his discussion of the religious ambiguity of the universe, I do not believe that such a level of certainty could ever be available. However, in this context, as distinct from the earlier ones, this is not a very significant critique of Hick, since it looks rather unlikely that many of the disputed truth-claims will ever be positively confirmed, even to the level of being shown to be more probable than not. Hence there seems much to be said for Hick's contention that these disputed points will in many cases be recognized as mythological rather than as factual assertions, and that increasingly an awareness of the limitations of human knowledge will lessen the influence of dogmatic and exclusive defences of traditional claims.

However, I am sorry that in his discussion of conflicting truth-claims concerning a life after death Hick's modesty prevented him from developing once again his own exploration of a way in which the insights of both East and West might be drawn together to form a single coherent speculation of what our future destiny might entail. A truly open and pluralist approach to religion encourages the view that perhaps the truth may lie not in any one tradition, but in insights drawn from all traditions. The best example I know of this being worked out in relation to any one doctrine is the global theology of death presented in John Hick's classic *Death and Eternal Life*. Although, in *An Interpretation of Religion*, Hick alludes in passing to this work, he does not develop its argument, and consequently no resolution of the apparent divergence between the world's traditions is in fact offered. I think this unfortunate because it seems integral to Hick's thesis that "The cosmic optimism of post-axial religion expects a limitlessly good fulfilment of the project of human existence."[14]

And, if this is the case, it would seem a pity not to spell out how this might be, and simultaneously give an example of a truly global and pluralist theology in operation. However, as Hick has already done this elsewhere, this is not a significant criticism.

An Interpretation of Religion is a fitting summation of a career wholly devoted to the detailed and exacting exploration of the coherence and meaning of the human response to the transcendent. No one could read it without being enriched and stimulated by it, and I know of no other approach to the questions posed by the new awareness of religious pluralism which so fully faces up to its challenges and implications.

NOTES

1.   Extracts from Lord Gifford's will establishing his lecture series in 1888. Cited in Bernard E. Jones, *Earnest Inquirers After Truth: A Gifford Anthology* (London: Allen and Unwin, 1979) pp. 45, 67, 81, 140.
2.   *Interpretation of Religion*, p. 1.
3.   Ibid., p. 236.
4.   Ibid., p. 269.
5.   Ibid., p. 337.
6.   Ibid., p. 11.
7.   Ibid., p. 10.
8.   Ibid., pp. 73–125.
9.   Ibid., pp. 316–37.
10.   Ibid., pp. 362–76.
11.   Basil Mitchell, *The Justification of Religious Belief* (London: Macmillan, 1973) p. 39ff.
12.   *Interpretation of Religion*, p. 136.
13.   Ibid., p. 369.
14.   *Interpretation of Relgion*, p. 361.

Critical Response

The Glitch in *An Interpretation of Religion*

L. STAFFORD BETTY

John Hick's *An Interpretation of Religion* is a work of impressive scholarship and consistently enlightened perspective. It deserves to be placed alongside his two other enduring works, *Evil and the God of Love* and *Death and Eternal Life*. Never before has the pluralistic hypothesis been made generally so plausible and attractive to thoughtful, well-informed people. Yet the work, as I see it, has a glitch, and it is this glitch that I want to examine here.

The glitch is Hick's claim that the Real *an sich* is *totally* beyond the range of our myths and theologies, and that the truth of a religious myth or theological system "consists in the appropriateness or inappropriateness of the practical dispositions which they tend to provoke".[1] This claim has been challenged in one way or another by each of the authors whose papers in this collection are primarily devoted to Hick's latest book.

Let us begin by reviewing the challenges put forward by each of them. First Gavin D'Costa:

> This Kantian revolution has come full circle. The cognitive claims upon which many of the religions are founded are no longer significant [in Hick's latest thought]; only the apparent effects of these claims on the believer are . . . . Religious truth-claims are forced into agnosticism.[2]

Chester Gillis writes,

> my contention is that myths do disclose something that is either true or false and that they are not merely linguistic tools for the proper orientation of attitudes or dispositions. They are not simply practical, as Hick insists, but make truth-claims like other forms of language. Myths, like literal language, also make cognitive claims.[3]

C. Robert Mesle argues,

> [Hick] now views his entire theodicy as "mythically true" but
> not "literally true". Yet he still claims that there is the "assu-
> rance" that "all shall be well".[4] How can there be such an
> assurance? How can immortality be mythically true if not
> literally true? . . .
>   What happens to the ability of the religious traditions to offer
> salvation to all if immortality itself is only mythically true and
> not literally true?[5]

Julius Lipner asks, "how can we grow as persons in a religious
context (which for HickWick is a vital dimension of human
existence) unless we *really*, not only imaginatively, enter into a
two-way personal relationship with the Real?"[6] And Paul Badham
states, "It is . . . at first sight surprising that at such crucial points
in his argument [Hick] should relapse into a kind of positivism
which says that, since alternative views are possible, no justifiable
conclusion can be drawn."[7]

In one way or another each of these authors is troubled by
Hick's refusal to take sides. Do we have any grounds for saying
that the Real *an sich* is conscious as opposed to unconscious,
purposive as opposed to non-purposive, good as opposed to evil?
Hick says no. Is a divine persona or a divine impersona a better
approximation of the Real? Hick declines to take a side. Is one
religion perhaps superior to another? Hick says that the major
religions seem on balance to be more or less equal in their ability
to lead their followers to human transformation, and he seems
relieved to find it so. Are naturalists and Marxists on balance less
in touch with the Real than earnest Christian theists or Hindu
Advaitins? Hick declines to say that they are.

It is tempting to believe that Hick, in his passion for what Mesle
calls "an interpretation of religion – including humanism – which
leads us toward a world of mutual respect", bent over backward to
accommodate contending points of view that are finally incompatible; that he, in other words, wanted to have it too many ways at
once. But I do not believe this to be the case. I suggest that Hick's
transcendental agnosticism, to use D'Costa's phrase, is grounded
on his immense respect for, and perhaps experience of, the Real's
utter mysteriousness. "None of the descriptive terms", says Hick,
"that apply within the realm of human experience can apply
literally to the unexperienceable reality that underlies that realm."[8]

I would like to say at once that these words ring true. Undoubtedly the Real is ineffably mysterious, as the mystics of all the great religions make clear; and I am glad to see Hick take the apophatic traditions of these religions so seriously. But what troubles me – and apparently many of my colleagues – is the *degree* to which Hick has carried this insight. It is one thing to say, as Hick says in chapter 15 of *An Interpretation of Religion,* that "a divine *persona* arises at the interface between the Real and the human spirit, and is thus a joint product of transcendent presence and earthly imagination, of divine revelation and human seeking";[9] I think that most of us agree with him here. But it is quite a different thing to say that the real is "totally" beyond the range of our conceptions, as Hick claims.[10] This last claim, it seems to me, really does land us in the transcendental agnosticism that D'Costa pointed out. Speaking personally, such a view would be the undoing of any faith I had in the Real. If the Real isn't the apotheosis of beauty, truth, goodness, wisdom, love and power, if the Real's nature is not more in alignment with these qualities than with their opposites – ugliness, falsity, wickedness, stupidity, hatred and ineptitude – then religion has no meaning for me. When I pray to or meditate on the Ultimate, it is of the utmost importance for me to believe that the Real really *is* all that is good – though exactly how this goodness disports itself I of course do not know; nor is it important for me to know.

I believe that Hick errs when he tries to go beyond Aquinas's mode of analogical predication when speaking of the Real. In the past Hick has used Aquinas's great insight as a bulwark of his own thought, and I wonder why he has deserted it now. Why, for example, would he refuse to grant that the Real is more aligned to consciousness than unconsciousness? What is closer to the truth? "The Real is a mass of consciousness", as the Upanishads say? Or "The Real is a mass of unconsciousness"? Why would Hick refuse to take a side on so basic a question?

The most Hick will allow is that, to take but one example, those who believe that God is Love would be far more likely to be transformed into saints than those who believe that God is Hate. Indeed, it is this sanctifying ability that constitutes the idea's truth. That is what Hick means when he says that "the various systems of religious thought [are] complex myths whose truth or untruth consists in the appropriateness or inappropriateness of the practical dispositions which they tend to evoke".[11]

But what a peculiar way of speaking. It is one thing to say that a particular theology or a particular religious myth *results in* or *encourages* human transformation, but a very different thing to say that it *consists in* or in some sense *is identical to* human transformation. I think Hick is correct to say that a religion's truth is *indicated* by the practical dispositions that it evokes in those who follow it, but incorrect to say that a religion's truth *consists in* those practical dispositions. This is to confuse one domain – shall we call it the ontological? – with another, the ethical. It is to confuse, in this instance, the cause with the effect. More to the point, this way of speaking is unintelligible. I simply do not know what it means to say that a religion's truth is the believer's transformation. The truth of a claim resides in the claim's congruence with the way things actually are, not with the claim's soteriological effect.

This is what I think Hick should have done: to have pointed out that, when we make claims about ultimate Reality, the Real *an sich*, we are two steps removed from our usual mode of univocal predication. When we say, for example, that a mother loves her children, we speak in the ordinary (univocal) sense: we know what the word "love" means. When we say of a divine persona that that persona loves his or her creatures, we speak analogically; we understand what we mean by the word "love" in an analogous sense. We are one step removed from the ordinary meaning of love. What do we mean when we say that "the Real" loves his/her/its creatures? Is this legitimate discourse? Can we at this most ultimate level speak even analogically? I don't see why we can't. It is true that we are one more step removed from knowing what we are talking about, but we are not proceeding altogether blindly either. In his *Philosophy of Religion* Hick labelled the statement "God is love" an analogy upwards. Why can't we label the claim "the *Real* is love" an analogy *all the way* upwards? Hick is like a kite-flyer who, in order to allow his kite maximum height and freedom, cuts the string. What I think he should have done – what would have *really* caused the kite to fly higher and freer – is to let out more line, indeed all that he had.

But look what would happen if he had! If we let the kite fly as high as it can go but without ever letting go of it, if we, to put the metaphor aside, give qualities to the Real by some upgraded analogical procedure, then we find ourselves eventually having to take sides on the question of whether the Real is better approximated by a divine persona or a divine impersona, for these qualities will fit one better than the other. That being the case, we are then logically forced to say that a theistic religion such as Christianity or Islam is superior to a non-theistic religion such as Advaita Vedanta or Theravāda Buddhism, or *vice versa*. Furthermore, since the Real has qualities in keeping with either theism or non-theism, and, since humanists and Marxists deny the reality of an Ultimate understood either theistically or non-theistically, as having this or that assignable content, humanism and Marxism will have to be regarded as seriously deficient at the most critical point. Moreover, since the Real has qualities, it will be possible to make comparisons between religions not only on the basis of their soteriological competencies, but also, and more basically, on the basis of their cognitive claims about the Real – that is to say, their theological and mythic competencies. I wish I could say that the glitch in Hick's thesis exists in isolation, but it does not. To remove the glitch, I fear, is to recast much of the overall argument.

That is what I hope Hick would be prepared to do. Not only would I be glad to see sides taken – for that is what living in an ambiguous world entails; it would please me immensely to see Hick reorient himself in such a way that his wonderfully illuminating insights about evil, eschatology and religious pluralism could be saved from the entropy of transcendental agnosticism that I'm afraid his new thesis implies. If Hick's Irenaean theodicy, to take but one example, is not in some analogical sense true, if it is not a cognitive claim about the way things ultimately are, then doesn't it amount to a sweet mythic seduction? And wouldn't a philosopher be better off avoiding it entirely?

It is somewhat painful for me to speak in this way, for John Hick has had more influence on me than any other living theologian. I hope that he can show me I am being blockheaded and that my criticism, as well as Paul Badham's charge of "total relativism",[12] misses the point. But, even if he can't, I hasten to say that my appreciation of his new work remains profound. Whatever the deficits, there are many more excellences.

NOTES

1.   *Interpretation of Religion*, p. 353.
2.   Gavin D'Costa, above, p. 7.
3.   Chester Gillis, above, p. 38.
4.   *Interpretation of Religion*, p. 360.

5. C. Robert Mesle, above, pp. 66–7.
6. Julius Lipner, below, p. 225.
7. Paul Badham, above, p. 93.
8. *Interpretation of Religion*, p. 350.
9. Ibid., p. 266.
10. Ibid., p. 353.
11. Ibid.
12. Badham, above, p. 96.

Reply

JOHN HICK

Paul Badham and Stafford Betty both represent a current in contemporary Christian thought with which I feel in sympathy – one which is theologically liberal, and yet conservative in its basic affirmation of the reality of God and of human immortality, and which is actively open to the presence of the other world religions and to all relevant information from both the natural and the social sciences. I thus have much in common with them. There are, however, some points that require discussion.

Badham prefers to speak of God rather than of the Real when referring to the ultimate Reality to which the world religions are (on a religious interpretation of them) responses. I grant that "God" is the most widely used term; and also that it is possible explictly to use it simply as referring to the Ultimate, without the implication that this is a personal deity. But, although it is possible to do this, I fear that most people will still assume that "God" means a divine person; and most Buddhists and some Hindus will very naturally feel that a basic issue on which they differ from theistic believers has been covertly settled in favour of the latter. I therefore still prefer a more neutral term, such as "ultimate Reality", "the Ultimate", or "the Real" – between which there is I think little to choose. Further, the *Interpretation of Religion* (IR) hypothesis hinges upon a distinction between, on the one hand, the God figures and the Absolutes of the different traditions, and, on the other, the postulated noumenal Reality of which these are phenomenal manifestations. Given this distinction, it would be anomalous to use the same term "God" both for some of these manifestations and also for that more ultimate Reality which lies behind them.

Turning to epistemology, Badham is not happy with the recognition in the IR hypothesis of undecidability at several important points. The first is the ambiguity of the universe – its capacity to be thought and experienced in both religious and naturalistic ways. By "undecidable" here I mean of course "objectively undecidable", or undecidable by methods or criteria that are generally accepted by reasonable persons. Badham, on the other hand, evidently thinks that it is possible to show by the kind of cumulative argument advocated by Basil Mitchell that a religious interpretation of the universe is more probable, or more rationally believable, than a naturalistic interpretation. But, if that is the case, why do not all reasonable people who apply their minds to the question agree about this? One could of course say that the sceptics are blinded by sin. But this does not strike me as a plausible response. Rather it seems to me that the universe *is* religiously/naturalistically ambiguous to us – not in the sense that it has no definite character, nor in the sense that if we could see its entirety we should not see what its character is, but in the sense that from our present limited vantage point the universe can be construed by reasonable people in both religious and naturalistic ways. And the principal evidence for this is that it *is* in fact so construed by different reasonable persons.

The second area of undecidability is the relative overall moral worth of the great world religions. Here I do not suggest, as Badham seems to suppose, that we cannot make any ethical judgements at all. We can, and should, make moral assessments of such specific phenomena as suttee in India, or the subordination of women in many Muslim societies, or past Christian persecution of the Jews. But the question is whether we can weigh up all the many different positive and negative aspects of the traditions to arrive at an overall objective moral ranking. We have a common basic ethical criterion in the principle of universal goodwill, love and compassion.[1] But to reach an objective quantification of the often very different goods and evils of different religious histories, although theoretically possible, seems not to be possible in practice. And, once again, the evidence for this is that no one has succeeded in doing it, except by predictably proclaiming the moral superiority of his or her own faith community.

On the third set of undecidables, the conflicting trans-historical truth-claims of the religious traditions, Badham and I seem to be largely in agreement; and I need not pursue this further here.

Stafford Betty is troubled by the suggestion of the IR hypothesis that the ultimate Real lies beyond the scope of our (other than purely formal) concepts. The root of his concern is, I think, religious: "When I pray to or mediate on the Ultimate, it is of the utmost importance for me to believe that the Real really *is* all that is good . . . ."[2] But is he not here forgetting the distinction, central to the IR hypothesis, between the noumenal Real and its experienceable manifestations? We do not pray to or meditate upon the Real *an sich*. We pray to the heavenly Father or to Allah or to Shiva, and so on; and we meditate (if our meditation has a specific object) upon Brahman or the Tao, or whatever. There is thus no cult of the Real in itself. But we rightly relate ourselves to the ultimately Real by rightly relating ourselves to one of its divine personae or metaphysical impersonae.

However, Stafford Betty thinks it important for us to know whether the Real is, for example, "a mass of consciousness" or "a mass of unconsciousness".[3] He is here assuming that these concepts formed by the human mind fit the ultimate ground and source of the universe. But is there not a residual anthropomorphism here? In contrast to this way of thinking I am impressed by the Buddhist insight – supported by work in modern Western epistemology– that we construct our experienced and understood reality in accordance with our own system of concepts, but that Reality in itself is not subject to these human cognitive procedures. It is therefore spoken of as *śūnyatā,* the Void, Emptiness, beyond the range of our human thought forms. This possibility is missed by Stafford Betty when he wants to "take a side" on the questions of whether the Real is personal or impersonal, conscious or unconscious, and so on. According to the IR hypothesis, these pairs of concepts do not apply to the Real in itself, but only to the Real as humanly thought and experienced. The result of Stafford Betty's rejection of the ultimate ineffability of the Real in itself is, as he says, that "we are then logically forced to say that a theistic religion such as Christianity or Islam is superior to a non-theistic religion such as Advaita Vedanta or Theravāda Buddhism, or *vice versa*".[4]

It seems to me, however, that the more or less equal value, so far as we can tell, of the fruits within human life of these two groups of traditions leads us to question the conclusion that one must be superior to the other; and this leads us back to question the initial assumption which led to that conclusion. Thus what Stafford Betty sees as a "glitch" I see as a virtue!

On a related matter, it would not be correct, from the standpoint of the IR hypothesis, to say as Stafford Betty does that "a religion's truth is the believer's transformation".[5] Indeed it does not seem to me to be appropriate to speak of religions, any more than of civilizations, as being true or false. But the propositions affirmed by a religious tradition are true or false; and those beliefs that are to be understood mythologically rather than literally are mythologically true or false, i.e. true or false in the practical sense of orienting us rightly or wrongly in life. I wonder why Stafford Betty has no place for the practical truthfulness of mythology as well as for the literal truthfulness of straightforwardly factual and analytic propositions.

NOTES

1. See *An Interpretation of Religion*, ch. 17, section 5.
2. L. Stafford Betty, above, p. 100.
3. Ibid.
4. Betty, above, p. 102.
5. Betty, above, p. 101.

Part II
Theodicy and Life after Death

5

Paradox and Promise: Hick's Solution to the Problem of Evil

WILLIAM ROWE

John Hick has written extensively concerning the problem of evil.[1] His writings on the problem are set within two general restraints. First, he holds constant the conception of God as omnipotent and perfectly good. Hick does not pursue the question of whether the facts about evil necessitate some drastic revision of our conception of God. In my discussion of his work, I shall accept this restraint. Secondly, Hick distinguishes the question of whether the existence of God is logically consistent with the facts about evil from the question of whether the facts about evil render belief in God unreasonable or irrational. It is the second of these questions that is the focus of Hick's attention. Some philosophers hold that the facts about evil do not provide any rational grounds or evidence for disbelief in God. Thus, for them, the only serious problem is the question of logical consistency. I side with Hick on this issue. The proposition that a given man is seventy-five years old and has an arthritic knee is logically consistent with his winning the next Boston marathon. But surely the fact that he is seventy-five and has an arthritic knee gives us good rational grounds for believing that he won't win the next Boston marathon. So too, although the free-will defence may establish that the facts about evil are logically consistent with the existence of God, there remains the serious problem of the extent to which the facts about evil render it unreasonable or irrational to believe in God.

Before we begin our examination of Hick's proposed solution to the problem of evil, I want to make explicit an assumption of mine, which I believe Hick shares, and note several different forms the problem of evil may take for us. The assumption is that, although we may have difficulty in defining "intrinsic good" and "intrinsic evil", this does not preclude us from knowing that certain things are intrinsically good and other things are intrinsically evil. We know, for example, that pleasure, happiness, love, the exercise of virtue, good intentions, and so on, are intrinsically good. We also know that pain, unhappiness, hatred, the exercise of vice, bad intentions, and so forth, are intrinsically evil. The problem of evil, then, is the problem of explaining why an omnipotent, perfectly good being would permit intrinsic evils to exist, or to exist in such abundance.[2]

But just how are we to conceive of our problem? Are we asking why an omnipotent, perfectly good being would permit *any* evil at all in our world? If this is our problem, then we can solve it by explaining how such a being would be justified in permitting just one instance of the evils that exists in our world. Are we asking why an omnipotent, perfectly good being would permit the various *kinds* of evil we find in our world? If this is our problem, then we can solve it by explaining how such a being would be justified in permitting an instance of each of these kinds of evil to exist in our world. Are we asking why an omnipotent, perfectly good being would permit the *amount* of evil (of these kinds) that we find in our world? If this is our problem, then we can solve it only by explaning how such a being would be justified in permitting *all* the evil (in its various kinds) that exists in our world. Or, finally, are we focusing on some *particular* evils and asking why an omnipotent, perfectly good being would permit these particular evils to occur? If this is our problem, then we can solve it only by explaining how such a being would be justified in permitting those particular evils to occur. So, once we think about the problem of evil, we come to see that there are four distinct problems of evil. And, as we shall see when we look at Hick's soul-making theodicy, what will solve one of these problems may be wholly inadequate to solve the rest of them.

To any of the four problems of evil that I have just distinguished, a theist may make one or more of four different responses. First, as we have already noted, the theist may insist that the facts about evil that are noted provide no rational grounds at all for rejecting belief in God. The argument from the facts of evil to the non-existence of God may be stated as follows. No good we know of is such that obtaining it would justify God in permitting evil (these kinds of evil, the amount of evil, these particular evils). Therefore, it is reasonable to believe that no goods at all would justify God in permitting the evil in question. But, if no good at all would justify an omnipotent, perfectly good being in permitting the evil in question, then God does not exist. To this argument, theists who make the first response typically reject the reasoning as fallacious, involving an illicit inference from "we don't know of any such good" to the conclusion that there aren't any, or from "no goods we know about would justify such a being in permitting the evil in question" to the conclusion that no goods we don't know about would justify such a being in permitting the evil in question.[3] A second response would be to acknowledge that the argument does provide rational support for disbelief in God, but to go on and argue that our rational grounds for believing in God are stronger and, therefore, *outweigh* the grounds for disbelief provided by the facts of evil.[4] A third response, like the second, may acknowledge that the argument, as stated, does provide rational grounds for disbelief. But this response goes on to suggest that there are other things we know or have reason to believe which, when conjoined with the premise of the argument ("No good we know of is such that obtaining it would justify God in permitting the evil in question"), gives us something that does not provide rational grounds for disbelief. Unlike the second response, however, the additional thing appealed to is not itself a reason for belief in God. For example, suppose one had good reason to believe that, *if* there are any goods that would justify an omnipotent, perfectly good being in permitting the evils in question, they would be goods we do not know. Now this information by itself is not a reason for belief in God. But, when we conjoin this information with the premise of the argument, the conjunction does not provide rational support for the conclusion that no good is such that obtaining it would justify an omnipotent, perfectly good being in permitting the evil in question. So here, instead of saying that our reasons for disbelief are outweighed, we can say that they are *defeated*. Finally, one may directly challenge the premise of the argument by arguing that there are goods we know (or can imagine) the obtaining of which would justify God in permitting the evil in question. It is this final response that Hick gives to the problem of evil; in common with other theodicists, he endeavours to single out some good or goods which can be plausibly believed to justify an omnipotent, perfectly good being in permitting evil.

In evaluating Hick's proposals about the justifying goods, it would be incorrect to require that he must show that the goods in question will obtain. A theodicist does not have to establish that, but it must be argued that we do not have any good reasons to think that the goods will not obtain. It would not be helpful, for example, to propose that the good in question is every human being achieving moral perfection, or even moral competence, before bodily death. For we have very good reason to think that such a good does not obtain. To the extent that the good in question is one that we have reason to think will not obtain, we have reason to think that the good proposed does not justify any omnipotent, perfect being in permitting the evil in question.

There are two good states that figure in Hick's theodicy. The first is the state in which all human beings freely develop themselves into moral and spiritual beings.[5] The second good state is that in which all such beings freely enter into an eternal life of love and fellowship with God.[6] In order for these goods to be an omnipotent, perfectly good being's reasons for permitting moral and natural evil, something like the following two principles must be true: a person's freely developing into a morally better being is intrinsically more valuable that a person's being made to be a morally better being; a person's freely coming to love another being is intrinsically more valuable than a person's being made to love another being. I believe both principles are true. But we should be wary of questionable inferences that may be drawn from such principles. First, it would be a neglect of Moore's principle that the value of the whole need not be the sum of the values of the parts (the principle of organic unities) to conclude that freedom itself is of great intrinsic value.[7] Secondly, to admit that freely developed goodness is intrinsically better than ready-made goodness does not imply that it would *always* be permissible to obtain the former rather than the latter. This would be so only if the degree to which the former is intrinsically better than the latter is *infinite*.

By appealing to the two good states just mentioned, Hick proposes to explain why, if there is an omnipotent, perfectly good being, it would be true that (1) human beings are not immediately aware of his existence, (2) human beings exist as morally immature beings, (3) the world is a place where real harm can be inflicted by one person on another, and (4) the world operates with a fixed structure in which real pain and suffering occur. For only in an environment in which (1)–(4) obtain can human persons freely come to know and love God, and freely develop themselves into mature moral and spiritual beings.[8]

Is Hick right about all of this? So far as (2), (3) and (4) are concerned, I think reason is on his side. My only real doubts concern (1) and Hick's claim that unless human beings existed at an "epistemic distance" from God they could not freely come to know and love God. And, even on this point, I am not clear as to the extent of my disagreement with Hick. If all Hick means to say is that, in order to come *freely* to *know* God (or to *believe* in God), one must exist at an epistemic distance from God, then I grant him his point. If God is directly present to me in all his power, glory and love, my intellect compels my assent to the proposition that he exists; there is no room for free assent. The problem is that Hick does not stop with this point. He sometimes says that, in order to be a *a person*, in order to be *morally free*, in order to be free with respect to *loving God*, we must exist at an epistemic distance from God. My difficulty here is twofold: I cannot find compelling reasons in Hick's writings for these further claims, and these claims do not seem to me to be true. Does Hick make such claims? Consider the following passages:

In such a situation [existing directly in God's presence] the disproportion between Creator and creatures would be so great that the latter would have no freedom in relation to God; they would indeed not exist as independent autonomous persons . . . . In order to be a person, exercising some measure of genuine freedom, the creature must be brought into existence, not in the immediate divine presence, but at a "distance" from God.[9]

Within such a situation [epistemic distance from God] there is the possibility of the human being coming freely to know and love one's Maker. Indeed, if the end-state which God is seeking to bring about is one in which finite persons have come in their own freedom to know and love him, this requires creating them initially in a state which is not that of their already knowing and loving him.[10]

. . . if men and women had been initially created in the direct presence of God, who is infinite in life and power, goodness and knowledge, they would have had no genuine freedom in relation to their Maker. In order to be fully personal and therefore morally free beings, they have accordingly (it is suggested) been created at . . . an epistemic distance [from God].[11]

I take it as evident that *a person* could exist in a state of epistemic immediacy with God. Could a person be genuinely free and exist in a state of epistemic immediacy with God? Clearly such a person could not be free with respect to coming to know or believe in God's existence. But could such a person be free with respect to developing morally in relation to other human beings? I don't see why not. Of course, this person would know that God exists, loves all his creatures, and so on. But knowledge is one thing; developing moral character and acting out of a sense of duty toward your neighbours is something else. It is very hard to see how the knowledge of God would destroy one's freedom with respect to moral development in relation to one's neighbours. But what about loving God? Would one still be free with respect to loving God? In the second of the three passages quoted above, Hick, after noting, correctly, that epistemic distance would leave the person free to come to love God, points out that, were God to *create* the person in a state where he or she (from the moment of creation) already loves God, the person would not be free *to come* to love God. This is certainly true, but somewhat irrelevant to the point at issue. The question at issue is whether a person can exist in epistemic immediacy with respect to God and still be free to come to love God. Such a person would know God's power and greatness, be aware of God's immense love for all his creatures, and so on. But isn't all this quite compatible with the person not responding to God's love with love of his or her own? To say that a person's freedom to come to worship and love God would be destroyed in such a situation is, I think, to confuse coming to have a very good reason to worship and love God with being compelled to worship and love God. It is, alas, part of the very nature of freedom to have the power not to do what one has a very good reason to do. So, while I fully agree with Hick that epistemic distance from God is necessary to cognitive freedom in relation to God, I can find no good reasons in Hick's writings to support his further claims that epistemic distance from God is necessary for the very existence of human persons, for their being free to develop morally, and for their being free with respect to coming to love God. And, if I am right about this, one must wonder about what good is served by our state of epistemic distance from God. Of course, without epistemic distance we would come to know God of necessity, not freely. And perhaps Hick would add a third to the two principles concerning intrinsic value noted earlier:

freely coming to know of a being's existence is intrinsically better than coming of necessity to know of the being's existence. But it is far from clear that this third principle is true.

Let us, however, put aside these qualms about what epistemic distance is required for, and return to the thread of the argument. So far, I think, Hick has built a reasonable case for the hypothesis that (1) if we believe there is an omnipotent, perfectly good being, it would not be unreasonable for us to believe that this being might have the realization of the two goods noted above as his goal, and (2) if such a being did have the realization of these two goods as its goal, it would permit the existence of moral and natural evil in the world. For, unless there are real obstacles in nature to overcome, and unless human beings are capable of doing real harm to one another, freely attained moral and spiritual growth would be practically, if not theoretically, impossible.

Has Hick, then, provided a reasonable solution to the problem of evil? As we have already seen, this is not just one question but four, for there are (at least) four distinct problems of evil (or four distinct levels of the problem of evil). The answer to our question depends, therefore, on which problem of evil we have in mind. My own view is that Hick has provided a reasonable answer to our first question: why an omnipotent, perfectly good being would permit *any* evil in the world. Moreoever, if we limit kinds of evil to natural evil, moral evil, human pain and suffering, and so on, I also think that Hick has provided a reasonable answer to our second question: why an omnipotent, perfectly good being would permit instances of the various *kinds* of evil to occur. But thus far nothing has been said that would explain why such a being would permit the *amount* of evil (of these kinds), or certain *particular* evils that exist in our world.

The plain fact, as Hick recognizes, is that evil occurs in such massive amounts in our world that it often as not defeats the development of moral and spiritual growth. Why then does God permit evil in such massive amounts? If the excessive amounts of evil were to fall on those humans who are particularly recalcitrant to moral and spiritual development, we might reason that God allows it to fall on them to enable them to become more sensitive to their need for such development. But incredible amounts of pain and suffering fall equally on the innocent and the guilty. Moreover, evil falls so unrelentingly on some people (whether saints or sinners) that it can only be seen by us as destructive of the soul-making enterprise. And, when we look at particular evils, it seems ludicrous to suppose that, had God prevented any one of these evils, someone's moral and spiritual development would thereby have been prevented or in some way frustrated.

That Hick recognizes the need for theodicy to address the amount and intensity of evil in the world is clear from the following remark:

> It [theodicy] attempts to explain how it is that the universe, assumed to be created and ultimately ruled by a limitlessly good and limitlessly powerful Being, *is as it is,* including *all* the pain and suffering and *all* the wickedness and folly that we find around us and within us. (Emphasis added)[12]

What then is Hick's response? So far as I can determine, Hick takes the remaining difficulties to be principally three: (1) the sheer amount and intensity of evil in the world; (2) the fact that this evil falls randomly and haphazardly on both the just and unjust; and (3) the question of whether the postulated goods for the sake of which God permits such evils can be worth the price (Dostoevsky's question). My interest here is Hick's attempt to deal with the first two of these difficulties. That he takes these to constitute major difficulties for his theodicy is evident from the following:

> the problem does not consist in the occurrence of pain and suffering as such; for we can see that a world in which these exist in at least a moderate degree may well be a better environment for the development of moral personalities than would be a sphere that was sterilized of all challenges. The problem consists rather in the fact that instead of serving a constructive purpose pain and misery seem to be distributed in random and meaningless ways, with the result that suffering is often undeserved and often falls upon men in amounts exceeding anything that could be rationally intended.[13]

What seems obvious to Hick and to us is (1) that the amount and intensity of evil in our world far exceeds what is needed for soul-making, and (2) that the evils in our world are distributed in a haphazard fashion, apparently unrelated to anyone's stage of development in soul-making. In the light of this, how can anyone seriously propose the good of soul-making as the reason for God's permission of all the pain and suffering in our world?

Hick's persistent answer is to employ what he calls the method of "counterfactual hypothesis" and to emphasize the importance of mystery in soul-making. Let us see how the argument goes with respect to the fact that the amount and intensity of evil in our world appears far to exceed what could be rationally intended for soul-making. In response, Hick asks us to consider a world in which no evil occurs in an amount beyond what is needed to play a role in significant soul-making. Moreoever, he asks us to suppose that we all *know* that this is so. He then argues that the result would be that we would make no significant efforts to overcome evil. But it is precisely such efforts (or the need for them) that lead to significant moral growth and development.[14] A similar line of argument is developed for the haphazard distribution of evil among the just and unjust. In a world in which suffering by a person is permitted only if it is merited or needed for soul-making, then, if we further suppose that we all *know* this to be so, no one would make efforts to relieve the suffering of others.[15] Paradoxically, then, soul-making would be considerably limited in a world in which we all knew or rationally believed that suffering is permitted only as it is required for soul-making.

There is, I believe, real merit to this line of argument. To help us understand and assess Hick's argument, I shall use the expression "an excess evil", where "*e* is an excess evil" means that *e* is an evil that an omnipotent being could have prevented without loss of significant soul-making.[16]

The point of Hick's argument seems to be this. Significant soul-making requires not only the existence of evils, but also that it be *rational for us to believe* that excess evils exist; it must be rational for us to believe that evils occur that omnipotence could have prevented without loss of significant soul-making.[17] For, if we were to believe that each evil that occurs is one that even an omnipotent being could not prevent without loss of soul-making, we would make no significant efforts to overcome such evils. And, as we have noted, it is precisely such efforts that are crucial to significant moral growth and development. Significant soul-making, then, has two requirements. First, it has a *factual require-ment*: there must be real evils to be overcome. Secondly, it has an *epistemic requirement*: it must be rational for us to believe that excess evils occur in our world. This second requirement has the air of paradox. It seems to say that evils not needed for soul-making are, after all, needed for soul-making. But it does not say this. What Hick's paradox says (roughly) is that rationally believing that there are evils not needed for soul-making is, after all, needed for soul-making. And, although paradoxical, such a claim is not incoherent.[18]

How does Hick's argument strengthen his theodicy? Well, having noted that soul-making requires real evils to be overcome, the problem was that it seems obvious to us that the amount and intensity of evil is far in excess of what an omnipotent being would have to permit for significant soul-making to occur. Hick's ingenious response is that, if it were not rational for us to believe that excess evil occurs, soul-making would be significantly diminished. Some might reject his claim. I am inclined to accept it. And what this implies is that the amount, intensity and distribution of evil in our world must be such as to create and sustain our belief that evils occur in excess of what an omnipotent being would need to permit for our moral and spiritual growth.

Suppose we grant the force of Hick's argument. My objection to it is that it does not really solve the problem of the amount and intensity of evil in our world. For it not only seems obvious to us that evil occurs far in excess of what an omnipotent being would have to permit for soul-making; it also seems obvious to us that evil occurs far in excess of what an omnipotent being would have to permit for us to be rational in believing that excess evil occurs. Clearly, if there is an omnipotent being, such a being could have prevented a good deal of evil in our world without in the least altering the fact that the amount and intensity of evil makes it rational for us to believe that evils occur in excess of what an omnipotent being would need to permit for our moral and spiritual growth. Hick's argument does show that our world must have enough evil to support the belief that there are excess evils. But, since it is clear that evil occurs far in excess of what is necessary to support such a belief, Hick's argument does not solve the problem of the amount, intensity and distribution of evil in our world.

Hick's argument has the defect of being an "all-or-nothing argument" or a "where will it all end argument". Let me illustrate this defect by an example. When I first taught at Purdue many, many years ago, the teaching-load was twelve hours a week (four courses a semester). I recall a discussion with a Purdue administrator in which I suggested that the quality and quantity of research might be improved by reducing the teaching-load to nine hours a week. He looked at me with a shocked expression, and then proceeded to point out that, if we were to reduce the teaching load to nine, the same reasons would apply and we would then have to reduce the load to six hours a week. But, again, the same reasons would apply and we would eventually have to reduce the teaching load to no hours, with the result that the university would close. "And so, Professor Rowe," he triumphantly concluded, "you see that the teaching load must be kept at twelve hours a week." This argument is a "where will it all end" argument, or an "all-or-nothing argument". If it were a good argument, which it is not, it would have justified a teaching-load of fifteen, eighteen, twenty-one, twenty-four or even more hours a week. (I refrained from pointing out to the administrator this possible extension of the argument.) And I cannot help but believe that Hick's argument suffers from the same defect. We look around our world and observe massive amounts of evil, enormously beyond what anyone would expect in a world governed by an omnipotent, perfectly good being bent on providing its creatures with an environment in which they could grow morally and spiritually. We say to Hick, "Surely this is not a world governed by an omnipotent, perfectly good being bent on providing its creatures with an environment in which they can grow, morally and spiritually." In reply Hick says, "But don't you see: if the apparently excess evil were cut in half, the same objection would still apply. So the only real alternative to the actual situation is one in which the amount of apparently excess evil is reduced to zero, one in which it is *obvious* to all of us that no evil or degree of evil is permitted unless its permission is absolutely essential to moral and spiritual growth. But, if that were the way of it, none of us would actively seek to prevent or overcome evil, with the result that significant moral and spiritual growth would be thwarted."[19]

The mistake in this argument is the more-or-less implicit assumption that the same objection would be applicable until apparently excess evils were reduced to the level of zero. If Hick is right in holding that some measure of apparently excess evil is required for significant soul-making, then it must be acknowledged that a world fit for moral and spiritual growth would be one in which some evil appears to us as excessive and unrelated to soul-making. There would be a *threshold* below which the deity could prevent such evils only at the cost of limiting moral and spiritual development. But isn't it abundantly clear that we are far above that threshold? For Hick's argument to work he needs to contend that, were the amount and degree of evil in our world that we take to be beyond what could be "rationally planned" *any less* than it in fact is, there would probably be some loss in soul-making. What he in fact shows is that, were the amount and degree of such evil reduced to zero, there would be some loss in soul-making. In like manner, the Purdue administrator does show that, were the teaching-level reduced to zero, some unfortunate consequence would ensue. What he needs to show is that, were the teaching-load reduced to something significantly below twelve but significantly above zero, that same, or some other, unfortunate consequence would ensue.

Earlier I quoted Hick's statement that what a theodicy aims to do is explain, on the assumption that there is an omnipotent, perfectly good being, how it is that the universe "is as it is, including all the pain and suffering and all the wickedness and folly that we find around us and within us". I have argued that, if this is the aim of theodicy, we must judge Hick's own theodicy as falling substantially short of its goal. In terms of the four problems of evil I noted earlier, I think we can say that Hick's theodicy does seem to solve the first two problems: Hick provides a reasonable answer to the question of why an omnipotent, perfectly good being would permit any evil at all in the world, and he goes some way toward providing a reasonable answer to the question of why an omnipotent, perfectly good being would permit instances of the different kinds of evil to occur in the world. Moreover, I think his final argument enables us to see how an omnipotent, perfectly good being would be justified in permitting instances of pain and suffering that appear to us to be excessive and unrelated to the soul-making process. But, when we turn to our final two problems – the explanation of the amount and degree of intrinsic evil, and the explanation of particular evils – I believe Hick's theodicy, like all other theodicies, fails to offer any believable solution. And, since it is particular evils, and the amount and degree of evils, that are generally regarded as providing the strongest basis for rational disbelief in an omnipotent, perfectly good being, I conclude that Hick's theodicy, although perhaps the best we have, does not succeed in turning aside the strongest arguments for disbelief based on the facts of evil.

NOTES

1. See, for example, *Evil and the God of Love*, 2nd edn; *God and the Universe of Faiths; Philosophy of Religion*, 3rd edn, ch. 4; and Stephen T. Davis (ed.), *Encountering Evil: Live Options in Theodicy* (Atlanta: John Knox Press, 1981).
2. This statement is quite close to Hick's general formulation of the problem: "Can the presence of evil in the world be reconciled with the existence of a God who is unlimited both in goodness and in power?" (*Evil and the God of Love*, p. 3).
3. In "Evil and Theodicy", *Philosophical Topics*, 16 (1988) 119–32, I have argued that this response is inadequate.
4. In "The Problem of Evil and Some Varieties of Atheism", *American Philosophical Quarterly*, 16 (1979) 335–41, I labelled this response by the theist "the G. E. Moore Shift".
5. I hold that *freely performing act A* is logically inconsistent with being causally determined to do *A*. Hick holds a different concept of freedom. But he emphasizes *authentic freedom*, which in fact has implications similar to the implications of my concept of freedom.
6. The second of these good states (and probably the first) obtains only if God exists. But, as I have suggested, in order to be successful a theodicy need not *establish* that the good in question obtains.
7. See G. E. Moore, *Principia Ethica* (Cambridge: Cambridge University Press, 1903) pp. 27–31.
8. Several criticisms have been advanced against Hick's efforts to explain why God would permit (1)–(4) to obtain. Hick replies to some of these criticisms in chapter 17 of *Evil and the God of Love*, 2nd edn. For responses to further criticisms and a strong defence of soul-making theodicy see William Hasker, "Suffering, Soul-Making and Salvation", *International Philosophical Quarterly*, 28 (1988) 3–19.
9. *Encountering Evil*, pp. 42–3.
10. Ibid., p. 43.
11. *Philosophy of Religion*, 3rd edn, pp. 45–6.
12. *Encountering Evil*, p. 39. It would be a mistake, I think, to understand Hick to be here charging theodicy with the task of explaining why God would permit this or that particular evil – if to provide such an explanation is to show how God's permission of *that evil* is necessary for some particular exercise of human freedom, or some particular bit of moral and/or spiritual development. It would also be a mistake to take the passage quoted as implying that Hick thinks that a theodicy must explain the precise amount and precise degree of intensity of evil in the world – if to provide such an explanation is to show why God's permission of just *that amount* or *that degree of intensity* was necessary for optimizing moral and spiritual growth through free human choices and actions. Instead, I think Hick's view is that a theodicy need only *explain* why our world contains a considerable amount

of evil and why it sometimes appears to us that some evils could have been prevented by God without any loss of soul-making. In addition, I think he holds that it must not be *unreasonable* to believe that the goods proposed may well be the reason why an omnipotent, perfectly good being would permit the world to be as it is. (I take it, though, that Hick would hold that if God exists *there is* an explanation of why he permits particular evils, and why he permits the precise amount and intensity of evil in the world.)

13. *Evil and the God of Love*, 2nd edn, p. 333.
14. Ibid., pp. 334–5.
15. Hick also notes that, if punishment for evil doing were immediate and apparent to us, morality would be replaced by prudential self-interest. See *God and the Universe of Faiths*, p. 59; *Evil and the God of Love*, 2nd edn, pp. 333–6.
16. Perhaps there are two equally severe evils such that either could be prevented without loss of soul-making, but one must be permitted to prevent such a loss. I shall ignore such complications in order to keep the notion of an excess evil as simple as possible. A complete account of the notion would need to take account of such possibilities.
17. Actually, all the argument technically shows is that it must not be true that it is rational for us to believe that no excess evils exist.
18. An analogy to Hick's paradox might be the following. Suppose a marathon runner is such that, if he believes that he will win, he won't train and, therefore, won't win. But, if he has grounds for believing that he will lose, he will train to the utmost so as to come as close to winning as he can. Of such a person it might be correct, although paradoxical, to say, "rationally believing that he won't win is, after all, required if he is to win".
19. For examples of "all-or-nothing arguments", see *Encountering Evil*, pp. 49–50; and *Evil and the God of Love*, pp. 327–8, 333–6.

Critical Response

LINDA ZAGZEBSKI

William Rowe has written a probing paper on John Hick's defence of the claim that the existence of evil does not make it unreasonable to believe in the existence of an omnipotent and perfectly good God. Hick's position is a version of the view that God permits evil for the sake of a certain good. That good is the good of the state in which human beings develop themselves into full persons, which means full moral agents with the capacity to enter into a relationship of love and friendship with God. The process of development into a full person is morally better if the person contributes to it by his or her own free choices. Whatever evil such a person brings about is permitted for the sake of the person-making or, to use Hick's term, "soul-making" process itself.

Rowe distinguishes four different variations of the problem of why God permits evil. (1) Why does God permit *any* evil at all? (2) Why does God permit all the various *kinds* of evil? (3) Why does he permit the *amount* of evil there is? (4) Why does God permit the *particular* occurrences of evil which we find in the world? Rowe concedes that Hick has provided a reasonable answer to the first two versions of the problem, but not the third and fourth.

Rowe concentrates his attack on the third of these four problems. Why does a perfectly good and omnipotent God permit *so much* evil? Though Rowe agrees that some evil would be necessary for soul-making, the evil we see around us appears to be far in excess of that needed for the soul-making process, and in some cases it may even be destructive of such a process. Hick's answer is that, if there were no evil in excess of that needed for soul-making, we would all know that and would have no motivation to overcome evil. The soul-making enterprise would thereby be defeated. As Rowe realizes, what this argument defends is not the need for excess evil, but, rather, the need for us rationally to *believe* that there is excess evil. Presumably, rational motivation depends upon rational belief, not on what actually exists.

Rowe agrees that there is real merit in Hick's argument here. If the soul-making hypothesis is true, it is rational for us to believe that there is excess evil. In fact, it seems to me that he ought to agree that it is rational for us to believe that there is a great deal of excess evil, for consider the fact that many people are not motivated to overcome evil unless they believe that there is so much of it that it is impossible for them to ignore it. Even some people who would agree with Rowe on the amount of evil in the world are still not motivated to overcome it. Apparently it takes an extreme amount to get them to notice. If this is right, the soul-making hypothesis requires not only that we rationally believe that there is excess evil, but that we rationally believe that there is a tremendous amount of excess evil. Such a belief is required to motivate many of us to become responsible moral agents.

Even so, Rowe claims that the argument does not solve the problem of the amount of evil in the world, "For it not only seems obvious to us that evil occurs far in excess of what an omnipotent being would have to permit for soul-making; it also seems obvious to us that evil occurs far in excess of what an omnipotent being would have to permit for us to be rational in believing that excess evil occurs."[1] But it seems to me that we do not know this at all and that if the soul-making hypothesis is true it ensures that we don't know it. For the evil needed for soul-making includes whatever evil is necessary to make it rational to believe that there is excess evil. Thus, if the soul-making hypothesis is true, it is rational to believe that there is excess evil, and that means that it is rational to believe that there is evil in excess of what must exist in order to make it rational to believe that there is excess evil. But, if so, Rowe cannot, as a way of showing the falsity of the hypothesis, appeal to the fact that we believe that there is such a degree of evil, since such a belief is exactly what the hypothesis predicts.

Rowe may think that we know *for a fact* that there is much more evil than is needed to make it rational for us to believe that there is so much excess evil. But, if the soul-making hypothesis is true, there would no doubt be a disparity between the amount of evil which actually exists and the amount of evil which it is rational for us to believe exists. If so, we could not be so confident in the reliability of our rational beliefs with regard to evil, and could not rely on them to refute the soul-making hypothesis.

My point then, is that, if the soul-making hypothesis is true, it would be rational for us to believe that it is false. That is, it would be rational for us to believe that there is a great deal of excess evil beyond that needed for soul-making. It *is* rational to believe that.

But, since this is precisely what is predicted by the hypothesis itself, it cannot be used to disconfirm it. May we conclude that the fact that it is rational to believe that the hypothesis is false *confirms* the hypothesis? That would be too hasty. It would also be rational to believe that the hypothesis is false if Rowe is right that it *is* false. The rationality of the belief that there is much excess evil, therefore, neither confirms nor disconfirms the soul-making hypothesis.

I would like to turn now to another point made by Rowe and suggest a variation on the soul-making defence which I believe bypasses this and a large class of objections made to most theodicies. As Rowe understands the soul-making solution, evil is permitted for the sake of good – the good of soul-making itself, and this is probably what Hick himself has in mind. However, I find the soul-making hypothesis much more convincing if we focus on Hick's analogy with the purpose of loving parents for their children. I deny that evil is ever permitted for the sake of good, but suggest instead that parents do not permit wrong-doing in their children for the sake of good. A good parent loves her child and wants him to develop into a full person. Gradually giving the child autonomy is necessary to that end, but the parent does not do it because doing so makes the child morally better, or because the loving relationship she wants to have with her child is good. Still less does she do it because the overall amount of good in the world will increase if she does so. If any of these reasons were her motivation, she would be treating her child as a means to an end – the end of producing good. It seems to me, however, that the parent would want this for her child even if the child did not use his autonomy to do good and even if much less good were produced in the world overall. She acts this way because she loves her child. It is also true that her love is good. But she does not act this way *because* her love is good. Goodness does not figure in her motivation at all. Instead, she loves her child as an end in himself and would continue to do whatever contributes to the development of his personhood whether or not it leads to good. What parent would ever agree to turn her child into a non-person or even less of a person because her child is bad?

The fact that the parent is so motivated in no way detracts from her goodness. This means, I believe, that doing good and preventing evil is not necessarily part of the motivational structure of a good being. Instead, I submit, it is possible, even probable, that a perfectly good being would be willing to allow any amount of evil, not for the sake of some good, but for the sake of the love of persons. To love a person logically requires permitting that person *to be* a person. To allow a person to be a person requires that he be allowed to contribute to his own soul-making through his free will. This is justified not because the existence of free persons is good, nor because love is good, nor for the sake of good in any other way, but simply because loving persons is something good persons do and loving persons in such a radical way that any evil is permitted for the sake of their personhood is something a perfectly good person would do.

I claim, then, that the acceptability of the soul-making defence does not depend upon the truth of the two principles Rowe proposes.[2] He says that the soul-making defence requires that freely developed goodness and freely given love is better than forced love. He says he believes that these principles are true but rightly notes that they do not justify the conclusion that it is always permissible to obtain the former rather than the latter. That would be so only if the degree to which freely made goodness and love is better than the forced kind is infinite. But, if I am right about the motivation of a parent in permitting a child autonomy, it does not depend upon the superior goodness of the free over the forced anyway. It depends instead on the fact that only a free person is a person, that loving a person entails permitting him to be a person, and the reason why one person loves another is independent of the goodness of the person and even of the goodness of the love itself.

I suggest, then, that the soul-making hypothesis be modified to fit the parent–child analogy more closely. I suggest that the hypothesis need not be defended on the grounds that soul-making is good. This leads to the trap of permitting a comparison of the goodness of soul-making with other alternatives. Instead, it seems to me that soul-making is something a good being would be motivated to produce, not for the sake of any good, but simply because a good being is loving and a loving being acts in that way.

If this is right, it suggests an answer to a serious difficulty raised by Rowe. The evil needed for soul-making sometimes seems counterproductive. Evil may encourage some persons to become responsible moral agents, but it can also lead to discouragement, bitterness, hatred, even despair. While I agree that these evils are a terrible price to pay for soul-making, I do not see that they actually prevent or even inhibit soul-making. Souls are made in various ways and a soul in despair is no less a soul than one which is happy in its friendship with God. If one of my children did not know I loved him I would be deeply grieved and would do everything I could to reconcile him to me, but I would stop short of interfering with his personhood, even if I had the power to do so.

It seems to me that we cannot evaluate the soul-making hypothesis unless we are clear on what a soul actually *is*. If the existence of souls is impossible without the degree of free will which actually exists, it would also be impossible without whatever amount of evil such free will produces.

NOTES

1. William Rowe, above, p. 120.
2. Rowe, above, p. 114.

Response to Linda Zagzebski

WILLIAM ROWE

I want to discuss two points Linda Zagzebski makes: one in criticism of me and one she makes by the way. The point she makes by the way is one I agree with and constitutes, I think, the basis of another objection to Hick's efforts to support his soul-making theodicy. I shall return to this point. Let me begin, however, with her criticism.

1   Hick acknowledges that it appears reasonable to believe that there are evils an omnipotent being could have prevented without loss of soul-making. Let us call any such evils "excess evils". Since it is rational to believe there are excess evils, doesn't this make it unlikely that the following theses is true?

I   It is to achieve the good of soul-making that God permits the world (with all its evils) to be as it is.

In response to this objection, Hick proposes what I shall call *Hick's paradox*:

II   Unless it were reasonable to believe that evils occur in excess of what God would have to permit for soul-making, significant soul-making would be diminished.

I have noted the merit of this response but have pointed out that in setting it forth Hick uses an illicit "all-or-nothing argument". For it is rational to believe that evils that appear not to serve soul-making occur in far greater excess than what is required for it to be rational for us to believe that there are excess evils. (Who would say that if only 5 million had been permitted by omnipotence to perish in the Holocaust it would *not* have been rational to believe that evils occur that omnipotence could have prevented without loss of soul-making?)

Zagzebski argues that I cannot discredit thesis I by using the point that it is rational to believe that evils not needed for

130

soul-making occur far in excess of what is required for it to be rational for us to believe that there are excess evils. Her point is this. Since the evils required to render it rational for us to believe there are excess evils are, by that very fact, required for soul-making, *it follows that* "it is rational to believe that there is evil [not needed for soul-making] in excess of what must exist in order to make it rational to believe that there is excess evil". And, of course, if Thesis I implies

(a) It is rational to believe that there is evil [not needed for soul-making] in excess of what must exist in order to make it rational to believe that there is excess evil

then we cannot use (a) to discredit thesis I.

But does thesis I imply (a)? I don't think so. With the help of Hick's paradox, we can reason our way from thesis I to the claim

(b) It is rational to believe that excess evils occur.

But from thesis I we cannot infer (a). From thesis I it does follow that whatever evils are required to render it rational to believe there are excess evils are not themselves excess, for in making (b) true these evils serve the soul-making process. But nothing else about what *it is rational to believe* follows from thesis I. Perhaps Zagzebski is arguing as follows.

(1) It is rational to believe there are excess evils.
(2) If thesis I is true then the evils that make (1) true are not excess evils – they are needed for soul-making.

Therefore,

(3) If thesis I is true then it is rational to believe there are evils not needed for soul-making that are in excess of the evils required to make it rational to believe there is excess evil.

I believe this argument is invalid: (3) does not logically follow from (1) and (2). So I continue to hold that

(c) It is rational to believe that there are excess evils in amounts far
    beyond what is required for it to be rational to believe there is
    excess evil

counts against the soul-making theodicy (i.e. thesis I).

2   In the course of her penetrating discussion Zagzebski remarks,
"My point, then, is that, if the soul-making hypothesis is true, it
would be rational for us to believe that it is false. That is, it would
be rational for us to believe that there is a great deal of excess evil
beyond that needed for soul-making." I think she is exactly right
in this remark. Or at least she is right if Hick is right in holding
that soul-making would be diminished unless it were rational for
us to believe that there are evils not needed for soul-making. Her
point means, however, that thesis I has a peculiar feature: *it is true
only if it is rational for us to believe it is false.* Zagzebski hastens to
observe, however, that we cannot use

(d) It is rational to believe that there is evil beyond what omnipo-
    tence need permit for soul-making

to disconfirm the soul-making hypothesis (thesis I), for (d) is what
is predicted by the hypothesis. Again I agree. What I used to
disconfirm thesis I is not (d) but (c). But, although (d) won't
disconfirm the soul-making hypothesis, it will, I believe, *undermine* Hick's central purpose in proposing the soul-making hypothesis. For we must remember that Hick's purpose is more than to
state the soul-making hypothesis: it is to argue that it is *reasonable*
(or at least not unreasonable) to believe that the hypothesis is true.
What Hick aims to do is show that it is *reasonable* to believe that it
is to achieve the good of soul-making that God permits the world
(with all its evil) to be as it is. But, once we see that the
soul-making hypothesis is true *only if* it is rational to believe that
it is false, we cannot consistently go on to argue that it is *reasonable
to believe* the soul-making hypothesis.

The general point underlying the objection just presented is
this. If our aim is to show that it is reasonable to believe *p*, we
cannot consistently proceed to argue that the truth of *p* depends on
it being rational to believe that *p* is false. The trouble with Hick's
paradox is that, although it neatly disposes of a serious objection

("So much evil appears to be unrelated to, or even to frustrate, soul-making"), it does so at the enormous price of rendering it unreasonable to believe the soul-making hypothesis to be true.

Reply

JOHN HICK

William Rowe puts forward a characteristically challenging argument, pointing to a possible fatal flaw, not previously identified,
in the Irenaean theodicy. Before coming to that, however, let me
respond to his remarks about our epistemic distance from God. I
think Rowe is right that this cannot be a necessary condition of
our being persons; and the passages in which I suggested this
need to be revised. But nevertheless I think that the main point I
was making stands. This is that, whereas being compelled to be
aware of a fellow human being leaves us free to adopt any attitude
we like to him/her, being compelled to be conscious of God would
not leave us similarly free to adopt any attitude to God. To be
inescapably aware that we are in the presence of the ultimate
power of the universe, who is limitlessly good, who knows us
through and through, and who loves us with a limitless love,
would be a situation in which we could only respond by worship
and an answering love. This is, of course, not a matter of logical
necessity but one of a strong psychological inclination, given the
(God-given) structure of our human nature. And so in order that
we may be autonomous persons, capable of entering by our own
free will into God's spiritual "magnetic field", we have to be
created outside it, at an epistemic distance from God.

Now I come to Rowe's very interesting argument about the
notion of "excess evil". I had suggested that, if we could see that
the evils that occur serve a soul-making purpose, then, paradoxically, they would not be able to serve a soul-making purpose. For
the very fact that they do not *seem* to be soul-making is a necessary
condition of their in fact *being* soul-making. Thus far Rowe is
inclined to agree. But then he says that

> it not only seems obvious to us that evil occurs far in excess of
> what an omnipotent being would have to permit for soul-
> making; it also seems obvious to us that evil occurs in excess of
> what an omnipotent being would have to permit for us to be
> rational in believing that excess evil occurs. Clearly, if there is an
> omnipotent being, such a being could have prevented a good

deal of evil in our world without in the least altering the fact that the amount and intensity of evil makes it rational for us to believe that evils occur in excess of what an omnipotent being would need to permit for our moral and spiritual growth.[1]

In other words, not only are the evils that occur such that we cannot see that they serve a soul-making purpose, but, further, we *can* see (Rowe is saying) that they exceed what is required for us to be unable to see that they serve a soul-making purpose! This is Rowe's argument; and I must agree that in its own terms it is a good argument. But, on the other hand, I believe that it is cancelled by an equally good counter-argument. For evil is either, in the long run, soul-making or soul-destroying; and it is soul-destroying to the extent that it exceeds what is required for it to be soul-making. Rowe claims that the amount of evil in the world not only *seems* to us to be soul-destroying but actually *is* soul-destroying. He says that this is obvious to us. But how can it be obvious to us? It is not enough that it *looks* that way to us; for it will look that way to us if it is in fact soul-making! Since evil is going to seem to us to be soul-destroying whether it is in fact soul-making or soul-destroying, we cannot tell, from the way it looks, which it is. We are therefore not in a position to say, as Rowe does, that it is obvious that there is more evil than is necessary to serve a soul-making purpose. Here I am agreeing with Linda Zagzebski, whose reasoning seems to me to be entirely cogent.

In his response to Zagzebski, Rowe makes a further point. He says,

> What Hick aims to do is show that it is *reasonable* to believe that it is to achieve the good of soul-making that God permits the world (with all its evil) to be as it is. But, once we see that the soul-making hypothesis is true *only if* it is rational to believe that it is false, we cannot consistently go on to argue that it is *reasonable to believe* the soul-making hypothesis.[2]

The answer to this is provided, I suggest, by a distinction between two levels or orders of discourse. In second-order (or meta-) discourse we can say that, if the Irenaean hypothesis is true, it must be possible, in first-order discourse, to make the reasonable judgement that it is false. Thus the fact that it can reasonably be said in first-order discourse to be false does not prevent it from being reasonably said in second-order discourse to be true. Of course, the fact that in order to be true the hypothesis must seem (in first-order discourse) to be false is not itself a positive reason to think, in second-order discourse, that it is true. But neither is it a positive reason for thinking, in second-order discourse, that it is false. The merits of the hypothesis still have to be argued on other grounds.

Finally, Linda Zagzebski goes on to make the very interesting constructive suggestion that the Irenaean type of theodicy should not hold that evil exists for the sake of the good of soul-making, but should appeal instead to the divine love, in virtue of which God gives us a freedom which can result in evil as well as in good, in the unmaking as well as in the making of persons. Two comments occur to me.

The first is that Zagzebski's proposal only attempts to deal with the moral evil that flows from human free will. It does not attempt to deal with the pain and suffering caused by such natural evils as disease, accident, earthquake, flood, storm, fire, drought, hurricane, lightning, and so on, except to the secondary extent to which they are contributed to by human actions. It would thus seem that, even if we were to accept Zagzebski's proposals, an Irenaean theodicy will still have to account for these natural evils as existing for the sake of some good, such as person-making.

Secondly, I agree with Zagzebski's principle that "only a free person is a person, that loving a person entails permitting him to be a person, and the reason why one person loves another is independent of the goodness of the person and even of the goodness of the love itself".[3] Nevertheless it seems to me that the ideas of love and goodness are integrally connected, though in another way. For is it possible to separate love from a seeking of the good of the beloved? Does not love mean valuing another and seeking that other's good? Surely, if we remove its seeking-of-good aspect, love would have no content or substance, no reason to express itself in one kind of behaviour rather than another. To say that God loves us is, then, to say that God values us and seeks our highest good. And in that case theodicy properly appeals to the divine love as establishing the kind of world in which we find ourselves, and permitting us to produce within it evil as well as good, in order that we may eventually come to enjoy our highest good as fully realized "children of God". I therefore do not think that theodicy can after all abandon the justification of evil as being necessary for a justifying good end.

NOTES

1. William Rowe, above, p. 120.
2. Rowe, above, p. 132.
3. Linda Zagzebski, above, p. 128.

6

John Hick on the Self and Resurrection

FRANK B. DILLEY

There are two issues which I wish to explore, perhaps neither of them extremely important, and yet each is a serious issue in the interpretation of the work of John Hick. Fortunately for us teachers of philosophy of religion, Hick's early work is still before us in the form of successive editions of his justly popular *Philosophy of Religion*, which should be due for another update soon. The material I want to discuss was written during the first half of his career. His concern for world religions which was emerging then has led him to the further developments which have characterized his work since the middle 1970s.[1] His more recent repudiation of biblical conservatism and exclusivism had already been prefigured in his choice of an Irenaean theodicy, which, as he noted explicitly, was universalistic. When exclusivism fell, along with it went the notion that the biblical view was true in any absolute sense, and Hick has spent the rest of his career working out the details of that realization in a rather brilliant way.

The primary focus in my analysis will be the work culminating in *Death and Eternal Life*, which shows, I shall argue, that his previous synthesis was breaking down. In *Death and Eternal Life*, he had to confront for the first time, in a full-length work, the nature of the self, in both its pre-mortem and its post-mortem forms. In writing this work he came up with some different answers from those he had given before, but both the old answers and the new answers are contained in that volume in an interesting but inconsistent way, or so I shall argue.

Prior to writing this book, I suggest, Hick had found entirely satisfying a particular complex of ideas which I shall draw out for examination, and had brought those ideas together in such a way that both the justification of theism as a meaningful set of claims and the justification of the ways of God could be accomplished. However, in order to write *Death and Eternal Life* he had to take a more careful look than he had ever taken before at the nature of the human self, and at the question of what a *desirable* view of afterlife would require, and he found himself forced to go beyond biblical eschatology and Rylean views of the human self. To make my point briefly, he discovered the need for mind or spirit, repudiated by both the traditions that had formed his earlier thought, and he discovered that the notion of spirit *could*, after all, be made intelligible and could even be *grounded* in ways his earlier analytic training had decreed impossible.[2]

What has not been appreciated, as far as I know, is that the new directions his thought took made parts of his old solution unworkable *as written*. Whether it is important to redo that work I shall leave up to John Hick. The claim I will try to develop is that either the chapter "Body and Mind" in *Death and Eternal Life* and the later developments in his eschatology which allow both embodied and disembodied phases will have to be repudiated, or else the nature of eschatological verification has to be completely recast to allow for the complexities that arise once it is admitted that the physical body does not constitute the whole of the person.

The outcome of my analysis will be the suggestion not that he go back to the old John Hick, but that he clean up the untidy spots in *Death and Eternal Life*, which persist in *Philosophy of Religion* (3rd edn): the unsatisfactory treatment which he gives to resurrection replicas and to the issue of how personal identity between pre- and post-mortem selves can be established. What I want him to do is to affirm the new view of self that he worked out in *Death and Eternal Life* and go back and redo his treatment of those other two problems.[3]

THE EARLY HICK VIEW OF SELF AND RESURRECTION

The early John Hick produced a provocative combination of biblical theology and analytic philosophy, the two views which were the fashion in the late 1940s and 1950s in the Anglo-American intellectual world. Biblical scholars were reinterpreting biblical religion in such a way as to emphasize its materialism, the *goodness* of creation (in contrast to Greek suspicion of matter and body), and the Bible's rejection of the natural immortality of the soul in favour of views that the person is fully material and that any afterlife would come after a death which was total. The biblical view talked about graves being opened and dead bodies coming to life again. Humans came from dust, will return to dust, and if they live again it is because they have been re-created out of heavenly dust.

On the philosophical side, we had all been exposed to Ryle's *Concept of Mind* and other similar works, and had been urged to reject as unintelligible Cartesian dualism and its doctrine of the immortal ghost in the mortal machine. Philosophers were writing that the very notion of a spirit or mind separate from the body was unintelligible, and the considerable body of evidence gathered by parapsychologists for survival of death was simply dismissed. Survival of death was in principle impossible because that notion could not be made intelligible. John Hick creatively attempted to make the notion intelligible but in a different way, by adopting a thoroughly biblical *and* thoroughly modern view of self. At least, that is how it looked.

Given these two currents of thought, it seemed quite reasonable to find passages such as the following in the writings of John Hick. The interpretation of them could hardly be in doubt. (My quotations are taken from the second editions of *Faith and Knowledge* and *Philosophy of Religion*, but the views expressed are present also in the first editions.) In *Faith and Knowledge*, Hick commented favourably on both the views of Moritz Schlick (of the Vienna School) and Ryle's repudiation of the "ghost in the machine". Hick noted that the biblical doctrine of the self and of the resurrection of the body had affinities with their view, where "Mental events and mental characteristics are analyzed into the modes of behavior and behavioral dispositions of [the] empirical self".[4] Hick interpreted the biblical view as involving the notion that the human being is by nature mortal, that apart from divine action the person would die, except for the fact that God "either sometimes or always resurrects or (better) reconstitutes or recreates him".[5] He suggests that we should abandon the word "spiritual" used by St Paul to articulate this doctrine "as lacking today any precise established usage". He states explicitly that the biblical view of the resurrection of the body and the view of Ryle and Schlick are "consonant".[6]

Going on to discuss the question of how it is that two people who have appeared successively in two parts of this world, or in two different worlds, one a resurrection world, could be known to be the same person, Hick answers, "Resurrected persons would be in no more doubt about their own identity than we are about ours now, and would be able to identify one another in the same kinds of ways, and with a like degree of assurance, as we do now."[7] The specific appeals made are to memory and to the fact that external observers would recognize this person. Hick writes as though the situations of the person before death and after death would be so similar that the person would have to satisfy himself that he had not just woken up from what he only "thought" to be his death-bed. "But how does he know that (to put it Irishly) his dying proved fatal; and that he did not, after losing consciousness, begin to recover strength and has now simply awakened?"[8] He looks around him, finds old friends who have died, and so on.

In all this discussion Hick never once refers to the existence of a *mind*, nor speaks even once of the divine re-creation of the mind of the person. The talk is only of the divine re-creation of bodies "composed of a material other than that of physical matter, but endowed with sufficient correspondence of characteristics with our present bodies and sufficient continuity of memory with our present consciousness for us to speak of the same person being raised up again to life in a new environment".[9]

In *Philosophy of Religion* (2nd edn) he says the same things; he rejects Platonic and Cartesian conceptions of the soul in favour of Ryle's view, which is explicitly endorsed. "Man is thus very much what he appears to be – a creature of flesh and blood, who behaves and is capable of behaving in a characteristic range of ways – rather than a nonphysical soul incomprehensibly interacting with a physical body." He also cites the biblical scholar J. Pedersen: "the body is the soul in its outward form".[10] Never does Hick suggest anything about the need to re-create the mind of the person, or talk about the possession of the same *mind* as constituting the link between pre- and post-mortem persons. He does, it is true, speak of the psycho-physical person in both works, but he never talks about the continuity of *the mind* as well as, or in contrast to, the continuity of the body.

He does, in both works, refer to human persons as free in some non-compatabilist sense, and speaks of minds in *that* connection, but never when he talks about the nature of the self explicitly or about its resurrection. The two ideas of self and freedom are not related until later. When that happens, his old view of self breaks down.

So far the case looks straightforward. When he is talking about the self and its resurrection, Hick seems to be in full agreement with those modern analytic philosophers who regard notions of spiritual selves as nonsensical, and he seems clearly to reject Platonic and Cartesian souls which are naturally immortal. He has accepted the biblical doctrine of the resurrection of bodies and has repudiated the doctrine of the immortality of the soul. When it comes to post-mortem existence he has spoken of re-creation of the body, in which an individual who physically replicates a pre-mortem person and is an indissoluble psycho-physical unity can establish through memory his or her continuity with the pre-mortem person. This self-recognition can be validated by others who can *see* that this is the same person. There is no puzzlement about whether the outward body which so closely resembles the original could be concealing a *different* mind, or about whether some other mind could be using that body and be receiving false memories from this body which it now inhabits. All is simple and straightforward for Hick.

The person *is* the body, and the only issue that needs to be discussed is under what conditions two people who exist at different times and in different spaces can be the *same* person. If we were to suppose that a person contained *two* elements, then that would always raise the possibility that the unity was not indissoluble after all, that the mental element and the physical element could get separated from each other. If the body is not the whole person, then questions can always arise as to whether the body is there but not the rest of the person, and the criteria for identification of persons become much more difficult. Unless the person is the very same thing as the body, then an exactly similar body does not necessarily mean an exactly similar mind. Once the intelligibility of a disembodied soul is admitted, then the possibility that continuous personal identity requires possession of the same soul becomes real.

If it should turn out to be the case *either* that Hick has held all along without mentioning it a view which allows for the separation of mind and body, *or* later developed such a view, then I think that he would need to come back to this sort of discussion, which persists even into the third edition of *Philosophy of Religion*, as well as chapter 15 of *Death and Eternal Life*, and clear up the problem that a dualistic view of the human self would cause for the identification of resurrection replicas. In a moment I shall argue that his discussion of the problem posed by multiple copies of person's bodies could also be answered much more successfully with the introduction of the notion of separable minds or souls.

JOHN HICK IN 1976

Has the situation changed by 1976? Well, that depends where you look, in my opinion. First let us look at Hick's discussion of "The Resurrection of the Person" in chapter 15 of *Death and Eternal Life*. Here we find him repeating his talk about indissoluble psycho-physical unity, and about analysing mental events and character-istics in terms of modes of behaviour and behavioural disposi-tions:

> The concept of the mind or soul is thus not that of a "ghost in the machine" but of the more flexible and sophisticated ways in which human beings behave and have it in them to behave. On this view there is no room for the notion of soul in distinction from body; and if there is no soul in distinction from body there can be no question of the soul surviving the death of the body.[11]

By this time the discussion has advanced some way beyond the second edition of *Philosophy of Religion*, because Hick has been forced to deal with a new challenge. If one exact duplicate of a body can be re-created, could not God re-create *two* such bodies, perhaps even more? By this time Hick has developed his (I think) rather arbitrary "replica" theory as a way of articulating his views. My plan is to recapitulate his "replica" theory, show why it fails, and then point to a solution which can be accomplished by developing some thoughts about the self which he develops *earlier* in *Death and Eternal Life* but does not really use (I refer to his discussion of body and mind in chapter 6).

Admitting that to identify a post-resurrection "replica" with a pre-mortem person requires linguistic decision,[12] Hick argues for the plausibility of that decision by noting that the "replica" is exactly similar in all respects "except continuous occupancy of space".[13] Appeal is made both to the memories of the "replica" and also to the individual's identification by other persons. He remarks that we should be willing to accept this extension of our notion of personal identity:

> We should be extending our normal use of "same person" in a way which the postulated facts would both demand and justify if we said that the person who appears in New York is the same person as the one who disappeared in London. The facts inclining us to identify them would, I suggest, far outweigh the factors disinclining us to do so. The personal, social, and conceptual cost of refusing to make this extension would so greatly exceed the cost of making it that we should have no reasonable alternative but to extend our concept of "the same person" to cover this strange new case.[14]

Thus Hick establishes, he says, a bridgehead for the claim that the pre-mortem person and the exactly similar post-mortem person should be regarded as the same person. I note in passing that nowhere does Hick suggest that anything passes from the first person to the second person; rather, the first person dies and is, either instantly or after the passage of some time, re-created in another spot, "from scratch" so to speak.

He goes on to comment on two other matters in order to "strengthen this bridgehead" before venturing out upon it. Both these discussions are consonant with the interpretation that I have given of Hick so far, that he is still thinking in his Rylean mode, that the person simply is a body of certain complexity who can still by analysed in terms of behaviour and behavioural dispositions, and that Hick in no way distinguishes the mind from those behaviours and behavioural dispositions.

Norbert Wiener has claimed, according to Hick, that bodily identity through time does "not" depend upon the identity of the physical matter composing it. Let us pay close attention to what Wiener is cited as saying: "The individuality of the body is that of a flame rather than that of a stone, of a form rather than of a bit of substance."[15] Hick goes on to interpret this as meaning that the pattern of the body can be regarded as a message, and that you can code, transmit and then translate that message back into appropriate matter. Hick defends the appropriateness of consid- ering the resulting person as the same person as the original, just as "the rendering of Beethoven's ninth symphony which reaches my ears from the radio loud-speaker does not consist of numerically the same vibrations that reached the microphone in the concert hall; those vibrations have not travelled on through another three hundred miles to me".[16] It is more appropriate to say that I am hearing "this rendering" of Beethoven's Ninth than to say that I am hearing something else. The key point, Hick claims, is Wiener's "insistence that psycho-physical individuality does not depend upon the numerical identity of the ultimate physical constituents of the body but upon the pattern or 'code' which is exemplified".[17]

The passages cited do not in any way suggest that Hick means for us to think that his view of self involves any sort of separation of mind from body. The individual is simply a particular patterned modification of some substance – it does not matter which. To speak of a person as a psycho-physical unity is just to speak of that person as a patterned substance, a set of behaviours and dispositions to behave.

His other attempt to strengthen his bridgehead is by means of a discussion of "replicas". Here he distinguishes between his specialized use of the term, indicated by quotation marks, and the more conventional use. In the usual sense of the word, it is possible for the original, say a statue, and its exact replica to exist at the same time, and for there to be any number of replicas simultaneously. A "replica" (in quotation marks), however, cannot exist either simultaneously with its original or simultaneously with other exact copies of that original. It is possible, Hick says, for the *corpse* of Mr. X to exist simultaneously with the "replica" of Mr. X (presumably the corpse no longer displays the pattern that constituted Mr. X), but if Mr. X still lived we would not have a "replica" of Mr. X but rather a mere replica of Mr. X, and a replica of Mr. X is not Mr. X at all.

Why do I think that this move is strange? Well, consider Hick's criteria for, identifying the "replica" of Mr. X as Mr. X himself. He *looks* exactly like Mr. X and says, when asked, "I remember having the experience of gradually losing consciousness but now have suddenly awakened in a new place." The "replicas" of all of the friends of Mr. X gather around and say, "Oh, this *is* Mr. X – he talks like Mr. X, he walks like Mr. X, he remembers everything that Mr. X normally remembered and nothing else, except for this experience of apparently dying and reviving in a different world. This is Mr. X all right", and, when "Mrs. X", whom we presume has already passed over, is asked if this is her husband, she replies, "absolutely, no one else ever called me 'Chickie' – that's X all right". Now, a replica (without quotes) of Mr. X *will pass all those same tests.* He will think that he is Mr. X and so will everyone else, but, on Hick's strange view, *that* Mr. X and all of his friends will be mistaken, even though none of them can possibly know that they are mistaken.

Suppose, just to take only one of the bizarre situations that could happen, that a heavenly "Mr. X" (quotes) is correctly identified by everyone, and then suddenly Mr. X on earth unexpectedly revives. It seems that "Mr. X" would suddenly become a mere replica, which would make him an impostor. If Mr. X on earth recovers, then there cannot be a resurrection "replica" any more. What was really a *genuine* "replica" becomes a mere replica when Mr. X revives. A splendid parody of this view is provided by John Perry.[18] One of his points, and also mine, is that a person's identity surely cannot be determined by facts which are completely external to that person, such as whether there happen to be two of them simultaneously in different places or even in different worlds. Who you are depends on what you possess yourself, what you are, and cannot be undone by duplication.

Hick wants to consider the "replica" Mr. X who wakes up, remembers losing consciousness and awakens to find his friends all recognizing him, and the replica Mr. X, who pseudo-remembers the experience of losing consciousness and wakes up also to find his friends *mistakenly* proclaiming him to be the same Mr. X as they remembered, as *two different people.* The only difference between them is the fact that, without anyone's knowing it, the dying Mr. X was revived in another world, or else a second duplicate of Mr. X has been brought into being somewhere. There is not a single detail of difference between them, in memories or in external observables. We are to accept the identity in one case and not in the other, but why?

Before looking at Hick's reason, let me note that at this point a Cartesian dualist would have a ready answer. Whether an exact copy of Mr. X *is* Mr. X depends upon whether the *soul* of Mr. X, that thing which could have persisted after Mr. X's body died, animates the exact duplicate of X's body or not. Where the soul of X is, there Mr. X would be, and he would be there whether the body is an exact copy or not. If the *Star Trek* transporter, which would be a technological possibility on the Norbert Wiener view, were to malfunction and two exact copies were assembled (created?), there would be *two* Captain Kirks, both with Kirk memories and both recognized by the *Enterprise* crew as James Kirk their captain. On Hick's view there would not be *two* Kirks; there would be *no* Kirks, since there are now *two* exact copies, not one. Had the transporter not malfunctioned, there would have been *one* James Kirk; the "replica" would *be* James Kirk imprinted on different matter from the original. For the dualist, there would be only one James Kirk, the one whose body was being operated by James Kirk's soul. The other person would be an impostor, and it might take some time for the crew to realize from the lack of creativity of this soulless automaton that he lacked a mind. The automaton could not recognize it because on a dualist view he would lack consciousness.

Why did Hick offer this special restriction on what can constitute a genuine resurrection body as against a mere copy? Hick's argument is *not* that two persons cannot have the same soul but rather that our concept of personal identity cannot tolerate multiplicity. Personal identity can tolerate, he says, a great deal of change, and could, he has argued, even tolerate gaps in space and in time, but at multiplicity he draws the line.

> But one thing it will not tolerate is multiplicity. A person is by definition unique. There cannot be two people who are exactly the same in every respect, including their consciousness and memories. That is to say, if there were a situation satisfying this description, our present concept of "person" would utterly break down under the strain.[19]

There is an ambiguity in the statement just quoted. Is Hick saying that on the Norbert Wiener view it would be impossible to imprint two blocks of matter with the same pattern? Is he saying that it would be impossible for two people to hear the same Ninth Symphony? Presumably not, in either case. Then what he is saying is merely that our concept of person would break down, but why should that matter? The analytic philosopher rises to the surface here, but surely the change of a name should not change the reality which it names! The issue should *not* be what we decide to say, but what the reality of the situation is, and yet Hick makes the decision on linguistic grounds.

Hick tells us that the notion that God could eliminate Mr. X in London and re-create two Mr. X's in New York is absurd. "There would then be two Mr. X's – which is absurd."[20] The problem however cannot be that God would be unable to create two exact duplicates of Mr. X; of course God could do that. The problem is merely that we should not know *what to say* in such a case; we would be "linguistically helpless".[21]

Hick urges that the fact that two "replicas" cannot be created should not lead us to think that *one* "replica" cannot be created; hence he maintains that his view that there can be one resurrection "replica" has not been disturbed. What I think Hick should have said instead I have already published elsewhere[22] and will not repeat here.

One other feature of this discussion should be noted. Hick ends his discussion of resurrection "replicas" with the claim that in his view "full initial bodily similarity" is required:

> The reason for postulating full initial bodily similarity between the resurrected person and the pre-resurrection person is to preserve a personal identity which we are supposing to be wholly bound up with the body. If the person is an indissoluble psycho-physical unity, it would seem that he must begin his resurrection life as identically the person who has just died, even though he may proceed to undergo changes which are not possible in our present world.[23]

One wonders why "full" initial bodily similarity would be needed, since what matters should probably be just the brain (the locus of all personality characteristics, memories, ideas). Slight changes in body would hardly be noticed by friends, and even a radically different body with the same-patterned brain could in time show itself to be Mr. X as it recited Mr. X memories, chose the way X used to and demonstrated his quirky sense of humour. Also, Hick does not make even a passing reference to a demonstration that this fully similar body has X's mind, so he must not have thought "having the same mind" to be at all problematic.

So far everything that has been said is consistent with the notion that Hick came out of the double tradition of biblical theology and modern analytic philosophy, and that he found in those two traditions a way of saving what was important in Western theism. The two traditions agreed in discarding Cartesian and Platonistic dualisms with their separation of an immortal soul from a mortal body, and therefore some reconciliation seemed possible. The ideas of resurrection "replicas" provided an empirical grounding for theistic interpretations of reality, as well as a solution to the theodicy problem.

DEATH AND ETERNAL LIFE, CHAPTER 6

I have argued so far that Hick's position on eschatological verification and resurrection "replicas" in *Death and Eternal Life* is unchanged from the way it had earlier been presented. On the other hand I have suggested that his views changed drastically since his earlier work. I now need to substantiate that claim.

No warning is given of the change which is to be found in chapter 6 of *Death and Eternal Life*. In the chapter entitled "What is Man?" (ch. 2). Hick gives his reasons for rejecting all three of the traditional views of soul acquisition: pre-existence, traducianism and special creation. He gives a biological account:

> How has this embodied self been formed? The answer seems to be that a package of genetic information has programmed the growth of a living organism in continuous interaction with its environment – the developing self exercising throughout a measure of free creativity within the narrow limits of an inherited nature and a given world.[24]

There is no discussion whatsoever of what it is, if anything, that makes human beings different from other life forms, or about that which permits people to exercise a measure of free creativity. It has always seemed to me clear from his discussion of theodicy that Hick does not accept the compatibilist view of Flew and Mackie. Nor, now that he has turned to the examination of process views, does he seem to find a general indeterminacy of nature satisfactory.[25] This raises the question of just what sort of free creativity human beings have. In his discussion of "freedom as limited creativity" in "A Theodicy for Today",[26] Hick makes it clear that he agrees with C. A. Campbell's contra-causal notion of free will.

No Rylean that I know of would go beyond compatibilism to Campbellian "contra-causal freedom" of the sort which Hick endorses. Someone with a Rylean view might endorse indeterminacy, but Hick rejects *that* view of freedom. What is it about the Rylean, Wienerian self (the pattern imprinted on physical material) that gives human beings the ability to act *against* their conditioning, to act *against* their character? The traditional answer to that question has been "the soul". But, if mind or soul were Hick's answer, one would expect him to have discussed how mind arose out of matter, and whether lower forms of life have shown similar sorts of behaviour. He might have offered or rejected panpsychism, or at least have told us something different from what Ryle or Wiener might have been expected to say. He might have talked about "emergence", for example. What we get instead are reasons for *rejecting* all three of the traditional views on how human beings get souls, but no alternative explanation.

Now, there is one place in his earlier writings where Hick says some things which might lead us to expect the ideas he expresses in chapter 6 of *Death and Eternal Life*. In his discussion of "freedom" in *Faith and Knowledge* (but never in his discussion of self in *Faith and Knowledge*, or when discussing resurrection "replicas" in *Philosophy of Religion* or even later on in *Death and Eternal Life*), Hick talks of the language of mind or inner self, with reference to one mind communicating to another *only* through symbols, immunity from having thoughts imposed on the mind, and so forth. These ideas never carried over into his discussions of selves, pre- and post-mortem. It is not until "Mind and Body" (*Death and Eternal Life*, ch. 6) is written that Hick develops his view of the self, and what a surprising view it is after all we have discussed so far. Not surprising, however, is that his belief in freedom is the key.

What is there about "Mind and Body" that is so surprising? After what has been said about Ryle, about Norbert Wiener, about Pedersen, wouldn't you be surprised to find *this* statement in the first paragraph of Hick's discussion of mind and body? "And the remaining view is that body and mind are entities of different kinds, mysteriously locked together in our present existence, but that the mind may nevertheless be able to survive the death of the body. I am going to argue that this view cannot be ruled out."[27] He goes on to comment that philosophical argument can never establish this fact, but that "Inspection of the notions of mind and body and evidence of mind/brain correlation, I shall argue, leave the door open, or at least unlocked, to a belief in the survival of the conscious self."[28] And he does not stop there.

This chapter is truly astonishing, given the discussion up to this point. Hick proceeds to develop the standard arguments for mind–brain dualism, examining the identity theory and rejecting it on the grounds that mental states are private, that mental states cannot be located in the same place as brain states, and that the qualities of thoughts and the qualities of brain states are different. He points out that the empirical evidence which can be provided for *correlations* between mental states and brain processes only proves that there are correlations, and do not justify going beyond correlation to establish identity. In short, he endorses mind–brain separation.

Next he takes up epiphenomenalism, the view that mental states are just the passive by-products of brain processes. Here Hick connects up with his earlier discussion of freedom. He offers a nicely developed argument that epiphenomenalism cannot possibly be a rationally jusitified position. He argues that determinism in both its physicalistic and epiphenomenalistic forms is self-refuting: "The nerve of this claim is that the concept of rational belief presupposes intellectual freedom; so that a mind whose history is determined cannot be said rationally to believe anything or therefore rationally to believe that total determinism is true."[29] Epiphenomenalism, therefore, must be rejected in terms of a full-blown dualistic interaction. Lastly he discusses parapsychology and gives his reason for concluding that extra-sensory perception ought to be given a mentalistic interpretation.

This whole chapter is a masterfully compact presentation of the arguments for dualism. It has all the pieces, and, by making freedom the key to the rejection of deterministic systems, it links freedom, which has always been an important concept in Hick's system, with mind–brain dualism. The kind of freedom which Hick has always endorsed is *here* used *to eliminate* Rylean and Wienerian views.

To understand why "Body and Mind" comes as such a shock, one has to recall that just three years before the publication of *Death and Eternal Life*, Hick was apparently *rejecting* the view of "a metaphysical soul incomprehensibly acting with a physical body". Here, however, we find him talking about mind as a different kind of reality from matter, of mind and brain as independent but interacting realities, and of the relation between them as unique and "utterly mysterious". I can find no real preparation for this dramatic shift anywhere in his early work, except in his discussions of freedom, which were never presented in terms of a doctrine of the self.

As far as I am able to tell, this newly articulated dualistic position, which seems to have replaced the old monistic Rylean behaviourist and Wienerian identity views, had absolutely no impact whatsoever on chapter 15 of *Death and Eternal Life*, which simply repeats all the earlier things he had to say about the nature of the self and resurrection "replicas", as though the discussion in chapter 6 had not taken place. He talks about the self in the same old way, and he does not use his newly articulated view of the possibility of mind–brain dualism and survival of the *disembodied* self to prop up his rejection of the possibility of multiple Mr. X resurrection claimants. Also he continues to write as though the task of identifying resurrection persons would be the simple one of asking them who they are, asking their friends who they seem to be, and then having to check up on all this by making sure that there are not too many claimants.

It seems obvious that, once the intelligibility of mind–brain dualism has been admitted, and the possibility is introduced that the conscious self can survive in a state which is either disembodied (H. H. Price) or embodied (traditional Christianity), then the problem will inevitably arise of how one can identify the presence of that mind or soul. The answer cannot be given merely in terms of whether some exactly similar body is present. Once it is admitted that the mind and brain are only *correlated* with each other, then the relation between them becomes contingent. With that comes the possibility of mind- or soul-switching, and then the presence of the *same physical body even throughout this life* cannot be a guarantee of sameness of soul. Identification of souls by identification of bodies will become problematic and require a much more complex solution. I repeat that I think that a solution is possible; my point is that identification of persons becomes a much more complicated task and that the problem is not even discussed by Hick.

At only one point does his view of persons expressed in chapter 6 of *Death and Eternal Life* seem to influence subsequent chapters. In chapter 22 he introduces a possible eschatology making use of what has by this point of the work become a threefold analysis of human nature in terms of body–soul–spirit (the eastern version is body–mind–*atman*). He suggests that, although embodiment is needed for the early stages of the development of human character, a time may come when embodiment is no longer necessary, and when a last stage is reached consisting in timeless entry into the Vision of God, or *nirvāṇa*. He does not accept the view that the *atman is* Brahman, preferring views which separate the creator from the creation.

> Our eschatological speculation terminates in the idea of the unity of mankind in a state in which the ego-aspect of individual consciousness has been left behind and the relational aspect has developed into a total community which is one-in-many and many-in-one, existing in a state which is probably not embodied and probably not in time.[30]

A REQUEST

I should like to see what would happen if John Hick went back to his discussion of the nature of the human self as he developed it in chapter 6 of *Death and Eternal Life* and then applied it to recast his views about resurrection replicas. I think he would find that his dualism provided him with a much more satisfactory reply to the multiple-replica objection than the seemingly arbitrary notions which he first developed. Possession of the *mind* of X could now become the criterion of personal identity; he would no longer have to commit himself to the view that the first appearance of the resurrected Mr. X would have to be that of a dying man; and he would have a proper basis for considering both embodied and disembodied states in his eschatology. The complication that it would introduce is that Hick would have to face the question of how particular disembodied souls could be identified with specific private and hidden souls that had previously occupied physical bodies; but he will have to face that question sometime, since his current eschatological views involve the notion that the embodiedness of souls is only temporary, and that the final stage is a disembodied one. The question will arise whenever that transition occurs.

I hope that my suggestions might be welcome, since they will provide John Hick with the opportunity to rework his earlier views, which I have attempted to demonstrate are inadequate.

NOTES

Since this paper was written, the fourth edition of *Philosophy of Religion* has been published (see my remarks on p. 138). However, the work does not require me to alter the comments I make above.

1. Hick's concern for world religions begins to show itself by the second edition of *Philosophy of Religion*, published in 1973, the same year as his collection *God and the Universe of Faiths* appeared.
    One only wishes that the younger generation of non-process philosophers who have taken up the defence of religion had learned some of the lessons that Hick has learned. To see fundamentalism rearing its ugly head again is dismaying.

2. The turning-point on disembodied souls seems to have been an essay by his former professor, H. H. Price, whose piece on disembodied survival was included in an anthology which Hick published in 1970. In *Death and Eternal Life* (1976) he devotes a whole chapter to it, crediting Price with turning the idea of disembodied survival into an "intelligible hypothesis". Price was the first person to have done that, Hick claims. What I interpret that extraordinary claim to mean is that the Rylean scales had fallen from Hick's eyes. Ryle *never* was right about Cartesianism.

3. In this paper I pick up and develop an idea I suggested as an addendum in "Resurrection and the 'Replica Objection' ", *Religious Studies*, 19 (1983) 473–4. Correspondence with John Hick indicates that he thinks that I *was* mistaken in holding that he had changed his views in the way I indicated. That leads to this second, much more extensive attempt to explore the point that I was making.

4. *Faith and Knowledge*, 2nd edn, Fount pbk, p. 179.

5. Ibid., p. 180.

6. Ibid.

7. Ibid., p. 184.

8. Ibid.

9. Ibid., p. 195.

10. *Philosopy of Religion*, 2nd edn, p. 99.

11. *Death and Eternal Life*, p. 278.

12. Ibid., p. 280.

13. Ibid.

14. Ibid., p. 281.

15. Ibid., p. 282.

16. Ibid.

17. Ibid., p. 283.

18. John Perry, *A Dialogue on Personal Identity and Immortality* (Indianapolis: Hackett, 1978) pp. 36–7. Because the examples are so hilarious it is tempting to repeat the whole passage, but I restrain myself. The highlight comes when Gretchen Weirob imagines discovering that, because God had created *another* person exactly

like her, she is no longer Gretchen Weirob: "There would be here, in my place, a new person with false memories of having been Gretchen Weirob, who has just died of competition – a strange death if ever there was one."

19.   *Death and Eternal Life*, p. 292.
20.   Ibid., p. 293.
21.   Ibid.
22.   Dilley, "Resurrection and the 'Replica Objection' ", *Religious Studies*, 19, pp. 467–71.
23.   *Death and Eternal Life*, pp. 294–5.
24.   Ibid., p. 35.
25.   *Philosophy of Religion*, 3rd edn, pp. 49–56.
26.   *Evil and the God of Love*, pp. 298–327.
27.   *Death and Eternal Life*, p. 112.
28.   Ibid.
29.   Ibid., p. 117.
30.   Ibid., p. 464.

Critical Response

Hick and Dilley on Life after Death

STEPHEN T. DAVIS

As one who has long been stimulated and challenged by John Hick's thoughts about life after death, I enjoyed pondering the interesting and well-argued paper by Frank Dilley.

I believe Dilley is correct in his main claim about the change in Hick's anthropology. There are indeed some older paragraphs and arguments that need to be rewritten in the light of Hick's new opinions. I do not view the matter with quite the alarm that Dilley does, however. To me it is simply that Hick came to see something that he did not explicitly see early in his career: that dualism is defensible. I also agree with Dilley's point about Hick's criterion of "full initial bodily similarity" being needlessly strong. Strikingly bodily and especially brain similarity would seem to suffice.

I shall quarrel with Dilley at only two points, and both have to do with Hick on personal identity. Dilley's criticisms of Hick are incisive and thought-provoking, but I think both can be answered.

First, Hick does work with a criterion of uniqueness in his discussions of personal identity (though in some of Hick's writings the criterion is not explicitly mentioned). That is, a person P2 in the afterlife can only be numerically identical with (i.e. the same person as) the P1 whom we know in this life if there is, so to speak, only one P2 in the afterlife. There must be no other equally plausible post-mortem candidates for P1-hood; otherwise, P1 has not survived death. Following John Perry, Dilley points out a paradoxical consequence of this criterion: it specifies a property that P2 must have (i.e. uniqueness) that is wholly extrinsic to P2. It seems odd that whether or not P1 has survived death now depends not on P2 (i.e. not on any of P2's intrinsic properties) but on whether or not P2 has any competition for P1-ness. As Perry points out, this gives God an odd way of disposing of someone: in order to ensure that P1 has not survived death, God need not annihilate P1 or do *anything* to P1 – God need only create multiple qualitatively identical replicas in the afterlife. Then P1 has not survived death.

This is an odd result, but odd only – not incoherent. Presumably (though it rarely occurs to us) the identity of persons in this life depends on a uniqueness requirement too. Since God – so I believe – has the ability here and now to divide any human person into a thousand qualitatively identical (or nearly qualitatively identical) persons, the continued survival of the original person depends on God's refraining from exercising that ability.

Furthermore, it is clear that there are some perfectly innocuous cases where X's having a property or not having it depends not entirely on X but rather on the properties of some third person or thing. Possibly most properties of persons are not of this sort – they are much more straightforward attributes such as "being healthy" or "being a carpenter" or "being sixty years old". Whether or not X has properties like these depends, so to speak, on X's own nature and not on anyone or anything else. But what about properties such as "being the shortest player in the league" or "being the first person to climb K-2" or "being admired by Henry Kissinger" or "being a widow"? These seem to be properties such that whether or not X has them depends not entirely on X's intrinsic nature but in part on whether certain other people or things have certain other properties. God could easily make the shortest player in the league no longer the shortest player not by doing anything to her (making her grow, for example), but by bringing it about that an even shorter player joins the league.

People such as Hick, who defend uniqueness as a criterion of personal identity, can simply say that properties such as "having survived death" or "being numerically identical to P1" belong in the second category. Whether or not one possesses them depends not only on what happens to oneself but also on what happens to others as well. This is somewhat counter-intuitive, I admit; our intuition is to believe that whether or not the P2 before us in the eschaton is numerically identical to the P1 who died depends on the properties of P2 and not on the properties of some third person P3. In support of Hick, I would argue that this is simply one area (there have been others in philosophy) where our attempts to think clearly on some thorny problem have led us to surprising conclusions.

My second point against Dilley can be handled much more briefly. Dilley criticizes Hick's discussion of personal identity in chapter 15 of *Death and Eternal Life* for appearing to be oblivious to the dualism introduced in chapter 6. Once dualism is allowed, Dilley says, the door is open to reidentifying P2 in the afterlife on the basis of the presence or absence of the same soul as was possessed by P1. This also raises problems that will have to be addressed, Dilley says, but it is at least odd that Hick introduces dualism in chapter 6 but in chapter 15 speaks of reidentifying people in the afterlife on the basis of bodies, behaviours and replicas, as if chapter 6 had never been written.

But I see no inconsistency here. Hick may simply want to avoid dealing with all the Perry-like problems connected with identifying "the same soul" and try to solve the problem of personal identity in the afterlife on the basis of bodies and behaviours. This seems fair, does it not? Hick simply thinks (or thought, when he wrote *Death and Eternal Life*) that personal-identity problems in resurrection cases can be solved without reference to minds or souls. And this seems a viable position, does it not, for anyone who is a dualist, who believes in bodily resurrection, and who holds that God will eternally prevent any mind- or soul-switching?

Finally, let me make two points of my own about Hick's views on life after death. Both are more theological than Dilley's criticisms.

First, one of my central worries about Hick's thought is that I think it has become increasingly Pelagian in recent years. Hick no longer holds (with Paul, Augustine, Aquinas, Luther, Calvin, Barth) that our justification or reconciliation with God is something that God graciously accomplishes for us and that we merely acquiesce in. Of course Hick can say – when he is speaking as a Christian theologian and not as a global theologian – that God is at work in the world. But it seems that Hick now sees the attainment of salvation/liberation as follows: given the way the world is, i.e. given the nature of our spiritual environment, we achieve it ourselves. I oppose this view; I believe that all forms of Pelagianism are unrealistic: the firm grip that evil has on us and our inability to save ourselves are not appreciated.

A second, related worry is as follows. In his pre-global-theology days Hick argued for both continued human free choice in the eschaton and universal salvation. When asked how we could be sure that all people will eventually freely decide to say yes to God – especially since there seem to be some in this life who hate God so violently that they will never come around – Hick argued that in the eschaton God will have unlimited time and unlimited arguments with which to win people over; we cannot be logically certain but we can be practically certain that all will eventually be convinced.

The problem Hick now faces is this: only a personal being can do such things as *counsel* or *urge* or *persuade* or *create an environment designed to produce to spiritual growth,* and Hick the global theologian is no longer willing to affirm that God *an sich* is personal. So assuming Hick still wants to hold to both universalism and free human choice in the eschaton, we must again ask how we can rationally believe that all will eventually reach salvation/liberation. Hick's old argument is no longer available to him; we might wonder what he would now say. I frankly doubt that his new theory allows him to say *anything* that is meant to be literally (i.e. non-mythologically) true about what happens to us, if anything does, after death. But I shall leave it to him to correct my impression, if it is mistaken.

Reply

JOHN HICK

I greatly appreciate Frank Dilley's careful and constructive contribution, which requires me to be more cautious in future when writing about human personality and its possible survival of death. I am also grateful for Stephen Davis's remarks in defence, as well as for his further critical points. I had not in fact realized until reading Dilley that it was possible to think that I was once a Rylean-type upholder of mind–brain identity who subsequently came to reject this and to affirm instead the possibility of purely mental survival of bodily death. But looking again through his eyes I can see that such a reading is entirely possible. This is because the writings to which he refers were dealing with different issues and were addressed to different readerships. In spelling out the replica concept I was trying to show that the Christian doctrine of resurrection is not ruled out by the Rylean-type philosophy of mind and the more recent mind–brain identity theory. But at the same time, right from the first edition of the little *Philosophy of Religion* text in 1963, I have held that some of the parapsychological phenomena, particularly extra-sensory perception, demonstrate mental interaction independently of the brain, so that the mind cannot be equated with the functioning of the brain.

In *Death and Eternal Life* I tried to put these two strands together – the ideas of replica-style resurrection and of mental life independently of the physical brain. They come together in the hypothesis of a disembodied *bardo* phase immediately after death, followed in due course by re-embodiment in another space–time, and indeed possibly a succession of such re-embodiments separated by a succession of *bardo* phases. In the *bardo* phase we create our own mind-dependent world, and seeing our desires (including our unconscious desires) reflected in it we undergo a kind of psychoanalytic experience as a result of which our next embodiment becomes a relatively new start.

Now, concerning the multi-replica problem: I look at this differently from Dilley, and indeed from most of those who have written about it, including Davis. (The philosopher I am closest to

160

on this is Derek Parfit in *Reasons and Persons*.) If we speak simply of what is logically possible, there could be any number of indistinguishable replicas of a given physical organism, and also, I would add, of a given mental organism or stream of mental life – for why could not souls be replicated by omnipotence as easily as bodies? We can imagine a universe in which after death there are a plurality of psycho-physical replicas of each person. People would multiply into branching post-mortem successor selves who would begin by being identical but gradually develop along different lines in the different circumstances in which they live. Such a universe would need a different conceptual system, including a different notion of "person", from the one we have developed in our actual universe. But one must not try to use the same system of concepts across different possible universes requiring different conceptualities. However, the multiple-replica problems that have so intrigued and entertained the readers and writers of the philosophical journals during the last twenty or so years, in articles about personal identity, are generated by using the conceptual system appropriate to the actual universe to try to describe what could happen in other logically possible but importantly different universes. I therefore do not regard these as real problems. And so the Perry paradox, that God could abolish someone by creating another identical instance of that person, does not seem to me to carry any threat. A universe in which such things happen would have to be described by means of a partly different set of concepts from that with which we now operate; and to try to mix the two only creates needless conundrums.

7

Hick against Himself: His Theodicy *versus* his Replica Theory

DAN R. STIVER

John Hick's replica theory of the afterlife was first proposed in response to the verification challenge to religious language.[1] Since then, it has been put to rest and resuscitated several times.[2] Issues from the validity of eschatological verification to the importance of embodiment in the post-mortem state have been involved. Hick himself shifted the context of a replicative or reconstitutive afterlife from verification to the nature of life beyond death. Intermediate in that shift was his development of an Irenaean theodicy, of which his personal eschatology is part and parcel.[3] What I propose to show is that consideration of Hick's theodicy can provide a fresh perspective on the debate over the replica theory. Specifically, I argue that Hick's replica theory undermines his Irenaean theodicy. Conversely, if one affirms an Irenaean theodicy, one has further reason to reject the replica theory. This conclusion, furthermore, offers intriguing implications for other important issues involved in personal eschatology, such as continuity and dualism. I shall therefore first sketch out Hick's Irenaean theodicy and replica theory, then deal with the tension between the two.

HICK'S IRENAEAN THEODICY

Hick argued in *Evil and the God of Love* that Irenaeus provides the foundation for an important alternative to the dominant Augustinian theodicy, making it possible to reconcile the evolutionary development of the universe with the existence of a perfectly good and omnipotent God.[4] A basic difference is that perfection lay

162

only in the future for Irenaeus, as opposed to being in the past and the future for Augustine. The principal reason for this difference is that Irenaeus imagined that Adam and Eve were created as undeveloped and immature beings who must gradually mature into the likeness of God. The goal of the creation of human beings was for them to come freely to love God and each other – in New Testament language, to be conformed to the image of Christ. But Irenaeus apparently believed that God could not have created human beings with such full-blown perfection. He wrote, "God had power at the beginning to grant perfection to man; but as the latter was only recently created, he could not possibly have received it, or even if he had received it could he have contained it, or containing it, could he have retained it."[5]

Hick follows Irenaeus at this point. He acknowledges that God might have created beings who are perfectly obedient to God, but who are not free. Like other proponents of a free-will defence approach to theodicy, he argues that such beings would not be as valuable as free beings. He further acknowledges that free beings could have been created who would always do the good because they would have been given a finitely perfect nature and environment. He even concedes to J. L. Mackie that God could have created beings who would always freely do good in an imperfect environment, owing to a perfect nature.[6] Yet in the end he contends that such free beings are not *truly* free and are not as valuable as beings who at an epistemic and moral distance from God freely choose to become children of God. I shall call this the Irenaean intuition. Hick expresses this conviction in a brief statement of his theodicy in the book *Encountering Evil: Live Options in Theodicy* (edited by Stephen T. Davis, 1981):

But if God could, without logical contradiction, have created humans as wholly good free beings, why did he not do so? Why was humanity not initially created in possession of all the virtues, instead of having to acquire them through the long hard struggle of life as we know it? The answer, I suggest, appeals to the principle that virtues which have been formed within the agent as a hard-won deposit of his own right decisions in situations of challenge and temptation, are intrinsically more valuable than virtues created within him ready-make and without any effort on his own part. This principle expresses a basic value judgment, which cannot be established by argument but which one can only present, in the hope that it will be as morally plausible, and indeed compelling, to others as to oneself.[7]

For Hick, these are the virtues and this is the freedom that count as true virtues and true freedom. These virtues qualify one as a true child of God. Hick wavers by continuing to consider guaranteed use of freedom, such as Mackie espouses, as "freedom", but it is clear that its value pales in comparison with his more strenuous sense of freedom. At one point he says that Mackie's freedom reduces people to "mere puppets" and that love or trust based on such freedom is "self-contradictory".[8] At such times Hick's views are essentially those of Alvin Plantinga who argues that freedom in Mackie's conception is not truly freedom.[9] In short, I believe Hick's view can be more straightforwardly expressed as claiming that genuine freedom and genuine love are possible only in a world consistent with the Irenaean intuition.[10]

The Irenaean intuition is the linchpin of Hick's theodicy because it provides a plausible reason why God could not have attained the goal of creating children of God in any other way than through a difficult person- or soul-making process. When responding to Stephen Davis's contention that God can suddenly transform people into new persons, Hick argues that such a possibility undermines theodicy. For, if God could transform us at death at our various stages of development, it seems that he could have done so at the beginning and avoided the travails of this life.[11] The critical point is that, if God could have achieved the goal of persons conforming to the image of Christ without their having to risk evils of a world such as ours, then these evils would not be justified.[12] But the insight that Hick shares with Irenaeus is that God could not logically have avoided that risk. Using the strongest possible terms Hick argues,

> Indeed, if the end-state which God is seeking to bring about is one in which finite persons have come in their own freedom to know and love him, this requires creating them initially in a state which is not that of their already knowing and loving him. For it is logically impossible to create beings already in a state of having come into that state by their own free choices.[13]

It is this corollary of the Irenaean intuition, so essential to Hick's theodicy, that is irreconcilable with the replica theory, which is so important in Hick's eschatology.

HICK'S REPLICA THEORY

Hick's replica theory was proposed as a way of making sense of post-mortem existence, an existence in which one could conceivably verify the truth-claims of the Chrisian religion. His argument involved three stages.[14] If a Mr. Jones suddenly disappears from a professional gathering in New York and an exact replica appears the next moment in London, according to Hick one could justifiably say that the replica is the same person. "The factors inclining us to identify them", Hick urges, "would . . . far outweigh the factors disinclining us to do so."[15] The next stage calls for Jones certifiably to die and yet appear in London. The third stage involves Jones dying and appearing in another time–space. By this gradual progression, Hick argues that we could legitimately regard the replica in all three cases as the same person.

As mentioned above, numerous objections have been raised to this account. Most recently, the issue has been the central one of whether Replica Jones counts as the same person as Jones. For the moment, we shall grant Hick the point while noting that it apparently involves differences in basic intuitions about the self that are difficult to resolve. However, as this paper will attempt to show, the perspective of theodicy can throw fresh light on that issue.

Although the initial context of the replica theory for Hick was verification, in *Death and Eternal Life* the context was the nature of resurrection *versus* disembodiment and reincarnation as post-mortem states.[16] Hick offers the replica theory as an example of resurrection. He assumes that resurrection entails complete extinction, with God then reconstituting the person as a psychosomatic whole.[17] Because of emphases in biblical studies, psychology and philosophy on the psychosomatic unity of the self, resurrection along the lines of reconstitution has gained favour as the most adequate conception of the nature of the afterlife.[18] This assumption about resurrection is one reason why the replica or reconstitution theory is so important. If reconstitution cannot be sustained, this monistic view of the self as an aspect of Christian personal eschatology must be seriously qualified.

THE CONTRADICTION

The difficulty with the replica theory from the perspective of an Irenaean theodicy is that it offers the possibility of God creating beings who meet the criteria of the Irenaean intuition and yet who never actually have to suffer the evils of this world. If replicas count as the same persons as those they replicate, which Hick must assume, then God must be able to constitute whole-cloth, as it were, beings who have the same kind of character and love as beings who have been through the worldly process. Remember that he understands resurrection to imply that beings perish and then are reconstituted. Is it therefore possible for God to short-circuit the process and to create at the outset such beings without actual predecessors? God might have good reasons not to do so, but it certainly appears to be a possibility. These would be beings unlike Mackie's with preformed and pregiven natures that were not shaped by choices over time. They would be natures which are identical to those acquired over time in an ambiguous environment and thus would be consistent with the Irenaean intuition. The advantage of these beings is that they would have avoided all the *actual* suffering that constitutes such a grave problem of evil for theistic faith. As noted above, Hick implies that, if persons *could* have the desired character without enduring all the evil of this life, God would not be justified in putting them through the pain. The justification of God in the Irenaean theodicy is that God could not avoid running the risk of so much evil in order for there to be children of God. However, if God can constitute such beings *ex nihilo*, then evil could have been avoided and God is not justified in the creation of this world.

Hick said in the context of his theodicy that the creation of such a person consistent with the Irenaean intuition is "logically impossible". But how is such a person different from a replica? Call the replica of Jones "Jones A", and the instantaneous creation of Jones without the actual existence of Jones, "Jones B". Both have been created from nothing, except in the sense that they exactly reproduce Jones in another space–time. I see no way in which Jones B differs from Jones A except that Jones A has an actual predecessor and Jones B a possible predecessor. Hick himself cannot make much of this difference because his theodicy has not emphasized the intrinsic value of this world so much as its instrumental value as the necessary condition for soul-making. His point has been a teleological one – that is, the only logically possible way for one to have Jones A with his love of God and his likeness to Christ is to have an actual predecessor.[19] But Jones B is exactly like Jones A without having to have an actual predecessor. It appears that the actual world is *not* necessary in order to produce a Jones replica, and is not justifiable on any another grounds. If this line of reasoning is correct, then Hick's replica theory undermines his Irenaean theodicy.

How might Hick respond? He might argue that there is indeed great intrinsic value in having actual experiences and in making actual difficult, hard choices. But, if the person conformed to the image of Christ, identical in all respects except for an actual past, is possible, is the intrinsic value of the actual past worth the price of the actual suffering? All good actual experiences would be forfeited, and that would be a great loss. But *all* experiences of actual suffering in this world would also be precluded, suffering that is extensive and dysteleological enough to constitute, as Hick himself confesses, perhaps the gravest obstacle to faith in a theistic God.[20] If one could nevertheless have the benefit of persons conformed to the image of Christ without anyone having actually to endure suffering, would an actual earthly existence be worth it? If the problem of evil is as great as Hick thinks it is, the answer would have to be no.

Hick could argue that Jones B is simply not the same person as the Jones who lived an actual earthly life. That is, there has to be continuity between the earthly life and the heavenly for the formed character to have the same value. Obviously, though, this point counts against the replica theory itself in that Hick presupposes that the replica is the same person as the one being replicated.

One might argue that, without an original Jones, God could not constitute Jones B. This objection assumes, it seems to me, that God does not have what has recently been called middle knowledge.[21] In other words, God does not know what *would* occur if Jones were to exist. However, even if God does not have middle knowledge, one can suppose that God has knowledge of possibles, of what *could* happen. If there is not an actual earthly world, does it make that much difference if God constitutes possible persons as opposed to persons based on middle knowledge of what would have happened if there had been an actual world? The difference between such a possible person and Jones B would not lie in the basic nature of the character or the love or the faith; it would lie only in the accidents. The person would still be consistent with the Irenaean intuition. So it does not seem that the issue of the difference between Jones A and Jones B turns on the question of God's possessing middle knowledge.

The most substantial objection that Hick might raise is that Jones B is living a lie. If memories are an aspect of the afterlife, and Jones B is identical to Jones A, then Jones B will have the memories of an actual previous life. If that is true, God would be implicated in significant deception, which would be inconsistent with the premise of a perfectly good God.[22] So in such a case Jones B would have to realize that his past was the past he would have had (if there is middle knowledge) or could have had (if there is not) if he had lived an earthly life – not his actual past. In that case, Jones B would no longer be identical to Jones A but would be substantially different. Would the alternative heavenly world still militate against the necessity for an actually earthly process in order to produce persons in the image of God? I think it would. One would still have beings with the same kind of character and love. Jones B would still be conformed to the image of Christ. It might be that Jones B would not have any memories of the past, and that such an absence would not be significant, since such absence of memory may not be an aspect of heaven anyway. If some memories of earthly existence are constitutive of persons, Jones B would presumably be aware that his memories of past difficult decisions and past sufferings were not of actual decisions and sufferings, but he would also presumably be aware of the necessity of such memories, of their nature as the kind of past he would have had, and that, in God's goodness, he had the memories and was spared the actual suffering. Furthermore, he would know that his loved ones and ones he came to know in heaven, if such interaction is a part of heaven, were spared such suffering. To us, of course, such a state of affairs appears to be somewhat odd, but, to the question of preferring it over actual suffering, I think an affirmative answer can easily be justified.

On the basis of Hick's own reasoning, it seems that, if such an alternative, odd and unreal as it is, is possible, then God could hardly be justified in creating a world such as the actual world.

The Irenaean intuition can be accommodated for all practical purposes, and yet the actual suffering of this world can be avoided.

If indeed there is a personal God, it is clear that the deity was not faced with that option, for the theistic premise holds both that this world and all its evil do exist and that its evil is justified. But its evil cannot be justified on the basis of a replica theory of the afterlife conjoined with an affirmation of the Irenaean intuition.

In pointing out that contradiction between an Irenaean theodicy and a replica view of the afterlife, one uncovers an implicit presupposition about personal identity. From the perspective of an Irenaean theodicy, where does the replica theory go wrong? The most likely candidate is that a replica in truth is not the same as a person who actually or even possibly lives an earthly life. At this point, Antony Flew would be correct when he argues that a replica is similar but not the same.[23] Some continuity is necessary beyond similarity. In the context of an Irenaean theodicy, reconstitution is not a coherent approach to the identity of the person who lives beyond death. If it were, then God would simply have constituted perfected beings without subjecting them to actual suffering and evil. So one has further support from the perspective of an Irenaean theodicy that replication does not count as identity.

Hick himself, without acknowledging the inconsistency, moved in that direction in the very book in which he argued for a replica view of the resurrection, *Death and Eternal Life.*[24] When he turned to consider his own view of what happens at death, he opted for continuity of the self in some way apart from the body, more akin to many Eastern views and in many ways closer to Western views of a disembodied spirit. As Frank Dilley points out, Hick developed his replica theory in the context of the verification debate, long before his theology and views on the nature of the afterlife had shifted.[25] Hick's views of the continuity of the self espoused in the latter part of *Death and Eternal Life,* which presuppose not only continuity but a more dualistic view of the self, are more consistent with his Irenaean theodicy than is the resurrection view that he seems to espouse in the earlier part of the book and in his earlier thought. Moreover, if, because of the dissolution of the body, one infers some form of dualism as an implication of continuity between the earthly self and the post-mortem self, then the Irenaean theodicy implies dualism as well as continuity.[26]

CONCLUSION

In sum, the replica or reconstitution view of the resurrection undermines an Irenaean theodicy. What is more consistent with an Irenaean theodicy – in fact, what affirmation of an Irenaean theodicy seems to entail – is a view of the continuity of the self in some substantial form, which also may well entail a dualistic conception of the self.

NOTES

1. See John Hick, *Theology Today*, 17 (1960) 12–31. A fuller discussion is given in *Death and Eternal Life*, pp. 279–96.
2. In recent years Frank B. Dilley has defended the replica theory against some objections in "Resurrection and the 'Replica Objection' ", *Religious Studies*, 19 (1983) 459–74. (See also above, Ch. 6.) In turn, Gerard Loughlin has argued against it in "Persons and Replicas", *Modern Theology*, 1 (July 1985) 303–19.
3. *Evil and the God of Love* (1966; 2nd edn 1978).
4. Ibid., 2nd edn, pp. 211–15. A concise and helpful presentation including dialogue with critics appears in Stephen T. Davis (ed.), *Encountering Evil: Live Options in Theodicy* (Atlanta: John Knox Press, 1981).
5. Irenaeus, *Against Heresies*, IV.xxxviii.2.
6. *Encountering Evil*, pp. 43–4. Cf. *Hick and the God of Love*, 2nd edn, p. 271.
7. *Encountering Evil*, p. 44.
8. *Evil and the God of Love*, 2nd edn, p. 274.
9. Plantinga has made this point in several places. An extended discussion is in *The Nature of Necessity* (Oxford: Clarendon Press, 1974) pp. 164–95. See also Davis's contribution to *Encountering Evil*, pp. 69–83.
10. *Evil and the God of Love*, 2nd edn, pp. 265–91. In response to Mackie, Hick inconsistently grants that it is a coherent idea that persons can always freely do right and then denies that such a freedom is genuine freedom (pp. 274–5). It would be clearer if Hick would say that it is incoherent for God to create persons who are *genuinely* free and also guaranteed always to do the good. Hick would then be making the same point as Plantinga makes against Mackie: that is, that it is not in God's power to bring about and determine genuinely free choice to do the good and to love God. Hick's collapsing-together a minimalist type of freedom and genuine freedom causes him in the additional chapter of the second edition to claim on the same page that Plantinga does and does not rebut Mackie! (p. 369). In *The Miracle of Theism: Arguments for and against the Existence of God* (Oxford: Clarendon Press,

1982), Mackie argues that God could create persons who would always do the good even in a difficult environment (p. 165). However, his point is that God could determine the natures of the persons such that they always choose the good apart from external coercion (p. 166ff). Plantinga and Hick both oppose this idea. Plantinga argues that no sense of freedom allows for God to determine the outcome; Hick argues that no genuine sense of freedom allows for God to determine the outcome.

11. *Encountering Evil*, p. 66.
12. As I take it, this is an important assumption underlying Antony Flew's argument in "Divine Omnipotence and Human Freedom", in Antony Flew and Alasdair MacIntyre (eds), *New Essays in Philosophical Theology* (London: SCM, 1955) pp. 144–69, esp. pp. 154–5. He implies that, if there is any way for God to create beings with the benefits belonging to free will and yet avoid their actual suffering, God would not be justified in not doing so.
13. *Encountering Evil*, p. 43.
14. I have taken this account from Hick, *Death and Eternal Life*, pp. 279–88.
15. Ibid., p. 281.
16. Ibid., pt IV.
17. Ibid., pp. 278–9. Of course, that assumption has been challenged, for example in P. W. Gooch, "On Disembodied Resurrected Persons: A Study in the Logic of Christian Eschatology", *Religious Studies*, 17 (1981) 199–213. Gooch argues that disembodiment is consistent with Paul's use of "resurrection". Dilley points out in "Resurrection and the 'Replica Objection' ", *Religious Studies*, 19, p. 460, that theists have traditionally understood resurrection to be compatible with at least a temporary disembodied intermediate state. However, note Bruce R. Reichenbach's objection to Gooch in "On Disembodied Resurrected Persons: A Reply", *Religious Studies*, 18 (1982) 225–9, and Gooch's response in "Reply to Professor Reichenbach", *Religious Studies*, 18 (1982) 231–2.
18. In addition to Hick, see Oscar Cullmann's influential study *Immortality of the Soul or Resurrection of the Dead? The Witness of the New Testament* (New York: Macmillan, 1958). Cullmann argues that death means the actual cessation of the whole person, which is why death is so threatening. "Furthermore, if life is to issue out of so genuine a death as this, a new divine act of creation is necessary. And this act of creation calls back to life not just a part of the man, but the whole man – all that God has created and death had annihilated" (p. 26). Somewhat inconsistently, later in the book Cullmann posits an intermediate disembodied "inner man" that does live on in proximity to Christ (pp. 52–7). On the pervasiveness of a reconstitution or replica theory of resurrection as the only possible coherent view, see Dilley, "Resurrection and the 'Replica Objection' ", *Religious Studies*, 19, pp. 459–61; and Gooch, "On Disembodied Resurrected Persons", *Religious Studies*, 18, pp. 199–200.

19.   *Evil and the God of Love*, 2nd edn, pp. 231–3, 256, 351–2, 382–3.
20.   Ibid., p. vii.
21.   For an example of how the lack of middle knowledge might require actual earthly experience, see Flew's discussion in *New Essays in Philosophical Theology*, pp. 155–6 n. 18. Flew indicates that middle knowledge or subjective conditionals are valid. For examples of recent discussions of middle knowledge in general, see two articles by David Basinger, "Divine Omniscience and Human Freedom: A Middle Knowledge Perspective", *Faith and Philosophy*, 1 (July 1984) 291–302, and "Middle Knowledge and Human Freedom: Some Clarifications", *Faith and Philosophy*, 4 (July 1987) 330–6.
22.   Note that when discussing H. H. Price's conception of a solipsistic, disembodied existence which appears to be material but is actually a mental projection, one of Hick's major objections is that such a situation is deceitful and is inconsistent with a perfectly good God (*Death and Eternal Life*, p. 269).
23.   Antony Flew, *The Presumption of Atheism and Other Philosophical Essays on God, Freedom, and Immortality* (London: Elek/Pemberton, 1976) p. 107. See also Loughlin, "Persons and Replicas", *Modern Theology*, 1.
24.   *Death and Eternal Life*, pp. 399–414.
25.   Dilley in fact points out the suddenness and subtlety of the change in Hick in "Resurrection and the 'Replica Objection' ", *Religious Studies*, 19, pp. 473–4. Hick makes the shift without reconciling it with his earlier views. In fact, the tension exists within *Death and Eternal Life* itself. It is not clear just what view Hick espouses. When dealing with the alternatives between disembodiment, resurrection and reincarnation, he leaves the impression that the replica theory of resurrection is the view he prefers. When he later develops his view in relation to Eastern views, he presumes a dualistic view of the self and uses language which presumes continuity, not discontinuity as in the replica theory. See pp. 400, 404, 408, 414, 420–1. Loughlin reads *Death and Eternal Life* as assuming only a monistic view of the self: "Persons and Replicas", *Modern Theology*, 1, p. 304. After hearing this paper at the spring Eastern regional meeting of the Society of Christian Philosophers in 1988, Hick commented that the reconstitution theory is confirmed by Derek Parfit in *Reasons and Persons* (Oxford: Clarendon Press, 1984); see esp. pt III.
26.   H. D. Lewis is perhaps the most significant exponent of the connection between continuity and dualism. For a recent and concise statement of his views, see "Immortality", *Review and Expositor*, 82 (Fall 1985) 549–63. See Hick's favourable notice of Lewis in the Preface to *Death and Eternal Life*, p. 13.

Critical Response

In Defence of Hick's Theodicy

HAROLD HEWITT, JR

There is almost nothing I enjoy better than a well-written, carefully considered critique – except perhaps one devoted specifically to a favourite topic as addressed by a favourite author. Dan Stiver's deliberations for (one suspects) Irenaeus and against Hick's "replicas" therefore provided me with a good deal of mental refreshment! He raises familiar issues with new force and anticipates possible responses. In that same spirit of analysis I shall try to challenge his conclusions.

The paper associates with Hick's theodicy some ideas which deserve second thoughts: for example, it is suggested that Hick contradicts himself and has not explained the contradiction away. On the other hand, Stiver's argument seems to challenge what I must agree is a core component of Hick's theodicy, the Irenaean intuition – "the linchpin of Hick's theodicy".[1] I have always found the case for genuine freedom to be quite compelling, and shall respond to Stiver with a single argument rather than by rebutting each element of his paper; I hope to show at least that Hick does not contradict himself.

Stiver's argument can be summarized as follows. Since in *Death and Eternal Life* Hick admits that God is able to produce "replicas" of people following their demise from this world, he must also admit the possibility that God is capable of producing "replicas" *ex nihilo* while sparing them the evils of this world. If Hick concedes this latter possibility, then his replica-infested Irenaean theodicy fails. How could God be justified in allowing worldly evil if it is possible for God to produce beings who are laden with this-wordly memories but have not had to undergo suffering in this world?

Stiver anticipates in his paper what I believe is the strongest and only necessary response to the challenge – namely, that the concept of a "replica" without its specific this-worldly predecessor is logically impossible – or, cast slightly differently, that it is logically impossible to conceive that God would create such a being.

Consider the concept of "memories", which most people would apply to the mental phenomena associated in living beings with past experience. It does not make sense to say that there can be a "Mr. X" or a "Jones B", created in some other space–time, that at the instant of its creation is replete with memories of non-existent experiences. One can grant that it is possible for persons to use the concepts "replica" and "memories" in this way, and one can even grant the possibility that in some universe God could actually create such a "replica" with such "memories", but the concepts involved would be nothing like what we understand by them in this life. Stiver's application of the concept "memories" to a being without its identical antecedent and actual past experiences is therefore strictly illogical. That language game is not played!

The insurmountable problem of utilizing concepts outside of their usual framework of meaning deprives Stiver's potentially most damaging arguments of much of their force. I have focused my attention on "memories" as the key concept because I agree with Hick that it is fundamental to identity. In *Death and Eternal Life* memory serves as the cornerstone of identity through the many lives of an individual in the soul-making process. As Hick states, "in addition to the transmission of character traits . . . [it] is the link of memory that picks out, say A^{1843} as the unique individual whose history is continued in the life of B, out of the thousands of others in the same generation whose character profiles qualify them as pre-incarnations of B".[2] What does "identity through lives" mean without memory, and what does "memory" mean apart from actual past experiences?[3] In my judgement, Hick's position on this point is more than convincing. So, when Stiver writes, "I see no way in which Jones B [an instantaneous creation without an actual predecessor] differs from Jones A [the "replica" of Jones] except that Jones A has an actual predecessor and Jones B a possible predecessor",[4] I must disagree! There is a difference between the two: Jones B is logically impossible.

In sum, I am not convinced that Hick's own reasoning leads to the failure of his version of an Irenaean theodicy – even with the inclusion of the theory of replicas. This could result only if Hick used the concepts "replica" and "memory" in meaningless ways in *Death and Eternal Life* (or elsewhere), and I am not convinced that he does this. The interesting discussions about God's middle knowledge – or lack of it – and God's deception are thus not essential to the main argument. It follows also that Hick – and some of us with him – will not need to consider dualism as part of theodicy (which Stiver recommends). In my view this is fortunate, since dualism suffers from several long-familiar and thorny problems of its own (for instance, the classic Cartesian dilemma of explaining precisely how it is that "soul" and body relate).

NOTES

1. Dan R. Stiver, above, p. 164.
2. *Death and Eternal Life,* pp. 364–5.
3. See also ibid., pp. 290, 419–21.
4. Stiver, above, p. 166.

Reply

JOHN HICK

Dan Stiver's perceptive paper exposes a problem of which I had not previously been aware.

Suppose Mary has lived to the ripe age of eighty and has in the course of her long life grown considerably in wisdom and love. When she dies God resurrects her by creating a Mary replica in the resurrection world. This replica, created *ex nihilo*, has all the hard-won wisdom and love of the eighty-year-old Mary. It follows from this that it is possible for God to create someone *ex nihilo* in a state of moral and spiritual maturity. But, if God can do this, presumably God could create a Mary *ab initio* in the resurrection world, without an earthly Mary having ever existed. God can, in other words, create a resurrection Mary who is *as though* there had been an earthly Mary who gradually and freely acquired the mature characteristics of the resurrection Mary. But in that case why not create everyone in a morally and spiritually mature state, and indeed in a state of complete human perfection, without our present world having to exist as the environment for a difficult soul-making process?

We are agreed that the resurrection Mary, with no earthly predecessor, would not in fact have attained to moral and spiritual maturity by personal struggle, although she would be in a state as though she had. The question, then, is whether her *ad hoc* creation is compatible with what Stiver calls the Irenaean intuition – the intuition that goodness which has been developed through the free making of right choices is enormously more valuable than goodness created ready made. I think we have to agree that, if we did not know that the Mary created in the resurrection world had no earthly predecessor, we should have no reason to think her goodness to be of the inferior kind. But let us suppose that God shares the Irenaean intuition. God *does* know that Mary's goodness is of the inferior kind. And, therefore, whilst God *could* make the kind of being described by Stiver, God would never want to; for to do so would be contrary to the Irenaean intuition.

Thus I want to grant the logical possibility of (a) God creating morally mature beings *as though* they had come to this by means of

176

a lifetime of freely made moral choices; but – in agreement with
Harold Hewitt – not the logical possibility of (b) God's making
morally mature beings whose moral maturity *is* a product of freely
made choices. And I suggest that if God operates in accordance
with the Irenaean intuition, God would never want to do (a). Thus
God will not do either (a) or (b) – not (a) because this would,
assuming the Irenaean intuition, be pointless in the eyes of divine
omniscience, and not (b) because this is logically impossible.

Part III
The Doctrine of the Incarnation

8

Squares and Circles: John Hick and the Doctrine of the Incarnation

GERARD LOUGHLIN

The doctrine of the incarnation is just one part of Christology, when Christology is understood as attention in faith to the man Jesus of Nazareth. The gospels themselves are Christological attentions, faithful renditions of his life and death. It is in the life of the Church that the doctrine of the incarnation, like all doctrines, has its origin and function. The purpose of the doctrine is to delineate the shape and shadow of faithful attention to Christ.

John Hick, in more than thirty years of reflecting and writing on the person of Jesus, has made several notable contributions to Christology. But always his chief attention has been to the grammar of Christology – that is, to the doctrine of the incarnation – to how it should be expressed today and to what its expression implies for contemporary Christianity. However, in the course of his reflections Hick has been led from affirming the truth of the doctrine to denying its fundamental contention. He has moved from attempting to spell out its meaning to denying that it has any meaning to be spelt out. Hick now holds that to say of Jesus that he was also God is as absurd as saying that a circle is also a square.[1]

The contrast between Hick's earlier and later positions is sufficiently startling to warrant a careful consideration of his journey between them. That is what I attempt in this paper, though I do so with a purpose. While the difference between Hick's earlier and later positions is conspicuous, his later position can be read as a development of his earlier one, given his understanding of doctrinal use and his view of human knowing. I neither share Hick's epistemological convictions nor hold with his view of doctrinal purpose. Consequently my aim in this paper is to render explicit the theological cogency and philosophical rigour

181

of the doctrine of the incarnation, and thus also the possibility of its truth, in the face of Hick's criticisms.

I start by looking at Hick's position as adumbrated in his contribution to *The Myth of God Incarnate* because there one can determine the conditions making for his radical restructuring of Christology. I then proceed to offer an account of those conditions as discerned in Hick's earlier defence of Chalcedonian orthodoxy and the development of his *agape* Christology, which, in the estimation of the late John Robinson, is Hick's most notable and valuable contribution to Christology.[2] Finally I return to a more detailed examination of Hick's arguments against the intelligibility and plausibility of incarnational doctrine. By the end of my discussion I hope to have established two points: that the conditions making for Hick's later Christology were present in the earlier, and that the doctrine of the incarnation, far from being a confusion of squares and circles, is one of appropriate precision and clarity.

I

In 1978, the year following the publication of *The Myth of God Incarnate*, John Coventry published a short article in which he neatly and carefully pointed out almost everything that is theologically wrong with the case made by the contributors to that book, the "mythographers".[3] Chief among their faults he found a shared "empiricism", principally exhibited in privileging historical criticism over the mediation of Christ in the Christian tradition. The mythographers, Coventry noted, held that Christian faith is grounded in New Testament texts, and that it is through and behind them that one meets the object of Christian faith, the historical Jesus as disclosed to biblical criticism. From this starting-point the mythographers went on to argue that, if one but looks at Jesus of Nazareth, as he really was, one will see that he was not God incarnate.

However, as Coventry pointed out, this perception is not a contingent result of historical inquiry but a necessary implication of historical method. "Limitation of the inquiry to the historical Jesus *systematically* excludes considering him as in any traditional sense divine."[4] Historical criticism has a limited vocabulary; it is able to describe only certain things and certain aspects of things, and "divinity" is not one of them. Indeed, the "divinity" of Jesus, as this has been understood in the Christian tradition, is neither an aspect of a thing nor a thing itself; it is not one of the "characteristics" of Jesus nor a "fact" about him – it is *him*.

The mythographers believed that Christology should be done from "below", from the bottom up, by the way of "ascent"; and not from "above", from the top down, by way of "descent".[5] One should begin Christology with the historical Jesus of Nazareth, and with what it is about his life and death that compelled the first Christians to confess him as the Christ.

Doing Christology from "below" means, as Hans Küng has put it, "that we do not make ourselves equal to God and consider everything, as it were, looking down from heaven. It means considering Jesus and his history from an earthly standpoint, from the standpoint of people of his own time, and asking: what did people really see in him, how did Jesus' disciples understand him?"[6]

Christology from "below" takes "empiricism" – the belief, as Bernard Lonergan puts it, that the "real" is the "already-out-there-now-real" waiting to be sensed – and inscribes it within theological reflection on the person of Jesus.[7] If one takes a "good look" at Jesus of Nazareth, as he really was, one will see the truth about him. One will see him as the disciples saw him. Christology from "below" is naïve; it forgets that taking a "good look" is never innocent, but always, irreducibly, guilty of prejudice. The historical method, of its nature, can reveal only certain limited facts.[8] As Austin Farrer once pointed out, the historical method is like a net let down into the ocean of the past. It will catch only those fishes that a net with its sort of meshes will catch.

> No net will catch all the living matter in the water and no historical method will fish up the whole of live historical reality, unless we give to "historical reality" the tautological sense of "what our historical method fishes up". There is plenty of history that will forever elude historical inquiry and it is pretty obvious that the supernatural being of Jesus Christ is some of that. The Christian faith is not believed on historical grounds alone, that is, on grounds which unaided history can establish: it is believed on living testimony of a special kind.[9]

This is not to say that Christology can dispense with historical inquiry, that the doctrine of the incarnation can be affirmed irrespective of whatever else we believe about Jesus, even that he never existed. Christology refers to an actual individual – concrete, contingent and conditioned. Thus it is correct that theology use historical criticism in order to curb possible docetic tendencies as well as to act as a check on Christological affirmation, but not as more than a check, such that Christology is abused by it. Simply to give the truth about Jesus over to historical criticism, as in effect Hick and the mythographers did, is to forget that the truth about a person cannot simply be given by a methodology. It forgets further that it is precisely the Christian claim that Jesus was not simply a man who lived at a certain time in a certain way, but also, at the same time, the Christ, the Son of God. It is this claim that cannot be given by an irreducibly empiricist methodology. The incarnation of God in Jesus of Nazareth is not something that can be seen simply by using the tools of historical criticism; it could not be seen then by those who simply looked and stared.

There is no doubt that the development of the doctrine of the incarnation took place over a considerable period of time, even if, as Coventry believes, the essentials of the doctrine had been developed by the time Paul wrote to the Romans. But, as Coventry notes, one is either convinced that the development of the doctrine was providential or one is not. The mythographers took the latter view and therefore saw the development as, in Coventry's words, no more "than an imaginative construction out of . . . traditional religious imagery by an excited group, valueless to us today".[10] But this neither is nor can be a historical judgement. The "guidance of God's spirit" is not something that historical enquiry is equipped to discern.

The arguments employed in the *The Myth of God Incarnate* rest on a refusal to take seriously the claim that the Christian tradition truthfully (really) mediates the person and meaning of Jesus of Nazareth, which refusal results from privileging the products of historical criticism. If the incarnation of God in Jesus cannot be verified by empirical/historical means, then it is unbelievable.[11] This view is succinctly stated by one of the early mythographers, Frances Young: "If Jesus was an entirely normal human being, no evidence can be produced for the incarnation. If no evidence can be produced, there can be no basis on which to claim that an incarnation took place" (emphasis removed).[12]

II

Some of Hick's earliest Christological thought can be found in his essay "The Christology of D. M. Baillie", published in 1958.[13] In his justly famous book *God Was in Christ* Baillie had sugested that in experiencing the "paradox of grace" – the experience of having to say, "It was not I but God" – one has an insight into the incarnate life of God in Jesus, the man in whom the paradox was realized absolutely.[14]

Baillie attempted to ascribe a unique status and soteriological significance to Jesus by affirming that "God in some measure lives and acts in us . . . because first, and without measure, He lived and acted in Christ".[15] However, Hick argued that Christ could not be the "cause" of the "paradox of grace" because that paradox is universal and not merely Christian. One cannot ascribe the "good deeds" of non-Christians to the power of God's grace unless one is also prepared to say that they are causally related to the incarnation. But one cannot say that because they are not. Thus, Hick concluded, Baillie is left "occupying the unsatisfactory position that Christ's uniqueness is one of degree – degree of divinely enabled moral achievement". As Hick has more recently put it in his contribution to *The Myth of Christian Uniqueness*, incarnation, in Baillie's sense, "has occurred and is occurring in many different ways and degrees in many different persons".[16] On such an account as Baillie's, Jesus is but one among others.

For my purpose this argument is of interest because it displays Hick's "empiricist" tendencies. Hick argued that God's grace can be held to be effective only if it is possible to trace the causal mechanism by which it operates, a mechanism which must be empirically tangible. Hick's argument assumes that the connection between the "paradox of grace" – without measure – in Christ, and the "paradox of grace" – in some measure – in the rest of humankind, is possible only if people are "in Christ" as members of the historic Church. But it has never been part of orthodox Christian tradition that God's grace is limited to the confines of the historic Church, *pace* Hick's strictures on the teaching of *extra ecclesiam nulla salus.*[17]

Hick also tried to spear Baillie's account of the incarnation on the horns of a dilemma. Either God acts first and we respond, or we act first and God responds. In terms of the incarnation: either Jesus was *predestined* to live a good life, or this good man was *adopted* by God. Baillie is "simply saying that when, in the mystery of personal freedom, a man does choose rightly, what he has done is to allow the divine grace to operate within him. We can do wrong by ourselves, but we can only do right by surrendering to the grace of God; and this grace is always available, always the prior condition of man's good works."[18]

However, while the charge of adoptionism against Baillie is not incorrect, Hick's reading of Baillie misses the point. For Hick, the decision to surrender to God and accept his always already-proffered gift of grace is a wholly human one. That choice is not the fruit of God's grace. For Baillie, by contrast, the whole point of the "paradox of grace" is that the decision to surrender to God's grace is itself the gracious act of God. Again, Hick's misreading can be understood as the result of his "empiricism": a Humean distrust of "mystery", of that which can be said appropriately only by such strategies as those of dialectic or paradox.

One of the most notable features of Hick's early article is the stringency of his criteria for interpreting the doctrine of the incarnation. This stringency was short-lived. Fifteen years later he was to argue that incarnational theories were "category mistakes" and the cause of all Christological heresy.[19]

III

After 1958 Hick set himself the task of finding a contemporary idiom that would continue to do the work of "substance" in Chalcedonian Christology, for he believed that the assertion of continuity between Jesus and God need not employ the notion of substance. Moreover, while the idea of substance had once appeared "clear and adequate", it was now felt by many to have an "odour of ambiguity and metaphysical pretension", and had been dropped from the "working vocabulary of contemporary philosophy"! The concept would have to be either rethought or replaced.

In 1966 Hick contributed an article entitled "Christology at the Crossroads" to the *Festschrift* for H. H. Farmer, *Prospect for Theology*.[20] He reprinted a large part of it in his book *God and the Universe of Faiths*.[21] It is notable for a number of reasons. First, it inscribed the question of Christology within the larger problem of religious plurality, which Hick saw as "the most disturbing theological problem that Christianity is likely to have to face corporately during the next hundred years or so".[22] Secondly, it strengthened Hick's concern with Jesus as an ordinary human person like the rest of us. This concern – the result of Hick's abiding "empiricism" – had led him in the years since 1958 to be much more tolerant of degree Christologies such as those advocated by Norman Pittenger and Nels Ferré. He had come to hold that "neo-Arian" Christologies were genuine options, for he recognized their valid concern with the claim that Jesus was genuinely and unambiguously human.[23] Nevertheless Hick still wished to stand on the side of "historic orthodoxy", though he admitted to no longer knowing of any "knock-down" arguments against degree Christology.[24]

Hick attempted to restate Chalcedonian Christology in terms of *agape* rather than of substance. Between God and Jesus there was a dynamic identity of action. Such identity is true to Christian experience. The Christian claim concerning Jesus is that in him the divine *agape* has been "inhistorized". The "compassion and concern which was expressed in Jesus' dealings with the men and women he met were identical with God's *agapé* towards those particular individuals."[25] Jesus's *agape* was not merely a reflection or representation of God's *agape*; it "actually and literally was God's *Agapé* acting towards them". Hick argued that this way of putting the matter retained the intent of the Chalcedonian use of *homoousios*.[26]

> The eternal divine *Agapé* towards mankind "caused" Jesus' *agapé* towards the men and women whom he met, in a sense analogous to that in which the radiating energy of the sun "causes" the falling of its rays upon the earth's surface. That is to say, the sun radiating forth its light, and that light illuminating and warming the surface of the globe, form one continuous complex event; and likewise the divine *Agapé* exerting itself in relation to mankind, and operating on earth as the *agapé* of Jesus, form one continuous event in virtue of which we can say that Jesus was God's attitude to mankind incarnate.[27]

Hick acknowledged that his account of the relation between Jesus and God was no more "self-explanatory than the assertion that Christ was one substance with the Father". But he wished "tentatively to suggest that the continuity-of-agapéing formulation may today be more intelligible than the oneness-of-substance formulation. Let us proclaim the *homoagapé* rather than the *homoousia*! for we know, at least ostensibly (and what better way could there be?), what we mean by *agapé*, but, we do not know what we mean by substance".[28]

However it is possible to read Hick's *agape* Christology as yet another degree Christoogy. If Jesus's *agape* was identical with God's *Agape* (because the finite does not exclude the infinite), why can this not be said of everyone's *agape*? Further, if everyone's *agape* is not identical with God's *Agape*, then, by Hick's own argument, the finite does exclude the infinite, and God's *Agape* is not "all the *agapé* there is". If Hick's *agape* Christology is to be preserved from this interpretation one will have to say something to the effect that, though Jesus's *agape* appeared to be his, it was really God's. But then this is to move too far in the other direction. Consequently it would seem that Hick's *agape* Christology is either a degree Christology or a docetic one, and either way fails in the task of rendering the intention of Chalcedon.

Hick's *agape* Christology fails because Hick misconceived the nature of the task he undertook, the restating of "historic ortho-doxy" for today. Hick conceived the problem to be a matter of determining a new ontological category in which to express the relation between Jesus and God. He assumed that the point of the tradition is to assert that in some ontological category, whether of "entity" or "event", Jesus and God are the same ("numerically identical"). Either they are, in some sense, the same stuff (substance), or they perform the same act (*agape*).

In this Hick failed to appreciate fully the metaphorical use to which the language of substance was put in providing a *grammatical rule* for how one should and should not speak of Jesus and God together and apart. Rather, he treated them as descriptions. To speak of Jesus and God as being of the same substance, or their love as the same *agape*, is, for Hick, to describe literally the nature of their ontological (numerical) identity.

Hick did not discover, with Athanasius and Lonergan, the "fundamental little rule"[29] that all that is said of the Father is also said of the Son, except that the Son is Son, and not Father. This simple grammatical rule is, as Lonergan has brought out in his study of ante-Nicene theology, the point of the Nicene–Chalcedonian assertion of "consubstantiality". It is a proposition about propositions. "Whatever propositions are true of the Father are true of the Son also, except that the Father is Father and not Son and that the Son is Son and not Father."[30]

Hick appears to have been aware that the point of Chalcedon was not the assertion of consubstantiality as such, but the identification and distinction of God and Jesus, Father and Son. "The point of the *'homoousios'* ", he wrote, "was to insist upon identity in distinction from likeness, reflection, imitation, representation, or any other relation holding between entities which are numerically and ontically distinct."[31] He saw that it does not matter whether substance or some other category or language is used, so long as the intended identification and distinction is maintained. Hick pointed out that the "notion of 'substance' was *used* at Nicaea to insist . . . that between Jesus Christ and the Godhead there is an all-important identity" (emphasis added)![32] But this point was only half grasped, and not taken as one about *grammar*, about how one is to talk of God and Jesus. This much is clear from the fact that Hick felt it necessary to find a descriptive category in which to speak of identity. But it is also evident from the fact that he held that to speak of the consubstantiality of Jesus and God was "as though one were saying that Christ is made out of the same lump of divine substance as the Godhead and thus shares the divine nature, as two loaves of bread might be made from the same lump of dough and thus be composed of the same substance".[33]

Unfortunately, any insight that Hick may once have had into the Chalcedonian *use* of substance language, as a means of excluding misconceptions and directing the saying of Jesus in relation to God, has since been lost or abandoned. In a recent discussion of Rahner's Christology, Hick has argued that it is the Chalcedonian use of substance language which *necessitates* the ascription of uniqueness and absoluteness to Jesus.[34] Historically and theologically this is to get matters the wrong way round. Chalcedon sought only to safeguard the apostolic faith: the conviction that Jesus of Nazareth, in his life and death, was and is "God with us".

IV

A shift away from the seductions and misconceptions of "empiricism" appeared to have been presaged in Hick's 1973 essay "Incarnation and Mythology", in which he announced the intention of investigating the "logical character" of incarnational language. But in this and succeeding essays – "Jesus and the World Religions" and "Religious Pluralism and Absolute Claims"[35] – Hick continued to maintain that the object of Christian faith is

Jesus of Nazareth as he is known to biblical criticism. This is the mark of empiricist Christology. As I read Hick, there have been no fundamental developments in his Christological thinking since the early 1970s. All that he has written since has been a drawing-out of points established then.

Hick no longer holds, as he once did, that incarnational language, whether of substance or of *agape*, is descriptive of ontological realities. But this is not because he has come to see that such language is used heuristically or grammatically; he has come to see that it is merely "poetic" or "metaphorical". The traditional language of Christology does not literally describe the person of Jesus, but metaphorically expresses his significance for the believer.

Hick establishes sharp dichotomies between expression and description, myth and theory, metaphor and literal speech. For Hick metaphor points to, stands in or substitutes for, another thing, which, as its opposite, is literal. Indeed, one might think of myth as an "extended metaphor", within which discrete metaphors are placed and from which they are taken. But, however one draws up these relations and distinctions, the important point is that neither myth nor metaphor has cognitive content. They merely point to or substitute for something else that does, and at most express and/or evoke an appropriate attitude to that something else. They are at best secondary ciphers and at worst redundant decorations.

Janet Martin Soskice in her book *Metaphor and Religious Language* has provided a useful typology of theories of metaphor. She groups theories of metaphor according to how they understand "metaphorical achievement", how they explain the successful working of metaphor. She distinguishes between Substitutive, Emotive and Incremental theories: "those that see metaphor as a decorative way of saying what could be said literally; those that see metaphor as original not in what it says but in the affective impact it has; and those that see metaphor as a unique cognitive vehicle enabling one to say things that can be said in no other way".[36]

Hick's account of metaphor is both Substitutive and Emotive. It assumes, with the Substitutive theory, that "metaphor is a consequence of deviancy in word usage and that a given metaphor could be suppressed with no detriment to the cognitive content of the text in which it was found".[37] For Hick, to say that Jesus of

Nazareth is the Son of God does not tell us anything about who he is, but rather invites us to respond to him in a certain way. "It is suggested by the Emotive theory that, while the deviant usage loses any genuine cognitive content, at the same time it gains an unspecified emotional one."[38]

However, the Substitutive and Emotive accounts are deeply flawed. For they are unable to explain how a metaphor *appropriately* evokes an attitude without being guided by some cognitive content. Why is the metaphor of divine sonship appropriate to Jesus if not because he is in some sense (metaphorically or analogically) God's Son? There must, as Soskice reminds us, "be some guiding cognitive features to which the emotive response is the response. We cannot conceive of emotive 'import' apart from a cognitive content which elicits it."[39] If Jesus is in no sense the Son of God it is difficult if not impossible to understand why the attitude that such a statement might evoke could be in any sense appropriate to Jesus.

Further, the Substitutive and Emotive theories suffer from being prescriptive rather than descriptive. This becomes evident when one tries to dispense with metaphor and discovers that one has also thrown out a certain cognitive content. Hick's historico-critical and non-metaphorical account of Jesus simply does not have the same cognitive content as more traditional accounts. To say that Jesus was "intensely and overwhelmingly conscious of the reality of God . . . his spirit . . . open to God and his life a continuous response to the divine love . . . so powerfully God-conscious that his life vibrated, as it were, to the divine life".[40] is not the same as to say that Jesus is the Son of God, as that metaphor is located within the gospels and epistles. Indeed, the language of "experience", of being "overwhelmingly conscious" of God's reality, is wholly alien to the gospel accounts. It is, if not a misrepresentation of those accounts, at least a peculiarly modern interpretation of them.

It is not just that historical criticism presents a different person from that pictured by traditional Christology. The difference goes deeper than that. Historical criticism gives only a *representation*, a hypothetical picture of Jesus. But traditional Christology, as committed reflection on Jesus as the Christ, and as entrusted to a narrative rendition in the gospels, liturgy and life of the Church, actually *mediates* the meaning of Jesus as God's Word to and with the world. For it is not just a picture, a tentative representation, but a self-involving confession. Christology is an act not of representation, but of disclosure and mediation – as it were, a theatrical performance in which the distinction between representer and represented is overcome, and the division between stage and auditorium dissolved.[41]

Noting the failure of the Substitutive and Emotive theories to describe the achievement of metaphorical use is to become aware that Hick's assertions are no better founded than are the claims of logical "empiricism" about meaningful and meaningless statements. Hick does not provide, and makes no attempt to provide, reasons why one should adopt his account of metaphor rather than those of others.

If one refuses to be persuaded by Hick's prescriptive account of metaphor, and chooses instead to hold an incremental theory as descriptive of actual metaphorical use, one can happily accept his claim that incarnational language is metaphorical without being committed thereby to the view that it is meaningless. Instead one can, with Soskice, hold that metaphor is a way of "speaking about one thing in terms which are seen to be suggestive of another": a "form of language use with a unity of subject-matter and which yet draws upon two (or more) sets of associations, and does so, characteristically, by involving the consideration of a model or models".[42]

A metaphor – in its cognitive use – draws on at least two networks of associations in order to speak of its subject, and draws on them in view of an underlying model or models. These models are, as it were, the dominant associations in any particular reading or construal of metaphor. Thus, as Soskice notes, "in construing a metaphor like 'writhing script', one might associate with 'writhing' not only actions similar to writhing such as twisting and squirming, but also entities which are known to writhe, such as snakes or persons in pain".[43] The construal of metaphor depends upon an ability to see it as suggesting a model or models which enable one to go on extending its significance. Thus, if one says that a theologian's work "flows", "runs smoothly", is "full", "steady" or "deep", one understands that work is being spoken of in terms suggestive of a river. When the Church confesses Jesus as the Son of God, it speaks of him in terms suggestive of filiation, and the associations suggested by the model of sonship cannot be limited in advance. "It is the capacity of the lively metaphor to suggest models that enable us to 'go on' which gives the clue to the richness of metaphorical description."[44]

When the true depth of Christological metaphor is taken together with a grammatical account of incarnational doctrine,
Hick's strictures on the latter's cognitive vacuity and the former's
emotive force lose much of their persuasive power. To confess
Jesus as the Christ, the Son and Word of God, is to do more than
merely express *that* he is important; it is to say *why* he is
important. It is to say that in him one may have hope of having
found and finding that intimacy of humanity and divinity which
is the sign and promise of our own possibility.[45]

V

But why has Hick abandoned the richness of the traditional
metaphors for Jesus, and denied them cognitive content? Why has
he ridiculed the doctrine of the incarnation as unintelligible and
lacking in cogency, a misguided attempt to put together what for
ever must remain apart, a simple contradiction in terms, a failure
of elementary logic? He has offered two arguments. First, the
doctrine of the incarnation is historically compromised; it is
contingent upon the cultural context of its formation. Secondly, it
is logically incoherent, a matter of trying to fit different shapes –
"divinity" and "humanity" – into the same "space". The first of
these arguments rests on a number of historical parallels that Hick
draws between the "exaltation" or "deification" of Jesus in
Christianity and that of similar figures in other religions. Hick
insinuates that, if what was said of Jesus was said of others, one
should believe what was said of those others if one also believes
what was said similarly of Jesus.

Hick contends that "Buddhology and Christology developed in
comparable ways".

> The human Gautama came to be thought of as the incarnation of
> a transcendent, pre-existent Buddha as the human Jesus came to
> be though of as the incarnation of the pre-existent Logos or
> divine Son. And in the Mahāyāna the transcendent Buddha is
> one with the Absolute as in Christianity the eternal Son is one
> with God the Father. Thus Gautama was the *Dharma* (Truth)
> made flesh, as Jesus was the Word made flesh.[46]

In both Christianity and Buddhism one can see "at work a
tendency of the religous mind".[47] Hick does not want to say

whether the exaltation of Gautama in Mahāyāna Buddhism is right or wrong, but clearly he does want to suggest that it is a matter of the human mind, a process that, whether taking place within Buddhism or Christianity, can be fully understood without reference to anything other than the context of its formation.

A similar suggestion is implicit in the parallels Hick draws between the story of the resurrection of Jesus, and those of Lazarus, the widow's son and the daughter of Jairus.[48] These stories also display a common tendency of the religious mind which in the case of Jesus no more than indicates "that he had a special place within God's providence".[49] (Hick appears to ignore the fact that the Christian community has always read the stories of Lazarus, the widow's son and the daughter of Jairus in relation to the story of Jesus's death and resurrection, and thus as resonant reflections of the redemptive significance of that life and death.)

In sketching the parallels between various stories within the gospels and between different religious traditions Hick discerns the operation of a universal process which in the case of the Christian Church led it to break with the "unitarian monotheism" of its Jewish heritage and "worship a human being". He describes this as a common-enough movement of the religious mind in the "ancient world".[50] The doctrine of the incarnation is simply the product of cultural context, and that is that. It is not believable in our cultural context today.

I think that Hick, along with some of his fellow mythographers, has committed the genetic fallacy of supposing that, once one has said *how* a belief has come to expression, one has said all that is to be said. But to tell the story of a belief's genesis without also telling why it was so developed and for *what* it was developed is to tell only half the story. Thus in the case of Christological belief one must also pay attention to *what* the early Church was trying to say in drawing on the religious and cultural resources that it did. The suggestions implicit in the historical parallels that Hick draws are *non sequiturs*, and thus he has displayed little reason for assuming, as he does, that, whereas the Jews understood the ascription of divine sonship to be a metaphorical usage, the early Christians wished to affirm a literal, physical filiality between Jesus and God.[51]

There is a more interesting account to be given of the development of the doctrine of the incarnation than Hick allows, one which, taking belief in God's incarnation seriously, seeks to disclose the action of the spirit in the contingencies of history. It also has to be said that nothing follows from noting that the Christian confession of Jesus as the Son of God, consubstantial with the Father, is "very far from anything that the historical Jesus can reasonably be supposed to have thought or taught".[52] Hick appears to think that this somehow suggests the falsity of the traditional credal assertions of Jesus's relation to God. But he leaves the reason for this unclear. This unclarity, however, should not be surprising, because there is no reason to suppose that Jesus understood himself in terms other than those available to him in his cultural context – namely, those of his Jewish heritage. But from this it does not follow that he cannot be understood by others in terms drawn from other contexts, as indeed Hick himself does. Since in orthodox thought Chalcedon is the fruit of reflection in the power of the Spirit, its use of terms other than those available to Jesus does not imply that it thereby speaks other than the truth about him. "Through prayer and much argument, the Church *learnt* something – about itself, about its Lord, and about the adorable mystery which He taught us to address as 'Father'."[53]

Hick's second argument against the doctrine of the incarnation is the charge of incoherence. He contends that it has never been possible to give Chalcedon's diphystic Christology any meaningful content. "It remains a form of words without assignable meaning."[54] Here it is clear that Hick believes that Chalcedon was not merely safeguarding the faith of the Church against error, nor merely saying the *mystery* of Jesus Christ, but also attempting to render that mystery intelligible and comprehensible. This belief, I think, betrays a certain failure of historical and theological understanding. Though the Fathers at Chalcedon were concerned to preserve the Christian confession of Jesus, they did not presume to render God's act in his life and death comprehensible. They were properly aware that precisely because it was *God's* act it was an act beyond the powers of human rendition.

It is because Hick supposed that Chalcedon intended an intelligible *description* of the "God–Man" that he was led to deride its formulation as logically absurd: "To say, without explanation, that the historical Jesus of Nazareth was also God is as devoid of meaning as to say that this circle drawn with a pencil on paper is also a square".[55] From this observation Hick concludes that the "real point and value of the incarnational doctrine is not indicative but expressive, not to assert a metaphysical fact but to express a valuation and evoke an attitude".[56]

It is not entirely clear from Hick's text why he thinks that the doctrine of the incarnation is a logical mistake akin to asserting the existence of a square circle, but he appears to think that it involves God in doing the sort of thing that God cannot do. And, indeed, if one thinks that God is the sort of person that Hick takes God to be – a disembodied personal consciousness[57] – then there is a problem, one that has been well presented by Austin Farrer:

> "A" god could not also be "a" man, any more than a dog could be a cat. . . . We might have "a" god letting on to be "a" man . . . we might have a god who turned himself, or got turned, into a man so effectively that he just was a man, and couldn't help it, as the companions of Ulysses, perhaps, are to be taken to have become real pigs under the influence of Circe's wand . . . .[58]

Most theologians, and Hick himself at other times and in other texts, are not sanguine about human knowledge of God. Indeed, even Hick's fellow mythographer Maurice Wiles noted that it is "much harder to plot the border-line between sense and nonsense in talking about the mystery of God" than it is in talking about square circles.[59] But it appears to be just such putative knowledge of what God can and cannot do that lies behind Hick's criticism. This confidence is evident again in a more recent discussion of Rahner's Christology. Hick cites the following passage, in which Rahner attempts to say, after Chalcedon, the identification and distinction of Jesus and God:

> Only a *divine* Person can possess as its own a freedom really distinct from itself in such a way that this freedom does not cease to be truly free even with regard to the divine Person possessing it, while it continues to qualify this very Person as its ontological subject. For it is only in the case of God that it is conceivable at all that he himself can constitute something in a state of distinction from himself. This is precisely an attribute of his divinity as such and his intrinsic creativity: to be able, by himself and through his *own* act *as such*, to constitute something in being which by the very fact of its being radically dependent

(because *wholly* constituted in being), also acquires autonomy, independent reality and truth (precisely because it is constituted in being by the one, unique *God*), and all this precisely with respect to the God who constitutes it in being.[60]

Hick comments, "But the tortuous complexity of [Rahner's] argument conceals the simple proposition that God, being God, can do anything, and therefore can become a genuinely free and independent being whilst remaining God."[61] It is clearly this proposition that Hick cannot accept.

Not only can he not accept it, he cannot even accept that one could accept it without talking nonsense. However in order to advance this claim – that the doctrine of the incarnation is manifestly absurd – Hick has to know a lot about God and about what it is to be a human person. But the implicit claim to so much knowledge is highly questionable. What does Hick know about human nature that makes him so confident that God could not be incarnate in Jesus of Nazareth?

> Can it be said, without qualification, that we "know" man, that man is known to man, that man is transparent to himself? How are we to account for the profound disagreements that exist among men concerning man's meaning, nature and destiny? Is not fear breeding intolerance at the root of much human conflict? And is not one of the grounds of this fear the fact that we experience the irreducible otherness of people very different from ourselves as a threat to our own fragile achievement of identity and self-understanding?[62]

Must one not say with Lash that the "paradox and tragedy of man is that he is unable to attain his own nature because he is unable, and knows himself unable, fully and with complete transparency to "express" himself"?[63] Must one not admit that we are a mystery to ourselves? And, if one must, how can Hick deny *a priori* the possibility of the Christian claim to recognize in Jesus of Nazareth the "initial healing of the gap between expression and the reality that seeks expression"?[64]

Again, what does Hick know of God that means that God could not be incarnate in, consubstantial with, Jesus of Nazareth? To know this much implies that Hick knows something about the sort of thing that God is, and thus about the sort of thing that God cannot do; he knows that God and Jesus are mutually exclusive. But how does he know this? What are his warrants? However he knows it, it is not by way of Christian faith which starts out from, and only from, God's self-saying in Jesus Christ. And the God who thus speaks, lives and dies, is not a thing which could be exclusive of any other thing. "It may", as Herbert McCabe reminds us, "be part of the *meaning* of man that he is not any other creature; it cannot be part of the *meaning* of man that he is not God. God is not one of the items in some universe which have to be excluded if it is just man that you are talking about. God could not be an item in any universe."[65]

As Austin Farrer puts it, the "combination of God and man in Christ is not the combination of two determinate sorts of being, the divine and the human, either compatible with one another or incompatible".[66] Rather,

> The infinite energy who creates the human Jesus fortifies and redoubles his creative act in living, or being, that man by personal identification. And God, infinite God, no more ceases to be God by thus being Jesus than he ceases to be God by making Jesus. But neither, on its side, is the humanity of Jesus forced, altered, or overborne. For God's incarnation consists precisely in being the man Jesus and not in being anything else. God, becoming incarnate, does not first become a non-human angelic form and then go and force that form on Jesus. Jesus is the form his incarnation takes, and Jesus is a man.[67]

The doctrine of the incarnation cannot be denied on theological grounds. For theology – as the self-understanding of the Christian faith – must accept, as a truth of the life it serves, that its own knowledge of God is God's self-saying in the life and death of Jesus Christ. Thus it is a sufficient *theological* refutation of Hick's assertion to say that, if God was incarnate in Jesus of Nazareth, then that is what God could (and did) do.[68] And it is a sufficient *philosophical* refutation of Hick's criticism to indicate that the Christian doctrine of the incarnation does not assert a logical impossibility – that two different things are the same thing – but rather points to the definitive locus for "knowing" the world's mystery. The doctrine of the incarnation does no more than insist on an identification and a distinction in Christian speech about Jesus and God; an identification and distinction appropriately given in the metaphor of filiation. The charge of logical incoherence that Hick brings against the doctrine of the incarnation is plausible only if one first assumes an understanding of God and human nature for which there is no warrant in Christian faith or, indeed, anywhere other than in the Enlightenment perspective properly characterizable as rationalist and "empiricist".

No doubt Hick would not be satisfied with this answer. For it does not say *how* God was incarnate in Jesus of Nazareth. But it is a *non sequitur* to suppose that, because one cannot say *how* Jesus was and is the mystery of God with us and for us, one must deny *that* he was and is the mystery of human redempton and salvation. Human infirmity does not render the doctrine of the incarnation meaningless.

However, it would be fair to say that, in so far as one were unable even to begin to understand, however dimly, that Jesus of Nazareth was and is God incarnate, this might suggest that the doctrine rested on a mistake. Thus it is a legitimate theological task to try to say how the mystery of God with us in Jesus of Nazareth may be thought, spoken and lived. But such saying must also at the same time be an unsaying, a dialectic that alone may preserve us against supposing that we have grasped and possessed the mystery of our freedom as it is given to us in the person of Jesus the Christ.

VI

"At the heart of the Christian faith is the conviction that God has expressed himself concretely in our history, has become part of the form and meaning and texture of that history, as a man."[69] I cannot sketch here how this truth may best be said. A sketch of the doctrine of the incarnation, if it were to be comprehensive, would be driven back, as MacKinnon notes, to the "doctrine of the trinity, and in particular the easily dismissed question of the relation of the essential to the economic trinity".[70] It would have to mention such matters as the pre-existence of the Son and the ascension of Jesus to the right hand of the Father. But I can suggest how such a sketch would look in the face of Hick's criticism of the doctrine of the incarnation.

Clearly it must insist that God is not that which can be known to be incapable of doing what Christian faith believes God is

revealed as having done in the very act of doing it. That is a large
task to undertake, but its necessity must be a persistent theme,
evident in a continuing stress on the incomprehensibility, mystery and transcendence of God, as the one who is hidden and
"wholly other".

In just the same way as we are led to consider the incomprehensibility of God when we reflect on sin and suffering, death and
eternal life, so also we are led to do so when we seek to understand
the doctrine of the incarnation, to "grasp in faith the mystery
which is Jesus".[71] Just because theological reflection starts out
from and returns to the life and death of Jesus, it is forever
returning to and starting out from the mystery and incomprehensibility of God. For the "mystery of Jesus is, like all mysteries, the
mystery of what 'God' means".[72]

It is precisely because God is utterly transcendent that he can be
and is God for us and with us, the absolutely immanent. This
point is made by Rahner in the passage I have already quoted:
God is able to constitute Jesus in being as "radically dependent"
on and yet independent of himself, precisely because he is the one
"unique *God*".

> In the incarnation, the Logos creates by taking on, and takes on
> by emptying himself. Hence we can verify here, in the most
> radical and specifically unique way the axiom of all relationship
> between God and creature, namely that *the closeness and the
> distance, the submissiveness and the independence of the creature do
> not grow in inverse but in like proportion.* Thus Christ is most
> radically man, and his humanity is the freest and most indepen-
> dent, not in spite of, but because of its being taken up, by being
> constituted as the self-transcendence of God. (Emphasis
> added)[73]

In order to speak of the mystery of God in Christ one is forced to a
paradoxical dialectic. (The point of Chalcedon is precisely the
preservation of this possibility.) To speak of Jesus Christ is to
speak not only of a man who lived and died, but also of a future
that is yet to come, but which in some sense is here already – a
permanent possibility.[74] If one says that the Word became flesh
one must also say that the flesh became Word.[75] One must say that
God is a man: a man is God. One can say this without contradiction because, as Farrer, McCabe and Lash, amongst others, have

said, there is no "logical space" common to both God and humankind. Yet language is always suggesting the opposite, allowing one to speak easily of God and humankind together – here is the root of the confusions on which Hick's critique trades. "In so far as we speak of God and man in the same breath, we are obliged to do so in sentences the form of which suggests that we have to choose: either (with Hegel) 'God' as subject, and human existence as predicate, or (with Feuerbach) 'man' as subject and God as predicated abstraction."[76] But this is a false dilemma, no matter how unavoidable it may appear. Thus one is forced to dialectic. What is said positively in one place must be denied in another, or at least corrected. This is a permanent task.

Once one has grasped that God is "wholly other", the absolute difference – and is revealed as such in the power of transcendence given over to the *flesh* of the world – one begins to see how it is possible to untangle the confusions engendered by "empiricism". One does not have to begin Christology from either "below" or "above", one does not have to solve a peculiar metaphysical conundrum. One can begin to see that, if God and humankind do not occupy the same "space", and yet Jesus is God, our concepts of divinity and humanity have been put "back into the melting-pot". "The Christological confession does not affirm the mysterious conjunction of two 'knowns'. The problems of Christology, of human history – man's making of man – read as the history of God's agency, do not reside simply in the conjunction ('divine *and* human') but also in both of its terms."[77]

The mystery of Jesus Christ is both the mystery of God and the mystery of ourselves to ourselves. This is why the Christian confession of Christ, the task of bearing testimony in word and deed to his life and death, has always been a self-involving enactment of trust in him as the truth of the mystery we are to ourselves and the mystery of the God who is for us in the man Jesus.

VII

Hick has brought other considerations to bear in his critique of the doctrine of the incarnation, most notably the interrogative presence of the world religions.[78] How can Christianity continue to maintain the identification and distinction between Jesus and

God that is the rule of the doctrine of the incarnation when other faiths similarly claim an absolute allegiance and devotion? How can it be the case, as the doctrine suggests, that Jesus is the unique appearing of God and thus the definitive and absolute reality, when other religious traditions, not obviously deleterious to human flourishing, teach contrary "truths"? These and other questions represent considerations arising, as it were, from "outside" the Christian tradition and thus outside the limits of this paper. I have sought to combat only those "internal" criticisms that Hick has advanced from within Christianity against the cogency and intelligibility of the doctrine of the incarnation.

It has not been my brief to consider how theology may respond to the interrogation of the doctrine of the incarnation by the world religions. Elsewhere I have tried to show that Hick's argument from the reality of other religions to the need for abandonment of traditional Christian self-understanding is inconclusive.[79] Here I no more than hope to have shown the following: that the doctrine of the incarnation is not logically incoherent – it is not a matter of fitting different shapes into the same hole; that it is not historically compromised – the formation of the doctrine does not decide the matter of its truth; and finally, that Hick's antagonism to the doctrine is born of his inability to give it a foundation within an irreducibly "empiricist" or "positivist" conceptuality. The doctrine of the incarnation cannot be proved, only prayed.

NOTES

I acknowledge the invaluable help afforded me in the writing of this paper by my friend and fellow theologian Gavin D'Costa.

1. John Hick, "Jesus and the World Religions", in Hick (ed.), *The Myth of God Incarnate* (London: SCM, 1977) p. 178.
2. Personal comment to the author.
3. John Coventry, "The Myth and the Method," *Theology*, 81 (1978) 252–60.
4. Ibid., p. 255.
5. On Christology from "above" and "below" see Nicholas Lash, "Up and Down in Christology", in S. W. Sykes and D. Holmes (eds), *New Studies in Theology I* (London: Duckworth, 1980) pp. 31–46.
6. H. Küng and P. Lapide, *Brother or Lord? A Jew and a Christian Talk Together about Jesus*, tr. E. Quinn (London: Collins, 1977) p. 23.
7. On Lonergan see David Tracy, *The Achievement of Bernard Lonergan* (New York: Herder and Herder, 1970).

8. For simple, friendly, but devastating criticism of critical method see F. G. Downing, "Towards a Fully Systematic Scepticism – In the Service of Faith", *Theology*, 89 (1986) 355–61.

9. Austin Farrer, *Interpretation and Belief* (London: SPCK, 1976) p. 127.

10. Coventry, "The Myth and the Method", *Theology*, 81, p. 256.

11. Cf. John 20:24–9.

12. Frances Young in Michael Goulder (ed.), *Incarnation and Myth: The Debate Continued* (London: SCM, 1979) p. 62; emphasis removed.

13. John Hick, "The Christology of D. M. Baillie", *Scottish Journal of Theology*, 11 (1958) 1–12.

14. D. M. Baillie, *God Was in Christ: An Essay on Incarnation and Atonement* (London: Faber and Faber, 1948).

15. Ibid., p. 128.

16. John Hick, "The Non-Absoluteness of Christianity", in John Hick and Paul Knitter (eds), *The Myth of Christian Uniqueness*, (Maryknoll, NY: Orbis, 1987) p. 32.

17. See Gavin D'Costa, "*Extra ecclesiam nulla salus* Revisited", in I. Hamnett (ed.), *Religious Pluralism and Unbelief: Studies Critical and Comparative* (London: Routledge, 1990).

18. Hick, "The Christology of D. M. Baillie", *Scottish Journal of Theology*, 11, p. 9.

19. *God and the Universe of Faiths*, pp. 170–1.

20. John Hick, "Christology at the Crossroads", in F. G. Healey (ed.), *Prospect for Theology* (London: James Nisbet 1966) pp. 137–66.

21. *God and the Universe of Faiths*, pp. 148–64.

22. Hick, "Christology at the Crossroads", in Healey (ed.), *Prospect for Theology*, p. 139.

23. Ibid., p. 150.

24. Ibid., p. 149.

25. Ibid., p. 154.

26. Ibid., p. 155.

27. Ibid., p. 164.

28. Ibid., p. 165.

29. Bernard Lonergan, *A Second Collection*, ed. W. F. J. Ryan and B. T. Tyrrell (London: Darton, Longman and Todd 1974) p 250.

30. Ibid., p. 251.

31. Hick, "Christology at the Crossroads", in Healey (ed.), *Prospect for Theology*, p. 150.

32. Ibid.

33. Ibid., p. 151.

34. *Problems of Religious Pluralism*, p. 57.

35. John Hick, "Religious Pluralism and Absolute Claims", in L. S. Rouner (ed.), *Religious Pluralism* (Notre Dame, Ind.: University of Notre Dame Press, 1984) pp. 193–213.

36. Janet Martin Soskice, *Metaphor and Religious Language* (Oxford: Oxford University Press, 1985) p. 24.

37. Ibid., p. 27.

38. Ibid.

39. Ibid.

40. Hick, "Jesus and the World Religions", in *The Myth of God Incarnate*, p. 172.

41.   See further Gerard Loughlin, "Myths, Signs and Significations", *Theology* 89 (1986) 268–75.
42.   Soskice, *Metaphor and Religious Language*, p. 49.
43.   Ibid., p. 50.
44.   Ibid., p. 51.
45.   For a critical treatment of Hick's account of metaphor that draws on the work of Paul Ricoeur see Chester Gillis, *A Question of Final Belief: John Hick's Pluralistic Theology of Salvation* (London: Macmillan, 1989).
46.   Hick, "Jesus and the World Religions", in *The Myth of God Incarnate*, p. 169.
47.   Ibid., p. 170.
48.   John 11: 1–44: Luke; 7:11–17; and Mark 5:35–43.
49.   Hick, "Jesus and the World Religions", in *The Myth of God Incarnate*, p. 171.
50.   Ibid., pp. 173–4.
51.   Ibid., p. 175.
52.   Ibid., p. 171.
53.   Nicholas Lash, "A Leaky Sort of Thing? The Divisiveness of Michael Dummet", *New Blackfriars*, 68 (1987) 556.
54.   Hick, "Jesus and the World Religions", in *The Myth of God Incarnate*, p. 178.
55.   Ibid.
56.   Ibid.
57.   *Problems of Religious Pluralism*, p. 132.
58.   Farrer, *Interpretation and Belief*, pp. 129–30.
59.   In Goulder (ed.), *Incarnation and Myth*, pp. 5–6.
60.   Karl Rahner, *Theological Investigations*, 20 vols (London: Darton, Longman and Todd 1961–84) I, 162; quoted in *Problems of Religious Pluralism*, p. 57.
61.   *Problems of Religious Pluralism*, p. 58.
62.   Lash, "Up and Down in Christology", in Sykes and Holmes (eds), *New Studies in Theology I*, pp. 40–1.
63.   Ibid.
64.   Ibid.
65.   Herbert McCabe, "The Myth of God Incarnate", *New Blackfriars*, 58 (1977) 353.
66.   Farrer, *Interpretation and Belief*, p. 137.
67.   Ibid., p. 130.
68.   E. L. Mascall, *Theology and the Gospel of Christ: An Essay in Reorientation* (London: SPCK, 1977) p. 131.
69.   Nicholas Lash, *A Matter of Hope: A Theologian's Reflections on the Thought of Karl Marx* (London: Darton, Longman and Todd, 1981) p. 143.
70.   D. M. MacKinnon, " 'Substance' in Christology: A Cross-Bench View", in S. W. Sykes and J. P. Clayton (eds.), *Christ, Faith and History: Cambridge Studies in Christology* (Cambridge: Cambridge University Press, 1972) p. 296.
71.   McCabe, "The Myth of God Incarnate", *New Blackfriars*, 58, p. 352.

72. Ibid., p. 353.
73. Rahner, *Theological Investigations*, IV, 17.
74. Lash, *A Matter of Hope*, p. 143.
75. Ibid., p. 144.
76. Ibid.
77. Ibid., p. 186.
78. *An Interpretation of Religion*.
79. See Gerard Loughlin, "Noumenon and Phenomena", *Religious Studies*, 23 (1987) 493–508. The task is carried through more systematically in Gavin D'Costa, *Theology and Religious Pluralism: The Challenge of Other Religions* (Oxford: Basil Blackwell, 1987).

EDITOR'S NOTE. There is no "Critical Response" to Loughlin's paper, as he was unable to attend the conference at Claremont and his paper therefore was not discussed.

Reply

JOHN HICK

It may seem strange to suggest that so persistently polemical a critic as Gerard Loughlin does not differ as much as he supposes from the positions he is attacking. And yet his arguments are often directed not against what I have written, but against his own misperceptions of what I have written. Perhaps a better way to put it is that he imposes his own agenda on texts that he is discussing and sometimes treats them as though they were dealing with different concerns from those which they profess to address. And, of course, the meaning of a philosophical suggestion depends in part on the question to which it is offered as an answer.

Thus it is high on Loughlin's agenda to oppose empiricism – a term which he uses in a flexible and undefined way. I am an empiricist in the sense of holding that we come to know "what there is and how things are" through experience: sense experience, moral experience, aesthetic experience and religious experience – all of these, as I have argued, being "theory-laden" in that they involve the use of concepts. Loughlin supposes that as an empiricist I must believe that, if Jesus was God (or God the Son) incarnate, historical research would be able to establish this. Lumping the seven contributors to *The Myth of God Incarnate* together as a single persona, he attributes to them, and hence to me, the view that "If the incarnation of God in Jesus cannot be verified by empirical/historical means, then it is unbelievable."[1] However, I do not hold any such view. Certain subsidiary related matters are, of course, open to historical inquiry. For example, whether Jesus was throughout his life sinless is a question of historical fact, though one which we do not have sufficient information to be able to settle. But whether Jesus was God incarnate is obviously not "something that can be seen simply by using the tools of historical criticism";[2] and to attribute this view to me is a misplaced projection on Loughlin's part.

But, while historical criticism could never establish that Jesus was God incarnate, it might reveal, at least as a judgement of high probability, that he was a humanly, morally and religiously very impressive person who claimed to be God incarnate. If historical

investigation *did* reveal this, the traditionally orthodox Christology would have a historical basis. In fact, however, historical
research reveals a humanly, morally and religiously very impressive person who did *not* claim to be God (or God the Son) incarnate.
Loughlin implicitly grants this when he locates the central issue
not in the historical person of Jesus, but in the question of whether
the development of the Church's Christology was or was not
providentially guided.[3] It is worth noting that this is a fairly recent
move within traditional orthodoxy. For some seventeen centuries
it was believed that Jesus did claim to be God incarnate, and
Fourth Gospel sayings such as "I and my Father are one", "He that
hath seen me hath seen the Father", were treated as historical
sayings of Jesus. Today even conservative (other than fundamen-
talist) exegetes grant that this cannot be sustained. There has thus
been a major shift from believing that Jesus was God because he
said so, to believing it because the New Testament is sometimes
close to saying so, to believing it because the Church came to say
so.

Moving to a related issue, Loughlin thinks that, according to me,
"neither myth nor metaphor has cognitive content".[4] This is a
misunderstanding. For an utterance to have cognitive content is, I
take it, for it to be either true or false. It is clearly possible to make
true and false metaphorical statements (for example, "Hitler was a
demon" and "Hitler was an angel"); and to make true and false
mythological statements (for instance, "Jesus was God incarnate"
and "Hitler was God incarnate"). I have argued that the doctrine of
the incarnation is metaphorically or mythologically true, although
lacking in any precise literal content. The incarnational metaphor
is a natural and effective one: "Joan of Arc incarnated the spirit of
France in 1429"; "George Washington incarnated the spirit of
American independence in 1776"; "Winston Churchill incarnated
the British will to resist Hitler in 1940." In these cases we are
dealing with expository myths which are capable of being trans-
lated (though less effectively) into literal terms, in distinction from
myths which are responses to "questions to which no answer is
possible in a literal use of language".[5] I regard the incarnational
myth as a myth of the former kind, one that is capable of being
spelled out non-mythologically. Its non-mythological meaning is
something like this: that Jesus was so open and obedient to God
that God was able to act through him in relation to those whom
Jesus encountered. Jesus could have said what the *Theologica*

Germanica (ch. 10) tell us that all Christians should learn to say: "I would fain be to the eternal Goodness what his own hand is to a man". This, in my view, is the concrete meaning of the mythological statement that God was incarnate in Jesus. It is interesting to see Loughlin moving in this same direction when he says that "one can happily accept [Hick's] claim that incarnational language is metaphorical without being committed thereby to the view that it is meaningless".[6] Since I have never held that it is meaningless (I have suggested above, and in many places, what I think the incarnational metaphor means), perhaps Loughlin does not after all differ from the view he thinks he is criticizing! Indeed, there are indications that he takes further than I do the thesis that incarnational language is metaphorical; for he says that "Hick failed to appreciate fully the metaphorical use to which the language of substance was put" at Nicaea and Chalcedon.[7] Loughlin thinks that the creed writers intended their formulations to be understood metaphorically. I am doubtful about this: I think it more likely that the Nicene and Chalcedonian creeds were intended as literal–metaphysical rather than as metaphorical statements. But I welcome nevertheless Loughlin's perception that a metaphorical interpretation of them is much more readily defensible than a literal interpretation.

One can ask concerning incarnational language whether a literal (non-metaphorical, non-mythological) construal of it is capable of being spelled out in any clear and acceptable way. The kinds of literal spellings-out of "Jesus was God the Son incarnate" that have been attempted have been in terms of identity of substance, of two natures, of two minds, of a divine mind in a human body, and of kenosis. I have argued that none of them is successful. All that is then left, other than metaphor, is "a form of words without assignable meaning". Loughlin comes fairly close to this when he translates the idea of divine incarnation into such vague (and metaphorical?) terms as that "Jesus was and is the mystery of God with us and for us".[8] This could well mean much the same as my own translation in terms of Jesus's openness and responsiveness to God's loving will for humanity. Neither translation requires us to solve the insoluble problem posed by traditional orthodoxy of a being who is both divinely omniscient and humanly fallible, divinely omnipotent and humanly limited, eternal and yet born in time, omnipresent and yet locally physical. In abandoning that traditional nest of problems, arising from a literal understanding of incarnational language, and opting instead for a metaphorical construal, Loughlin seems, without noticing it, to have joined those who speak of the myth of God incarnate.

NOTES

1. Gerard Loughlin, above, p. 184.
2. Ibid.
3. Loughlin, above, p. 195.
4. Loughlin, above, p. 190.
5. *Interpretation of Religion*, p. 349.
6. Loughlin, above, p. 192.
7. Loughlin, above, p. 188.
8. Loughlin, above, p. 199.

Part IV
On *An Interpretation of Religion:* A Concluding Narrative

9

At the Bend in the Road: A Story about Religious Pluralism

JULIUS LIPNER

In his essay "Seeing-as and Religious Experience", John Hick quotes Wittgenstein as follows. "I should not like my writing to spare other people the trouble of thinking – but, if possible, to stimulate someone to thoughts of his own."[1] Hick uses this statement as a basis for extrapolating Wittgenstein's idea of "seeing-as" in a context not considered by Wittgenstein. I too should like to use one aspect of Hick's multifaceted writings, no doubt with his approval, to stimulate thought of my own. This is the aspect concerned with religious pluralism. This paper is intended as a critical tribute to a thinker whose writings on this and other topics have become of seminal importance in contemporary philosophy of religion. In true Hickoid tradition, let me resort to narrative.

A small band of travellers is walking along a broad, winding road. It is the only such road there is, and passes through terrain that is sometimes perilous for one reason or another and sometimes safe enough; in fact no one knows what each new turn in the road will bring. The travellers have no choice but to go on; a nameless dread threatens to overpower anyone who backtracks or remains in one place for too long. The company comprises a Hindu, a Muslim, a Jew, a Buddhist, a Christian, someone called a Religious Pluralist, and an Atheist. (There was a time when each walked alone, pausing occasionally to scoff or look on indifferently when another traveller encountered a hazard of the road. But of late, I am glad to say, they have begun journeying together, conversing with one another and helping each other to cope with the vagaries of the road. Even Atheist, surprisingly you may think, is one of the band – now amused, now repelled by the reactions, squabbles and agreements of the others. Perhaps Atheist is in need of entertainment on an otherwise tiresome journey, or even derives moral support from the situation. I don't know. Anyway, it is a homogeneous little band from the standpoint of its members' interest in and knowledge of one another's views about life, and this makes for some interesting conversations along the way.)

Each religious member of the group interprets the road as terminating eventually at a Celestial City – the goal of the journey. But each understands the goal differently. For Hindu, the Celestial City is a place where all earthly differences – of sex, personality, even individuality itself – vanish like mists in the noonday sun in a blissful identity of being: there, all is the One and the One is all. Muslim, Christian and Jew, on the other hand, agree that the Celestial City is ruled by an infinitely wise, benign and powerful king (Christian actually believes in a Trinity who act as one, and who, helpfully for the purposes of this story, may be referred to in the singular). This divine king watches over the progress along the road of each member of the group, ready unobtrusively to protect, encourage and comfort, as and when the situation requires. But the three disagree about other features of the Celestial City, its ruler and his relationship towards them. This often leads to heated debate among the company, for it is generally held not only that it is necessary to put one's beliefs about the goal into practice in order to arrive safely, but also that, the closer one's beliefs about the goal are to the truth, the more securely can one interpret the potentially hazardous signposts along the road. (Here I must mention that from time to time the group comes across signposts with signs pointing to shortcuts leading off in different directions and purportedly joining up with the main road some way ahead. Many of the signs seem to be "personalized", inviting the way-farer to take a shortcut along, for example, "Brahman's Walk", or "Nirvāṇa way", or "Prophet's Pass" or "Via Thomistica". Some of these signs are supposed to be genuine, but ever since Rank Relativist, a former member of the band, broke away down a path called "Sceptics' Delight" and vanished from ken – Rank Relativist had promised to await them on the road ahead – no one has dared to take the same risk.)

Buddhist, who is not a theist, believes, like the other religious members of the group, that one's attitude to the goal has an important bearing on progress along the road, but is unhappy with the tendency of the theists to speak confidently about what the Celestial City is like. Particularly irksome is the way the theists all claim that the imposing gates of the Celestial City display the distinctive symbol associated with their own particular faith. Buddhist, on the other hand, prefers to talk of the goal in negative terms as a place where there is no suffering, no yearning, no death, no change, no conditions. Occasionally Buddhist will speak of the Celestial City as a place of peace and bliss – no more.

Perhaps this consistent reticence is the reason for a curious rapport with Atheist, who maintains that there is no such thing as a goal to their journey, Celestial City or otherwise. The road, says Atheist, is aimless and no one can speak with certainty of the end; perhaps the road goes on forever, or perhaps it terminates abruptly on the lip of a precipice beyond which lies utter darkness. Like the others, who carry their particular authoritative texts with them, religious and/or otherwise, which each consults from time to time for comfort and guidance (and, alas, also for purposes of argument), Atheist too, you may be sure, carries works of reference and uses these to justify a non-religious interpretation of the various features of the road.

All, however, are puzzled by Religious Pluralist. No one is quite sure how to make sense of this character. This is because Pluralist espouses two alternate sets of beliefs about the Celestial City and the different religious interpretations concerning it. Pluralist prefers to talk about the beliefs of each set somewhat vaguely as beliefs about the "Transcendent" or the "Real" or the "Ultimate", and in discussion deploys one or other set apparently as and when the occasion demands it. I hasten to add that Pluralist is not called a "Pluralist" because of this espousal of more than one set of beliefs about the Transcendent – in fact, this just happens to be a peculiarity of the Pluralist in our story. No, Pluralist is so called because of the *kind* of beliefs held, and it is to this that we now turn briefly.

The others, of course, through their association with Pluralist, are becoming familiar with both sets of beliefs. It will be as well for me to explain their gist, however, the better to enable you to appreciate this story. In essence, the first set of beliefs is derived from the great guru, HickWick; the second from the spiritual Master, Cobbwebb.

Guru HickWick taught that there is but one Celestial City – or Transcendent/Real as he preferred to call all that this City stands

for – whose impact on responsive human consciousness is mani-
fest through the different, complex, culturally conditioned religions we know as Hinduism, Buddhism, Islam, Christianity,
Sikhism, Judaism, and so on. One cannot prove by purely logical
or rational processes that the Transcendent exists; this would be to
work with too naïve an understanding of "proof" or, indeed,
"reason". So far as belief in the Transcendent is concerned, the
world in which we live is systematically ambiguous, putative
evidence for the existence of the Transcendent engendering as
equally plausible and rational the alternative faith-responses of
the atheist and the religious believer. It is what lies at the end of
the road, if there is such an end, that will decide the issue. Here it
is reasonable to suppose that we shall have a cumulative experience   which   verifies   beyond   rational   doubt   either   the
naturalistic/atheistic or religious interpretation of our journey
through life. Rather grandly, HickWick called this decisive experience "eschatological verification".[2] (I may add that, while some
of the religious members of the group are grateful to HickWick for
the philosophical precision and contextualization of his concept of
eschatological verification, they point out that the idea underlying
it is religiously very old. For example, Christian likes to quote an
ancient seer called Paul, who said, "I consider that the sufferings
of this present time are not worth comparing with the glory that is
to be revealed to us."[3] And the others say the like.)

For HickWick, we cannot know the nature of the Real as it is in
itself (or *an sich,* as he would say): this noumenal reality transcends our consciousness. All we have are the various representative "faces" – better, interfaces – of the Real as it phenomenalizes in
this or that way through human experience, in the different
religious traditions. HickWick makes the point that this distinction between the Real *an sich* and the Real as humanly perceived is
common to all the major religions. A number of fragments of his
works have come down to us; some quotations might be helpful.
One statement has it that there is

> a distinction that is to be found in different forms and with
> different emphasis within each of the great traditions, the
> distinction between the Real *an sich* (in him/her/itself) and the
> real as humanly experienced and thought. In Christian terms
> this is the distinction between God in God's infinite and eternal
> self-existent being, "prior" to and independent of creation, and

God as related to and known by us as creator, redeemer and sanctifier. In Hindu though it is the distinction between *nirguṇa* Brahman, the Ultimate in itself, beyond all human categories, and *saguna* Brahman, the Ultimate as known to finite consciousness as a personal diety[4] [here the text becomes illegible] . . . . In Mahāyāna Buddhism there is the distinction between the *dharmakāya,* the eternal cosmic Buddha-nature, which is also the infinite Void (*śūnyata*), and on the other hand the realm of heavenly Buddha figures (*sambhogakāya*) and their incarnations in the earthly Buddhas (*nirmāṇakāya*). This varied family of distinctions suggests the perhaps daring thought that the real *an sich* is one but is nevertheless capable of being humanly experienced in a variety of ways. This thought lies at the heart of the pluralistic hypothesis which I am suggesting.[5]

Thus, the independently existing noumenal Real phenomenalizes[6] in the different religious traditions in distinctively personal or impersonal/transpersonal ways, which HickWick calls "personae" and "impersonae" respectively. In what we know as HickWick's major work on the nature of the religious enterprise, entitled *An Interpretation of Religion,* it is said, "A divine *persona* arises at the interface between the real and the human spirit, and is thus a joint product of transcendent presence and earthly imagination, of divine revelation and human seeking."[7] The same may be said, *mutatis mutandis* (for here, the Guru reminds us, we cannot speak in specifically *theistic* terms), with regard to the various impersonae of the Transcendent. Examples given of the personae are "God the Father" in the Christian tradition, "Adonai" in Judaism, "Allah" in Islam, and "Īshvara" in Hinduism; examples of the impersonae are *saccidānanda* in Advaitic Hinduism, the "Tao" in Chinese religion, and the *dharmakāya* in Mahāyāna. It is important to note that, for HickWick, personae are personal and impersonae are non-personal representations in human experience of the Transcendent; we shall see, when I take up the story again, that this becomes an important issue.

Finally, we may note that for the Guru these "many different perceptions of the Real, both theistic and non-theistic, can only establish themselves as authentic by their soteriological efficacy".[8] From general and particular evidence of human goodness in a global context, we must conclude that the major world religions, at least, are all equally soteriologically efficacious and that the various representations of the real, both personal and impersonal, are equally authentic. In this life, there is no way of telling which accredited persona or impersona of the Transcendent comes closest to capturing its nature; the truth, such as it is, can only be known eschatologically. Needless to say, as will become clear, some members of our little band do not accept that all religions are equally valid both soteriologically and veridically; indeed, they make the point to Pluralist that HickWick's position fails to distinguish adequately between the veridical and soteriological validity of religion. All of them maintain – and this is not unusual – that, though the adherents of other faiths may arrive at the Celestial City, it is in their own religious tradition that the nature of the Real has been grasped most veridically, not indeed by human effort alone but through some sort of gratuitous sovereign self-revealing of the Real. This revealed truth is of great aid to arriving safely at the goal. After all, even Hindu is fond of quoting the scriptural passage "This Self cannot be attained by discussion, or intelligence or by much scriptural instruction; it can be attained by the one whom it chooses. To such a one the Self reveals its own form."[9] More about this point later.

We come now to the second set of Pluralist's beliefs, the set deriving from Master Cobbwebb. In essence, the two sets of beliefs differ as follows: whereas according to the HickWickian hypothesis there is but one ultimate Real which interrelates with human consciousness in the different religious traditions in the way described, Cobbwebb proposed that there is more than one Ultimate, answering (in the existential or experiential order) to different *kinds* of sets of ultimate questions posed in the different religious traditions. Cobbwebb puts it like this:

> Why not allow, at least as a working hypothesis, that what is named by "Yahweh" and "the Father of Jesus Christ" is not the same as what is named by "Emptiness"? Such a hypothesis would not imply that one is real and the other not. Quite the contrary, it could mean that each has just the reality and character attributed to it by those who are recognized authorities in the two traditions. We could acknowledge that both are transcendent in very important ways without identifying them. And we could allow each tradition to define the proper mode of relating to that of which it has most experience. We could allow parallels and similarities to appear, but we would have no need to obscure differences at the most fundamental level.[10]

Only a few fragments of Master Cobbwebb's writings are in Pluralist's possession. From these it is not clear whether he taught (1) that there is only one "existential" Ultimate or that there is more than one such Reality corresponding to possibly different sets of ultimate questions in, say, the theistic traditions (that is, *as reals*, are some or all of the following examples different: the Adonai of Judaism, the God of Christianity, the Allah of Islam, the Īshvara of devotional Hinduism?); and (2) that there is a plurality of final states/experiences (corresponding to, for example, *nibbāna* in Theravāda, Emptiness in Mahāyāna, and the Tao of Chinese religion) or that there is only one Ultimate of *this* kind. At any rate, as the extract quoted shows, Cobbwebb suggested that at a fundamental level there is more than one Ultimate. Further, he believed that the Ultimates of religious experience are mutually compatible: 'I am convinced that the respective claims of the [text obscured here] scriptures are profoundly different and that finally they are complementary rather than contradictory.'[11]

This is an interesting hypothesis, and our travellers have begun to consider it. Christian remarked once that it was quite similar, in a parallel context, to the views of Yogi Zena on mystical experience. The Yogi had argued that the various kinds of mystical experience – the theistic, the monistic, the solipsistic – claimed by mystics in different religious traditions as ultimate are not fundamentally the same, as some thinkers have maintained. They do not "make contact" with the same (or same level of) transcendent being, remaining only inessentially different owing to different cultural influences on their experiences; on the contrary, they are intrinsically different kinds of ultimate experience. However, unlike Cobbwebb, Zena went on to evaluate and grade these experiences, placing the theistic at the top of his scale.[12] Now on with the story.

It had been a particularly tiring day, spent for the most part under a burning sun. The company had been hard put to it to cope with the vagariees of the road, in particular a signpost with the notice "To Each-their-own" which pointed down a little path running into a cool forest glade. The sign had generated a heated discussion with Pluralist at the centre, who argued, in Cobbwebbian mode, that the path was genuine. The others thought it treacherous. Eventually Pluralist was prevailed upon to stick with the group – not without some jostling and pulling, I might add.

It was now dusk. For some time the road had been winding its way up the face of a mountain, the first of a chain which stretched into the distance. The travellers were dispirited, weary and hungry, and had decided to pitch camp at the first suitable spot after the next bend in the road, visible some way ahead. In a short while they straggled up to it, Muslim and Christian in front. Abruptly, the two stopped short – open-mouthed. The mountain-side fell sheer at their feet, and valleys and distant plains stretched out before them. It was an awesome sight. But it was not this that had caused consternation. Almost immediately the others (except Atheist) came up, and looked and gasped. (Atheist, who had a plump sufficiency about the person which not surprisingly had a delaying effect physically, usually brought up the rear.) In the distance, under a dying sun, in a V-shaped swirl of hazy mist and cloud between two jagged peaks, something caught their eye. Dimly it shimmered for a few seconds more and then faded from sight. Even Atheist, who had joined the group, was staring intently in the direction to which some still pointed.

Eyes shining, Christian was the first to cry out, "The Celestial City! It's there. I saw it!" Then, turning sharply towards the others, Christian said triumphantly, "Now do you believe me? I was right, wasn't I?"

Muslim and Jew were equally roused. They too had seen something, something which seemed to be the silhouette of a great city glowing in the half-light.

Muslim replied, "Yes, I saw it!" Then, after a pause, "What do you mean, *you* were right? *We* were right! There *is* a City out there."

"But the symbol on the gates," cried Christian, "didn't you see? It looked exactly like the symbol of *my* faith!"

Before Muslim could reply, Jew said with spirit, "*Your* symbol? Nonsense! It looked exactly like *my* symbol."

"No mine!" cried Muslim.

The other four had remained silent. Now Atheist spoke. "You three are imagining things as usual. But we can't stand here arguing. It's getting late. First let's find somewhere safe to camp and eat, and when we're resting we can discuss what happened."

This seemed sound advice. It was now quite dark, and it would be wise to pitch camp as quickly as possible. Fortunately, after a few minutes' walk, they came upon a large hollow in the mountain-face; it was easily defensible and at the mouth of it they could light a small fire and cook some food. So they pitched camp there for the night and unloaded their backpacks in an air of excitement. It was only after a largely silent meal, and some calm had descended on the little band huddled round a crackling fire, that discussion started on what had happened at the bend in the road.

"I tell you I saw it," said Christian soberly, "the Celestial City, with its massive gates shimmering in the haze. All right, I'll admit the scene was indistinct, but I seemed to recognize that symbol at once."

"You thought you saw a Celestial City," said Buddhist slowly. "So did I. But I could make out no symbol. I realize now that what I saw was a cloud-formation – a transient image that came and went. We were exhausted, and saw a projection of our own expectations."

Hindu and Atheist agreed. "I saw no City," said Atheist.

"You're wrong!" said Muslim vigorously. "That was no mirage or projection of the imagination. It was real enough. Some of us were given a glimpse of the Celestial City by the Lord to encourage us at this point in the journey. Those of you who were not properly disposed thought they saw nothing or an illusion. Those whose religious beliefs are closer to the truth" (here Muslim looked towards Jew and Christian) "saw more of the reality, but not quite enough to recognize the true symbol on the gates. What they glimpsed in this respect was probably a projection of their minds. Say what you will, that was my symbol I saw at the bend."

"You've got the bends all right," said Atheist good-humouredly. (Atheist's jokes were not always very good.) "I saw nothing but mountains and mist and curling clouds in hazy light. There's certainly no Celestial City out there. If you don't like "the bends", let's just call this a clear case of creative imagination", and Atheist chuckled audibly.

Though both Christian and Jew agreed with Muslim about the veridical nature of what they had seen, neither was happy with the way Muslim claimed to have had the definitive vision. Before either could register a protest, a voice was heard. It was Pluralist's.

"That's just the point – the subjective nature of what we all saw. For consider: Christian, Muslim and Jew saw a Celestial City, with the symbols of their respective faiths. Hindu spoke earlier to me of seeing "something like a city", but it was pretty nondescript – no mention of symbols here! Buddhist claims to have seen a cloud-formation, while Atheist saw only clouds! As for me – I saw something too, but believe me when I say that I thought I could make out twin cities, one rather like a mirror image of the other! Well, don't you see?" Pluralist looked around. "It couldn't have been otherwise. There is no definitive view from where we stand. The theists caught sight of what corresponds to personae of the celestial Reality; the other believers saw impersonae (if Buddhist glimpsed anything of it at all!), while Atheist saw nothing celestial, of course. So I'm making two points really: first, that we saw what we've each been conditioned to see; secondly, that from where we are on the journey the view towards the goal cannot but be inherently ambiguous, hazy, "indistinct", as a philosopher[13] once said."

Christian said pointedly, "Pluralist, *you* believe there's a Celestial City out there, don't you?"

Pluralist considered. "Yes, I do; perhaps there's more than one. From this side there's no way of being more specific."

"The more you talk like that," said Christian with some bitterness, "the more like Buddhist and Atheist you sound. I'm never quite sure whether you're a believer or not, never mind the *kind* of believer you are! Look here, wasn't it one of your own Pluralist mentors, the sage Zorun, who criticized HickWick on this score? Zorun maintained that, the more you set aside specific religious doctrines, the more questionable it becomes whether a *religious*, as opposed to a non-religious, commitment is what gives life ultimate significance. As any religious hypothesis, he said, about the nature of reality is made more indefinite, more religiously agnostic, the available inductive evidence to support that hypothesis is not increased.[14] In fact, it decreases. You can't have it both ways," continued Christian; "you can't keep harping on the way a religious realist's interpretation of the world is supported inductively by the cumulative evidence of what passes for religious experience globally, and at the same time attenuate the existence of the Real behind the cognitively impenetrable phenomena you call personae and impersonae. So watch your step, Pluralist. Before long either you'll be forced to say that there's nothing behind the façade – no Celestial City, no Transcendent, no nothing – which means you'll have become a Cupittite" (Christian said this with some awe; clearly it was a terrible charge) – "or else, about that of which you profess to know nothing, you'll have to remain silent. Such silence will be bad for religion."

"But not necessarily for us," murmured Jew.

"Seems a pretty circular process to me," said Atheist, "relying on evidence derived inductively from religious experience in

order to affirm the existence of a transcendent Reality that's
supposed to provide the stimulus for this kind of experience in the
first place." Atheist took a measured swig from the large hip-flask
that was replenished periodically along the way. "Perhaps that's
why you need this eschatological verification lark."
    Buddhist, who had been staring into the fire, now spoke up.
"Christian said that Pluralist was beginning to sound like Atheist
and me. But I do not say that there's nothing at journey's end. That
would be a kind of nihilism, and I want to steer clear of both
nihilism and eternalism. All I say is that it's dangerous to
speculate about our goal. Dangerous because such speculation
gives people the wrong ideas about where we're going and how to
get there. It distorts one's perception of the road. As a result,
sooner or later one or other of us will follow a wrong signpost,
with disastrous consequences. Besides," said Buddhist sombrely,
"these beliefs about the Real also generate much divisive argument. Why are you theists in particular so in love with words and
ideas? You can't help allowing these to police your thought, your
behaviour, your very faith."
    Hindu spoke. "Buddhist has a point. The theists are too caught
up in the idols of their own conceptions. If words and ideas are
like policemen, they should point unerringly towards our destina-
tion, not arrest our progress. Our scriptures should lead away from
themselves towards our common end – the Absolute, in which all
difference vanishes; they must help us to see how provisional and
relative our ideas of the goal are. Then we shall be more ready to
help rather than quarrel with one another."
    Here Pluralist took heart and spoke again. "You speak of our
common end. As I say, there may well be but one reality behind
the relativistic personae and impersonae of it produced in the
different religions. But what if there's more than one end, each an
absolute in its own right? Or, to put it differently, what if there's
not one Celestial City, but several, each corresponding to a
different *kind* of religious conception or experience of what lies at
journey's end? One for Buddhist – let's call it the Abode of
Unconditioned Repose; another for Hindu, where Oneness
reigns; a third for Muslim, Jew and Christian, though I'll wager it
has more surprises in store for them than they've bargained for;
and perhaps one even for Atheist, where Atheist rules." There was
general laughter at this.
    But Jew was not amused and said, "Not so fast, Pluralist! Let's
proceed one step at a time. I'll take your HickWickian hypothesis

first. We'll get to Master Cobbwebb in due course. Now, doesn't
HickWick speak a great deal about human *response* to the Real in
the different religions? If he's used the word once, he's used it a
thousand times! Why, even his *magnum opus* on the subject was
subtitled 'Human Responses to the Transcendent'. Wait a minute,
I'll show you what I mean." Jew pulled out a slim wad of papers,
searched for one and peered at it in the light of the fire. "Listen!"
said Jew, and read: " 'All authentic religious awareness is a
response " (Jew stressed the word) " 'to the circumambient presence and prevenient presure of the divine Reality'.[15] Now let's
attend to words for a bit. Does it make sense to speak of a *response*
to the Transcendent without implying some sort of *initiative* on the
part of the Transcendent in the first place? Listen to your Guru
again." Here Jew quoted once more: "We are no longer speaking
of an intersection of the divine and the human which only occurs
in one unique case, but of an intersection which occurs, in many
different ways and degrees, in all human openness and response
to the divine *initiative'* " (again the word was stressed).[16] "Well
now, speaking properly, it only makes sense to talk of *persons*
taking the initiative, does it not? Doesn't HickWick thereby
covertly imply by his terminology that the Real behind the various
personae and impersonae is basically personal? And, further, that
in general personae represent the nature of the Real more authentically than impersonae?"

Pluralist smiled and said, "Not necessarily. But I'm glad you've
raised the question of terminology. We can lay it to rest once and
for all. Remember that HickWick started off, to use his own
expression, as a Ptolemaic Christian – that is, as a theist who
believed that the Real or supreme being had revealed its true
nature as personal in terms of what Christians generally said
about it. But, as the result of what he called his 'Copernican
Revolution' in theology – that is, placing *the noumenal Real* at the
centre of the universe of faiths, and not some phenomenal
conception of it, be it Muslim, Christian, Hindu, Jewish, or
whatever – HickWick sought increasingly to refer to what he
preferred to call 'the Real' in person-neutral language. This conscious attempt to be descriptively person-neutral about the Real is
noticeable in the *magnum opus* you mention, much of which has
come down to us, thank goodness. Nothwithstanding its subtitle, I
doubt if the book contains, in its discussion of religious pluralism,
any reference to responding to *initiatives* from the Transcendent,

as the earlier writings you quoted do. In fact, if my memory serves me right, HickWick states expressly that, if things known are known according to the mode of the knower, finite persons will naturally tend to be conscious of the Real as a divine person.[17] But, since personality is essentially interpersonal, he continues, we cannot say that the Real *an sich* is personal. For this would presuppose that the Real is eternally in relation to other persons.[18] Finally, my friend, aren't you being a little pedantic? We *do* sometimes speak of responding to things that are not personal. So, all in all, be fair to HickWick. Don't confuse what may well be residual traces of theism in his style with the *logic* of his philosophical position, which, I believe, remains intact."

Jew smiled and replied, "Fair enough, Pluralist! Your point is well taken. We'll leave terminological disputes on one side. However, I thank you for *your* response because it's going to sharpen my next objection." The others were listening attentively, not least Muslim and Christian, who realized that what Jew was about to say was likely to be of special relevance for the theistic position they held in common.

The night was cold. The little group sat huddled round the fire, faces dimly reflected in its flickering light. All of them looked curiously shapeless under their long, cowled robes.

Jew continued, "I'm not done with the idea of response yet. Consider the matter from another angle: who or what responds to the 'pressure' or 'presence' of the Real? Or, to put it differently, what makes religious consciousness, in all its much-vaunted global variety, possible? People do; human persons do. I'm sure I'm right in saying that Guru HickWick never tires of repeating that it is only through free and conscious response that human beings grow into mature personhood. This is what being *responsible* is all about. Well, how can we grow as persons in a religious context (which for HickWick is a vital dimension of human existence) unless we *really*, not only imaginatively, enter into a two-way personal relationship with the Real? All the experts – psychologists and sociologists and anthropologists and philosophers – say that on the human level, horizontally so to speak, we come to personhood precisely through relating with other persons. And do you mean to say that vertically, in our relationships with the Transcendent" (here Jew waxed somewhat oratorical), "at what HickWick himself says touches the deepest levels of our being, it could be otherwise? Surely those who respond to the

Transcendent within the parameters of an interpersonal relationship are in closer touch with the core of the Real than those who do
not, and, being thus closer, grow the more perfectly into full
personhood. What I have said is quite in accord with other facets
of the Guru's thought – his eschatology, for example, and his
answer to the problem of evil, both of which eventually incorporate a personalist understanding of the real as the rationale for
ultimate human well-being.[19] Thus you must admit, Pluralist, that,
by failing to affirm, in the context of a plural religious response to
the Transcendent, that the Real is ultimately personal in some
sense, HickWick's position becomes untenable."

"Jew sometimes gets it right," muttered Muslim to Christian.
Jew seemed not to have heard.

"But what about HickWick's claim," said Hindu, "that, since
personality is essentially interpersonal (as you yourself seem to
agree), we cannot say that the Real *as such* is personal, for this
would presuppose that the Real is *eternally* in relation to other
persons?"

"I have lots to say about it," said Jew. "In the first place, I'm
talking about person*hood*, not personal*ity*, which has psychological connotations. Personality – one's distinctive behaviour-
patterns, likes, dislikes, tastes, foibles, and so on – does seem to be
necessarily dependent on interpersonal relationships for its development. If we can speak with propriety of the Real as having, or
being seen to have, a personality, then this may well be what
personae, in the Guru's sense of the term, are all about. The Real's
personhood – philosophically, the character of being personal –
would then be masked by different personae, or indeed different
personalities, the product of the different cultural milieux in and
through which it is experienced. Thus we have Allah, the God
Christian calls Father, Krishna, who indeed has been called the
supreme personality of Godhead,[20] the Goddess, my own God,
and so on. In this context, it makes sense for HickWick to have
said, if I remember correctly, that a persona is a *social* reality living
in the consciousness, memories and continuing interactions of a
community.[21] That's the first thing I have to say about HickWick's
claim. In the second place, note that I said that it is the finite
human being who grows as a person through relationships with
other persons. But this does not mean that this kind of interpersonal context is necessary for personhood *per se*. In fact, it has
generally been agreed in the history of Western (and indeed

Hindu) philosophy that to be personal means, minimally, to exist with a certain quality of self-conscious freedom. I see no difficulty in saying that the supreme being, the Real, as infinitely perfect, has always existed as fully personal in this sense of the term, without in any way having had to depend, *qua* personal, on other personal beings. If it is reasonable for HickWick to suppose the eternal existence of the Transcendent in the first instance, I do not see why it is not equally reasonable to hypothesize the existence of such a Transcendent. Confusion arises because as humans we naturally tend to anthropomorphize the personhood of the Real – to give the Real a personality, a *persona*. It is not right to say, of course, that the real has always existed in this sense. Now," continued Jew expansively, "this is where I appreciate Hindu's distintion between the *saguṇa* and *nirguṇa* Brahman. In fact, the Guru got it wrong here too. The point of this distinction, as I see it, is not to claim that the *nirguṇa* Brahman is *impersonal*, as HickWick would have it, but to contrast the Absolute as transcendently personal with our devotionalized, mythologized, *anthropmor-phized* grasp of it as the *saguṇa* or qualified Brahman – the Lord/Goddess, or whatever, of historical consciousness. After all, does not the preceptor Śaṃkara, to whom Hindu defers, maintain consistently that, if we are to speak at all about the *nirguṇa* Brahman – the Brahman without human attributes – then on scriptural evidence the preferred epithets are *person* predicates such as 'consciousness' and 'bliss'? He explains the abstract forms of these terms as showing that the words are to be understood as stripped of all empirical imperfections. And the same may be said, I'm sure, for the Mādhyamika Buddhist description of the *dhar-makāya*. Indeed, even *nirvāṇa* has on occasion been described by Buddhist here as 'bliss', has it not?" Buddhist looked thoughtful.

"Where I disagree with Hindu is in the view that we are ultimately to realize our oneness with Brahman not in *communion* but in *identity*. This makes Hindu's Advaita or non-dualism an ultimately non-theistic stance, but not, as I hope I've shown, an impersonalist one. Guru HickWick has confused non-theism with impersonalism. Anyway, I think Śaṃkara went too far in his apophatic emphasis on the personal nature of the Real (not to mention his monism). I believe that, for all its undisputed tran-scendence, the Real has revealed itself to our historical conscious-ness in an act of sovereign freedom as an essentially personal God who demands a personal response from us – though some of us go too far by talk of Trinity, incarnation and so on." Here Jew looked reproachfully at Christian. "But that is not the point I'm making. The point I'm making is that, even with respect to the so-called impersonalist understandings of the Transcendent, HickWick's view cannot be defended, and that his distinction between persona and impersona breaks down. In fact, our various faiths *do* relate explicitly or implicitly to the real as personal, and the Real has indeed been encountering us in the great world religions as personal, though in different degrees and on different understandings of 'personal'. We may conclude *inductively*, then" (Jew relished the word), "that those religions which regard the Transcendent as personal seem more authentic, more true than impersonalist ones, should these exist."

"Well said, friend!" cried Muslim with enthusiasm. Jew looked pleased.

"Of course," said Christian before Pluralist could speak, "I should want to go on and say that, *within* the framework of an understanding of the real as personal, there are further degrees of truth. It is in this context that I should wish to make an *enlightened* defence of the doctrines of Trinity, incarnation, and so on. I believe that these doctrines properly articulated explain best the personal nature of the Real, and guide and perfect our relationship with it. For example, where the doctrine of the incarnation in particular is concerned, I should proceed in the manner of the Great Dean who argued that, if the personal God is to make himself known in the most personal and specific way possible by coming amongst us himself in person, to rescue us from our predicament, then that coming had to involve a particular story – a particular historical context, a particular tradition of faith, and a particular life history. There is no way, he said, in which this personal self-revelation, this specific atoning and reconciling act" – he was speaking of the Cross of Christ here – "could be equalled or replaced by a universally available set of general truths. Christian discourse, therefore, is bound, in the nature of the case, to reflect the *particularity* of divine self-revelation by way of the incarnation and the Cross.[22] But I mustn't disgress here from Jew's general defence of the Real as personal. In fact, I think that on the whole Jew has made some excellent points and I should like very much to hear what Pluralist has to say in reply."

There was a general murmur of assent. Once more Pluralist's mouth opened to speak; once more there was an interruption.

"Just a minute," said the normally placid Buddhist with some spirit. "I want to clear something with Christian first. Then we shall hear Pluralist. I can understand Christian saying that there is need for a particular revelation of the Real, but I hope Christian wouldn't go on to say, with the Great Dean, that Christianity requires there to be at all times and in all places some more general knowledge of God, expressed in the varied modes of religious discourse to be found in the world religions, in order to provide the necessary conditions for Christian events such as the incarnation, and their reception."[23]

"Why not?" said Christian.

"Because," Buddhist replied, "that would be an instance of religionism.".

"What do you mean?" asked Hindu.

Buddhist answered, "Well, you've heard of sexism, speciesism, and so on – ways by which one group discriminates against another for its own advantage. Religionism is where people of one faith discriminate, for their own advantage, against those of another religion, or against that religion itself. To argue that other faiths must exist so that in one way or another the superiority of one's own may become apparent, and that this may be put down to God's providence, hardly makes for an *enlightened* defence of one's religion. On the contrary, it throws one's faith and one's God into a very poor light indeed. I hope, Christian, that you are not going to adopt this religionist kind of argument."

"I should like some time to think about what you say," said Christian cautiously.

"And I, for my part, also wish to think about Jew's statement before I give my response," broke in Pluralist quickly. "I'll admit Jew has given me food for thought. In any case, it seems that Jew's general argument about the Real being personal could hold only if there is one Real with whom we enter into personal relationship in the different religions. The whole thrust of Jew's argument implied the existence of one supreme being which manifests itself more or less personally in the different faiths. But what about my alternative hypothesis – that there is more than one Ultimate answering to the different kinds of ultimate questions religions ask?"

It was Muslim who replied. "I doubt if that works either. In the first place, wouldn't Jew's argument apply in that these Ultimates would have to be acknowledged as being more or less explicitly personal? If that's so, how could there be more than one personal *ultimate* Reality interacting with us? But, secondly, this hypothesis hardly does justice to what the adherents of the different religions are on about as they seek the goal of their faith – precisely this, that they are relating to not one Ultimate among, as it may be, many, but to the only Ultimate there is, in the only way that brings ego-transcending fulfilment! To take an example from Master Cobbwebb himself, I seem to remember you mentioning his view that there is no reason in principle to assume that the Buddhist and Christian claims about the Ultimate exclude each other; that the fact that according to Śūnyavāda all things are empty does not directly contradict the claim that one should place ultimate trust in God.[24] But how can this be? It seems to me that, when the Buddhist claims that all things are empty, it is being claimed that in one way or another the God that Jew, Christian and I worship *as God* is, howsoever thoroughly we may try to demythologize and deanthropomorphize our understanding of 'God', ultimately empty of the character of what it means to be *ho theos*. And this isn't good enough! For then I, at any rate, could not be a *Muslim* since there would be no Allah – may He be exalted forever – to whose will I could wholeheartedly submit. Thus your Cobbwebbian hypothesis undercuts the religious enterprise as a whole. It fails to take account of the overriding commitment a religious person makes to his or her Ultimate precisely as *the* Ultimate rather than as *an* Ultimate. Śūnyavādins no less than theists make this commitment.

"Further, it seems to me wrong for Cobbwebb to go on and argue that there may be more than one Ultimate as the terminus of the different kinds of ultimate questions that religious believers ask. For instance, he says something to the effect that 'Emptiness' is the ultimate answer to the question *what* things are, whereas 'God' is the ultimate answer to questions concerning the *how* and *why* of things.[25] Surely we cannot accept such a distinction. For surely religious people everywhere are looking basically for the same kind of answer from the Ultimate that they so variously seek: an answer to what it means ultimately to be human, to transcend the ego in self-fulfilment – the better to cope with the vagaries of life, its joys and sorrows, evil and death, which as humans we all experience so emphatically. The contours and emphases of the questions asked in the various faiths may differ in important respects – for cultures differ – but the answer sought is invariably the same: an adequate account of the what and how and why of things, so that there is ultimate meaning to our lives."

"I dare say," said Christian, chipping in, "that, if you ask your

common-or-garden Śūnyavādin whether 'God' exists or whether
divine incarnation is possible, the reply will be "Don't know" or
"Don't understand the question." Quite understandably. Such
questions are too wrapped up in the concepts particular to one
faith; they are not sensitive to the religious ears of the Buddhist.
But, if you attempt to explain what you mean by 'God' and
'incarnation' in terms of ultimate human concern and meaning
and value (and possibly the concepts of Dharmakāya, *sambhogakāya* and *nirmāṇakāya*), the answer will probably be quite
different – at least both of you will be conversing on the same
wavelength. I quite agree with Muslim's splendid critique of your
Cobbwebbian hypothesis, Pluralist."
    Everyone looked expectantly at Pluralist.
    Pluralist said, "Clearly I've been given much to think about
today. And think about it I shall. So don't expect answers off the
cuff. In due course I'll have plenty to say!" – and then he stoked the
fire vigorously.
    "What it all boils down to," said Atheist in a fairly loud voice,
"is that the theists claim that *as theists* they are closer to ultimate
truth than poor Hindu and Buddhist here, who are non-theistic
believers, though the theists have managed to rope them into their
wider circle of believers in a personal Transcendent – implicit
believers, that is! Typical! I've always thought how much more
arrogant theists appear to be than non-theistic believers." Hindu
and Buddhist nodded slowly.
    It was Christian who responded. "I am sensible of your charge,
Atheist. I agree that it is very easy for us theists to appear arrogant.
No doubt theists often *are* arrogant, and I for one am very sorry for
this." Christian looked at Muslim and Jew, who both nodded in
agreement. Christian continued, "When one tries to live wholeheartedly in and through a personal relationship with God, and
tastes of its sweetness, it is very easy to think at times that one has
got it right in contrast to other kinds of relationship with the
Transcendent. And here I take to heart Hindu's admonition that
we theists are prone to make idols of our conceptions of God.
However, let me say something that I hope will mitigate the
charge of arrogance. I see it this way. First, I honestly believe that a
theistic perception of the Real is intrinsically more true than a
non-theistic religious perception, for reasons already touched
upon this evening, not least the experience of faith. The Real –
God – is personal. I cannot gainsay that. I further believe that,
within the framework of a theistic understanding of the Real, in

which we can include the faiths of Vaiṣṇavism, Śaivism, Sikhism, Islam, Judaism and so on, there are degrees of approximation to the truth. This stands to reason since the theistic faiths present conflicting truth-claims about the nature and revelation of God. These claims cannot all be true. But in my view it does not necessarily follow that a theistic faith is *de facto* salvifically more eficacious that a non-theistic one. For salvation crucially has to do with the sincerity with which one follows one's lights, with the way one knowingly or unknowingly co-operates with God's grace to become increasingly selfless in the service of one's neighbour. And in this respect an atheist" – Christian smiled – "may well be closer to God – in a more redeeming relationship with the Real, nearer true self-fulfilment (describe it as you will) – than a theist. This is a very large issue as you know; much more needs to be said. But it is already late, and we cannot go into it today."

"I appreciate the point you've tried to make," said Hindu. "No doubt there's much truth in it. What puzzles me is this. If salvation depends not on true belief but on sincere practice, what's the point of having the truth then – if you like, of being a theist rather than a non-theist?"

"That's a very difficult question to answer briefly," replied Christian. "It's part of the larger issue I've just mentioned. But I suspect that the answer has something to do with the greater resources that a theistic approach to the Real, as compared with a non-theistic one, makes available for coping with the road to journey's end – with, futhermore, *this* theistic approach proving more helpful than *that*. I'm sure I caught a glimpse of the Celestial City today, with the symbol of my faith on its gates. I feel refreshed, strengthened, enabled to carry on. I feel the closeness of my God's loving hand, and inspired to be of service to others along the way. The road has acquired a fresh significance for me. I feel that I understand better where I am and where I'm going. I hope this will make me a better companion on the road. In short, the relationship between my God and me has grown deeper and firmer and a little clearer – it is its own reward. I respect your truth, Hindu, and yours, Buddhist, and yes, yours, Atheist. But please respect mine, and my desire to share it with you. But perhaps we can discuss all this in greater detail some other time."

Suddenly Christian shivered. There seemed to be a strange chill in the night air. One or two of the group looked uneasily down the road. It was time to bed down for the night. They all realized that not long after first light they would have to be on their way. Yawning somewhat delicately, Atheist was the first to rise. "Need my beauty sleep, Celestial City or no Celestial City," Atheist said, trying to strike a light-hearted note. "Thanks for the discussion. It was not without interest, though you musn't be surprised if I say that parts of it made about as much sense to me as angels dancing on the head of a pin."

And there, as they settle down for the night, we must leave the members of our little band. We wish them well. There will be many more discussions along the way; perhaps we shall have occasion to listen in again.

For the present, I conclude my story. Perhaps this is the most profitable way to discuss such matters. If you think that for one reason or another the story was worth narrating, you must thank John Hick for providing the inspiration.

NOTES

1. *Problems of Religious Pluralism*, p. 18.
2. For more on this concept, see ibid., ch. 8, and *An Interpretation of Religion*, pp. 177–80.
3. Romans 8: 18.
4. In *An Interpretation of Religion* the idea of the *saguna* Brahman is enlarged to include the "Saccidānanda" of Advaita; see p. 283.
5. *Problems of Religious Pluralism*, pp. 39–40.
6. The use of Kantian terminology by Hick is deliberate and is discussed in *An Interpretation of Religion* in some detail; see pp. 240–46.
7. Ibid., p. 266.
8. *Problems of Religious Pluralism*, p. 44.
9. "nāyam ātmā pravacanena labhyo na medhayā na bahunā śrutena; yam evaisa vrnute tena labhyas tasyaisa ātmā vivrnute tanūm svām" (Katha Upanishad 2.23).
10. See John B. Cobb, "Christian Witness in a Pluralistic World" in John Hick and Hasan Askari (eds), *The Experience of Religious Diversity* (Aldershot: Gower, 1985) p. 156.
11. Ibid., p. 157.
12. See R. C. Zaehner, *Mysticism Sacred and Profane* (Oxford: Clarendon Press, 1957).
13. Wittgenstein, in another context.
14. Quoted from Joseph Runzo, "God, Commitment and Other Faiths: Pluralism *vs*. Relativism", *Faith and Philosophy*, 5, no. 4 (Oct. 1988) 354.
15. *Problems of Religious Pluralism*, pp. 97–8.
16. *Problems of Religious Pluralism*, p. 63.

17. Quoted from *An Interpretation of Religion*, p. 252 (substituting "person" for "Thou").
18. See ibid., p. 264.
19. See *Death and Eternal Life* and *Evil and the God of Love*.
20. By the founder of the International Society for Krishna Consciousness.
21. Quoted from *An Interpretation of Religion*, p. 265.
22. Quoted from Brian Hebblethwaite (Dean of Queens' College, Cambridge, and University Lecturer in the Philosophy of Religion), "Religious Language and Religious Pluralism", *Anvil*, 4, no. 2 (1987) 106.
23. Ibid., p. 111.
24. Cobb, "Christian Witness in a Pluralistic World", in Hick and Askari (eds), *The Experience of Religious Diversity*, p. 159.
25. Ibid., p. 158.

Critical Response

The Road Not Taken: A Story about Religious Pluralism, Part 2

JOSEPH PRABHU

In the best Hollywood tradition, I feel that such a wonderfully entertaining narrative as Julius Lipner's deserves a sequel – hence my title. And, in the same tradition, my response to Lipner takes the form of a play, possibly even a screenplay, if Hollywood is interested.

The play has three characters: HickWick; Lipsync, the narrator of Part 1 of the Pluralist Story, now no longer able to hide behind his authorial role but forced to speak in his own name; and someone called Plurad, a figure of some mystery. The scene is a room outside the Celestial City called "Scholars' Dungeon", a correctional facility for those chronically given to cerebration and unable to enjoy the simple pleasures of the city. The time: decidedly post-Copernican.

The door of the dungeon opens and we see the three characters flat on their backs, their feet in wooden stocks, on which is inscribed in large letters Wittgenstein's epigram, "Whereof you cannot speak, thereof you must be silent", and in slightly smaller letters Frank Ramsey's response to that: "Yes, and you can't whistle it either." Not to be deterred, however, our three characters feel that, if they can have one last go at it, they might finally get it right – a triumph which, if accomplished, would make the pleasures of the city outside the dungeon seem trivial by comparison. HickWick as the senior partner begins the conversation.

HICKWICK. Well Lipsync, your story was very interesting, but you should know, in these literary-theoretic times, that a narrative in itself establishes very little, but rather calls out for a meta-narrative, or at least for interpretation. You do not seem to me to have offered any serious arguments against my fundamental hypothesis of the Real *an sich* and its personae and impersonae, but only a caution against the danger of attenuating the Real by

235

putting it beyond human cognition. You then proceed to offer your preferred personalist view of the Real, implying that it is better able to explain the facts of religious consciousness and human growth. But, in response to your caution, I do not see that I am becoming agnostic about the Real simply because I make it transcendent to any but the most general human categories of thought. On the contrary, in a Kantian move I am attempting to make room for faith, by confining the scope of reason and conceptualization to the experiential sphere. In this way the radical transcendence of the Real is preserved, and the equal validity of different ways of responding to that transcendence acknowledged. The belief that a personalist – more precisely, a transcendently personalist – account of the Real offers the best way of conceiving it is something that I specifically make room for in my notion of "personae". Within a theistic world view, "God" as transcendently personal is a symbol whose truth is thought to be universal, and correctly so, because that is how the logic of the symbol "God" or any other Ultimate functions. This is valid, however, only within that world view. It is quite a different matter to claim universal validity for that world view.

LIPSYNC. But isn't this in a sense what you yourself are doing, except that you shift the universalism to a metaphysical level? Isn't the view that there is one ultimate Reality differently manifested in human communities itself a metaphysically particular view? I have attempted to articulate the universalism at a religious rather than a metaphysical level by arguing that the notion of "personhood" is a richer category than "personae" or "personality" and that it can accommodate within itself some of the aspects of the divine-human encounter that you call "impersonae".

HICKWICK. I am not sure that the purported distinction between non-theism and impersonalism makes much difference to my argument. The Buddhist experience of "nothingness", the Taoist of the "Tao", the Confucian of "heaven", the Upanishadic *neti, neti* all seem to me to have very little to do with either personhood or personality. And it is very doubtful whether Śamkara would regard "consciousness" and "bliss" as essentially person-predicates. They can be, and are, of course, enjoyed by persons, but that does not make the qualities themselves personal. If I might take a parallel from philosophical logic, Frege's *Gedanken* (propositions) might well be thought by minds, but the truth of the propositions is not itself mind-dependent. Thus, neither on empirical nor on logical grounds can I agree with your assertion that "Ultimates would have to be acknowledged as being more or less explicitly personal".[1] Of course, you are right that experientially we relate to what we consider to be the only Ultimate there is, but pluralism enters precisely at the point, where we must hold to that consideration while at the same time recognizing that there are other equally valid standpoints. The only way of getting around this difficulty is by making the truly Ultimate beyond human grasp and relativizing the humanly conceived ultimates, by showing that they are not ultimate in themselves, but only so for their partisans.

LIPSYNC. Plurad, you have been uncharacteristically quiet.

PLURAD. These stocks are terribly uncomfortable and are cramping my style. But another reason I've been keeping quiet is that, while I have my differences with HickWick, I find myself on his side as a pluralist responding to his "inclusivist" critics. As far as theoretical attitudes to other faiths go, I find the inclusivist position imperialistic, even if unintentionally so, in its claim to respresent the final, definitive and universal criterion for the truth of all faiths, and the assumption of absolute superiority that goes along with this claim. If my way is thought to be the only way, ultimately, through which Reality can be rightly understood and known, then the ways of other faiths cannot but be regarded as inadequate and even mistaken. And, as far as practical attitudes towards inter-religious understanding are concerned, I find the consequences of inclusivism disturbing.

First, there is the tendency to interpret the meaning of other traditions through the norms of one's own tradition, as in Lipsync's personalistic misreading, to my mind, of the impersonalism of at least some branches of the Hindu and Buddhist traditions, not to mention Taosim or Confucianism.

Secondly, no real dialogue is possible in such circumstances, because the assumption of the finality of truth in one's own tradition makes one see other faiths as interesting and perhaps profound but nevertheless as inferior in their grasp of truth to one's own, which alone provides the criteria for fully articulating the truth-claims of the alien traditions. Thus, not only are these latter not understood in their own terms, but what other traditions precisely in their radical otherness have to teach us is gravely undercut. The possibilty of what Cobbwebb has called "mutual transformation" in dialogue is, therefore, eliminated from the very start.

Thirdly, not only is this unfortunate as far as inter-religious dialogue is concerned, but its consequences for intra-religious dialogue are also unpromising. One could argue that one's own faith, far from being threatened, gets greatly enriched through the inter-religious encounter, if properly conducted with pluralistic openness. Here one could turn the tables on Lipsync and suggest that it is only when one gives up the "exclusively personal relationship with God and the taste of its sweetness"[2] that one can see new aspects to the Mystery of the Cross.

LIPSYNC. As you are waxing eloquent on Christian symbols, it is perhaps appropriate to ask you from what religious position, if any, you speak.

PLURAD. Like you Lipsync, I'm an Indian Christian trying to bring these two sides of our common heritage, our Indianness and our Christian faith, together so that they enrich, rather than serve as embarrassments to, each other.

LIPSYNC. How then would you reconcile the claim to universality inherent in the Christian faith with your relativization of it?

PLURAD. Well, that's a very large question or series of questions. Suffice it to say here that I agree with HickWick when he said earlier that the Christian can and must regard Christ as "universal saviour" and believe that the transformation to Reality-centredness is best accomplished in him. But at the same time I would say that as Christians we are required not to freeze that assertion into an absolute claim, but to acknowledge that there are other paths to salvation than that of historical Christianity and that these are equally valid, though, for reasons of our historical–cultural finitude, we Christians are unable to encompass them. When we do learn something of these other paths, we may as Christians include their salvific grace in the universal saving function of Christ. The Christ phenomenon, as I perceive it, vastly exceeds its appropriation in historical Christianity and extends to other faiths, even though it would not be called that in those faiths.

LIPSYNC. But if you open the door to such relativization, what prevents you from sliding down the slippery slope to relativism?

PLURAD. There are many different degrees and kinds of relativism, which I can't go into here. But in broad stroke I would distinguish between relativism and relativity. All our religious symbols and assertions are relative, both to one another and to the Absolute. That does not at all mean that at any one time we cannot from our own finite position arrive at what appear to us to be, at the present, the best available standards for cognitive and moral evaluation. As a scientific project, chemistry is superior to alchemy, but, of course, there may be other standpoints – social and spiritual, for example – from which people in the modern scientific world may be able to learn from alchemical experiences. Absoluteness and relativity stand, for me, in a creative tension. The religious symbols of our faith are as precious to me as to you, Lipsync, because it is through them that the Absolute is mediated, but that very fact also relativizes them. I therefore regret that you so quickly dismiss the relativist option, to which the title of this piece, "The Road Not Taken" presumably refers. That road is not a slippery slope or a dark alley where anything goes. All human religions have through history displayed their demonic sides. These can and must be criticized by standards that we take to be normative and binding, and yet relative to our own world view.

HICKWICK. Your position, Plurad, sounds very close to my own. How, then, do you think we differ?

PLURAD. To put it in a nutshell, you are, as Lipsync pointed out, a religious pluralist but a metaphysical universalist, in the sense that you hold to one, sovereign Ultimate, differently mediated in the religious traditions. I would regard myself as a radical pluralist – sometimes one's name can exert a certain tyranny – a pluralist both in religion and in metaphysics. I have difficulty with the very notion of one ultimate Reality, where "one" is taken as singular. Your position is plausible, if we accept the Kantian premises of your argument, because, if the thing known is put "in" the knower, then, given Kantian subjectivism, the only way in which the objectivity of knowledge can be preserved in the face of the diversity of human conceptualization is by way of a notion of a sheerly transcendent noumenon. In your Kantian framework, Jesus, Krishna and Amida are empirically real, i.e. actually "given" in the faith experience of the different religious communities, but transcendentally ideal, i.e. not existent as salvific figures apart from those experiences; while the

Real is empirically ideal or beyond our experiential grasp, but transcendentally real, i.e. actually existent quite apart from our experiences. The difficulties with this strategy – as with Kant's original project – are many. Let me just mention two.

First, if you regard the Real as *sheerly* transcendent, then we can't say anything at all about it, certainly not that the most general human categories of thought apply to it (an assertion which implies some knowledge of the Real). In that case we cannot know if we are actually related to the Real, rather than a figment or projection of our imagination.

Secondly, if there is a sharp dichotomy between noumena and phenomena, you open the gate to wholesale scepticism. Instead of appearances being made a function of the Real, the Real is made a function of appearances, and, given the epistemological status of appearances in your account, this subjectivism really does attenuate the nature of the Real.

At this point, perhaps at the mention of the "sheerly transcendent", thunder and lightning are heard and seen, illuminating the Wittgensteinian dictum about silence. Undeterred HickWick, whose blood is roiled by talk of radical pluralism, presses the issue.

HICKWICK. But what sense does it make to talk of plural ultimates? How can the Ultimate be other than one?

PLURAD. We often are, as Wittgenstein says, bewitched by language. The locution "the Real" inevitably makes us think of it as one. Here I would want to use your own intuition of the transcendence of the Real but articulate it differently. The infinite fecundity and creative power of the Real are such that they continually defeat our normal and irrepressible urge to impose unity on it. If we do want to have such unity – and without it our very language and discourse would be impossible – it would in Kantian language be a postulate. Such unity, if postulated, would still contain and display an internal plurality, as in the Christian doctrine of the Trinity, where the three are seen as one, because the one itself is intrinsically trinitarian.

The conceptual drive to thinking of the Real as one for us by no means warrants the conclusion that the Real in itself is one. Here I find myself closer to Cobbwebb. Each of the experienced ultimates of the religious traditions is different from the others, but still real. Neither singly, nor together, do they exhaust the power of the Real. That does not at all mean that our religious experiences have no purchase on the Real. Now we "see through a glass darkly", but we do see. The essential mystery of the real is revealed not in the complete inability of human thought to reach it, as in your Kantian picture, but in its ability continually to overreach our necessarily limited knowledge of the Real.

At this mention of mystery, the thunder that has been growing steadily louder now becomes deafening and the door of the dungeon closes. Not a sound is to be heard from inside. Is the slamming of the door a sheer coincidence? Or the punishment of a God, who finally loses patience at the incorrigible hubris of philosophical theologians? On this side of the grave we shall never know. The question awaits eschatological verification.

EPILOGUE

If I, Plurad, could, in a Pirandellian manoeuvre, shift from cha-racter to author, I should like in the latter capacity to offer this play to John Hick in admiration and gratitude. It was Heidegger who said that thinking is thanking, meaning by that that thinking arises in response to the giftedness of being. I hope that John Hick, alias HickWick, will accept this exercise of thinking as a token of thanks for a lifetime of thought.

NOTES
1.   Julius Lipner, above, p. 229.
2.   Lipner, above, p. 231.

Reply

JOHN HICK

Julius Lipner demonstrates that the dialogue is still an excellent format for exploring a variety of viewpoints, allowing one's own conclusions to arise out of the discussion. His story is a brilliant example, intellectually substantial as well as highly entertaining, of the art of philosophical dialectic; and Joseph Prabhu follows in the same happy vein.

Rather than attempt to imitate this method, I shall single out what I take to be Lipner's main contention. This is his claim that the ultimate Reality, the Real, must be personal. The first phase of his argument (expressed by "Jew"[1]) holds that, since we grow as persons through our responses to persons, the idea of growth in response to the Real presupposes the personal character of the Real. Although plausible-sounding this is very inconclusive. According to the *Interpretation of Religion* (IR) hypothesis the Real is present to us in and through everything, but most importantly, so far as personal growth is concerned, through other finite persons and the moral claims that they mediate. But it in no way follows that the Real is itself personal.

Lipner goes on to distinguish[2] between personhood (as self-conscious freedom) and personality (as the concrete character that develops in relationship to other persons). He needs this distinction in order to be able to hold that the Real has personhood but not personality, the particular divine personalties – Yahweh, Shiva, and so on – being formed (as suggested in the IR hypothesis) in interaction with different human faith communities.

But I cannot see that any such distinction can be sustained. In relation to what does the Real as free self-consciousness exercise its freedom? If such a self-conscious freedom is properly to be described as having *person*hood, must not that freedom be exercised in relation to other persons? Can we give any meaning to the idea of a personal free self-consciousness existing by itself, without any other free self-consciousness with whom to interact? Such a solitary self-consciousness might perhaps be said to be potentially personal; but, surely, in order for it to be actually personal there must be other persons with whom to be in personal contact.

The motivation behind Lipner's distinction is to support the belief that the ultimate Reality is a personal deity. But any line of argument that the Real must be personal, in order to bring out the spiritual transformation of human beings, runs up against what seems to me to be the fact that this transformation takes place as much within the non-theistic as within the theistic traditions. If this is so it can hardly be the case that only a personal ultimate can bring it about; and the basis of Lipner's argument evaporates. Further, his line of thought would lead us towards the unacceptable theistic imperialism that Prabhu so well exposes.

However, I cannot agree with Prabhu either when he seems to recommend postulating a plurality of Ultimates. That is an option that was, I thought, very effectively disposed of in Lipner's dialogue by "Muslim".[3]

NOTES

1. Julius Lipner, above, pp. 223–6.
2. Lipner, above, pp. 226–8.
3. Lipner, above, pp. 229–30.

Index